GRAMMAIRE ACTIVE DE L'ANGLAIS

GRAMMAIRE ACTIVE
DE
L'ANGLAIS

par

M. Delmas

Le Livre de Poche

Sommaire

Introduction

Le présent ouvrage contient **l'essentiel** de ce qu'il faut savoir pour s'exprimer dans un anglais **correct**. C'est à dessein qu'ont été éliminées des subtilités dangereusement encombrantes au niveau auquel nous nous adressons : élèves de troisième à terminale, des classes préparatoires, étudiants du premier cycle, adultes autodidactes désireux de se remettre à l'anglais.

Rédigée dans une langue simple, à la portée de tous, la **Grammaire active de l'anglais** tient le plus grand compte des **difficultés généralement rencontrées par les francophones**.

Chaque chapitre est composé de **courtes unités**, affectées d'un ou de deux astérisques.

Les unités à **un astérisque** (*) contiennent les **rudiments de base** qu'on ne peut ignorer.

Les unités à **deux astérisques** (**) proposent des **notions un peu plus « savantes »** (correspondant au second cycle des lycées et au premier cycle des facultés).

La **page de gauche** comporte l'exposé des **faits grammaticaux** à partir d'un rapide **contexte** (une phrase ou deux contenant les structures qui posent des problèmes). Les exemples y sont nombreux et traduits dans leur majorité.

La **page de droite** propose des **exercices** d'application **autour d'un même thème lexical**, ce qui permet, chemin faisant, de réviser un vocabulaire courant, résolument moderne, relatif à des champs d'activité très divers (les sports, le bricolage, le tourisme, les spectacles, les affaires...). Un **corrigé** de ces exercices figure en fin de volume.

Une exception est faite à cette démarche pour le chapitre 38, le dernier mais non le moindre (last but not least!). Il s'agit d'une liste des **mots de liaison** qui constituent l'ossature de la phrase. Ils sont présentés dans des exemples. Leur importance est telle que nous n'avons pas voulu les ranger dans les annexes.

Parmi celles-ci, qu'il ne faut d'ailleurs pas négliger, on trouvera :
— Des tableaux de conjugaison
— Les formes réduites ou contractées
— Les préfixes et les suffixes (formation des mots)
— Les principales modifications orthographiques
— Les verbes irréguliers
— Les corrigés des exercices
— Un index très précis de référence aux pages de gauche.

Cet ensemble fait de la **Grammaire active de l'anglais** un instrument de **travail autonome**. Il pourra servir soit à l'acquisition ou à la révision systématique des bases de la langue, soit à la consultation ponctuelle, pour résoudre telle ou telle difficulté.

Avertissement

Sauf cas particuliers, on trouvera, entre parenthèses, dans les exercices :

— les **mots anglais** au **singulier** ;
— les **mots français** au **pluriel**, le cas échéant ;
— la **base verbale** (infinitif sans **to**) des **verbes anglais** ;
— l'**infinitif** des **verbes français**.

En faisant les exercices, l'utilisateur veillera donc à opérer les transformations nécessaires.

1. Be, auxiliaire et verbe.
Différents emplois

A ■* I **am** English, you **are** American, he **is** Canadian. We **were** all in the Allied Forces... I **was** wounded *(blessé)*.

▷ **Be** a de nombreuses formes (conjugaison complète p. 172)
— trois au présent : I **am** ; you, we, they **are** ; he, she, it **is**
— deux au prétérit (cas unique dans la liste des verbes irréguliers p. 179) : I, he, she, it **was** ; we, you, they **were**
— **been** au participe passé, **being** au participe présent.

Be sert d'auxiliaire dans différentes constructions verbales :
1. La forme progressive à tous les temps (p. 172-173) :
   I **am going** to the town-centre.
2. La forme passive à tous les temps (p. 50) :
   This young artist **was encouraged** by the local authorities (p. 50).
3. Le futur proche et le futur imminent (p. 40) :
   I **am going to** wash (p. 40) I **am about to** go out (p. 40).
4. Le futur de projet (p. 40) (plan établi à l'avance) :
   We **are to** meet outside the restaurant.
   Nous devons nous rencontrer devant le restaurant.

N.B. : quelle que soit la nature de **be**, auxiliaire ou verbe ordinaire, verbe principal de la phrase (verbe d'état, « être »), on n'a jamais **do, does, did** aux formes interrogative et négative du présent et du prétérit ; on a simplement :
   You are happy → **Are you** happy? → **You are not** happy.
   On a par contre : **Will you be...?** (futur) **Would you be...** (conditionnel).

▷ *Emplois particuliers de* **be** *comme verbe ordinaire* :
1. Dans l'équivalent du *il y a* français (p. 14) :
   There **is** a book on the table. *Il y a un livre sur la table.*
2. Avec **how**, pour interroger sur l'âge, les mesures... (p. 144) :
   How old **are** you? I **am** twenty / How long **is** it?
   It **is** seven meters long / How far **is** it?
   It **is** ten miles away from here.
3. On a aussi : **be** cold, *avoir froid* ≠ **be** warm, **be** hot ; **be** hungry, *avoir faim* ; **be** thirsty, *avoir soif,* etc. (cf. exercice).

A' ■* I **am** English, you **are** American, he **is** Canadian. We **were** all in the Allied Forces... I **was** wounded *(blessé).*

VOCABULAIRE - **Health,** *la santé.*

Traduisez les phrases suivantes :

1. J'ai très chaud *(be hot),* j'ai de la fièvre *(have a temperature).*

2. Il n'est jamais malade *(ill).*

3. Quel âge a le malade *(patient)*? Il a soixante ans.

4. Cet homme était en pleine forme *(be as fit as a fiddle).*

5. Ils sont tombés malades *(be taken ill)* l'année dernière *(last year).*

6. La pauvre *(poor)* femme était très faible *(weak),* elle était sur le point de s'évanouir *(faint).*

7. Avez-vous faim *(be hungry)*? Non, j'ai soif *(be thirsty)* et je suis mal en point *(be out of sorts).*

8. Nous allons faire venir *(send for)* le docteur *(doctor).*

9. Le sida *(aids)* est une maladie infectieuse *(infectious).*

10. L'infirmière *(nurse)* s'occupait *(tend)* des malades *(patient)* pendant que *(while)* le chirurgien *(surgeon)* opérait *(operate).*

11. Vous serez opéré *(be operated on)* la semaine prochaine *(next week).*

12. Elle prenait *(take)* ses médicaments *(medicine)* quand l'infirmière-chef *(sister)* est entrée.

13. Le blessé *(injured man)* sera-t-il transporté à l'hôpital? *(take to hospital).*

14. Avez-vous peur *(be afraid)*? C'est seulement une piqûre *(injection)*!

15. A quelle distance se trouve l'hôpital?

16. Est-ce le cancer *(cancer)* ou la tuberculose *(tuberculosis)*?

17. Votre mère sera-t-elle toujours en bonne santé ?.▲ *(health).*

18. Seriez-vous ambulancier *(ambulance man)* par hasard? *(by any chance).*

19. Pierre avait-il honte *(be ashamed of)* d'avoir cette maladie *(disease)* contagieuse *(contagious)*?

**B ■* There is one book on the table...
No, there are two books!**

Il y a un (seul) livre sur la table... Non il y a deux livres!

▷ La traduction littérale de la structure anglaise (« là est un livre... ») aide à comprendre *l'accord du verbe,* qu'on retrouve notamment au prétérit (there **was** a..., there **were** two...) et au present perfect (there **has** been a..., there **have** been two...).

— La structure avec **there** existe *à tous les temps* :
There will be a change. *Il y aura un changement.*
There would be difficulties. *Il y aurait des difficultés.*

— Elle peut être combinée *avec les modaux* (p. 20) :
There may be a war. *Il se peut qu'il y ait une guerre.*
There must be a problem. *Il doit y avoir un problème.*

— On la trouve aussi avec **used to** (p. 58), **going to** (p. 40), **seem**...
There used to be a church here. *Autrefois il y avait une église ici.*
There is going to be an election. *Il va y avoir une élection.*
There seems to be a noise. *Il semble qu'il y ait un bruit.*

— La structure avec **there** s'emploie dans des phrases interrogatives, négatives, interro-négatives, elliptiques (p. 46) :
Were there any problems? *Y a-t-il eu des problèmes?*
There **won't be** any problems. *Il n'y aura pas de problèmes.*
Isn't there anything to do? *N'y a-t-il rien à faire?*
There is a problem, **isn't there?** *Il y a un problème, n'est-ce pas?*

N.B. : La structure avec **there** ne peut en aucun cas s'appliquer à l'expression de la durée, du temps. On a alors :
I **went** to America two years **ago** (p. 34).
Je suis allé en Amérique il y a dix ans.
It **is** ten years **since** I **went** to America (p. 34).
Il y a dix ans que je suis allé en Amérique.

B' ■* I **am** English, you **are** American, he **is** Canadian. We **were** all in the Allied Forces... I **was** wounded *(blessé)*.

Traduisez les phrases suivantes :

1. Il y a une épidémie *(epidemic)*.

2. Il y avait un service de réanimation *(intensive care unit)* très moderne dans cet hôpital *(hospital)*.

3. Il y a des maladies *(disease)* très graves *(serious)* comme le cancer *(cancer)*.

4. Y a-t-il beaucoup de jeunes *(young people)* qui souffrent de *(suffer from)* de maladies cardiaques *(heart disease)*?

5. Il y aura beaucoup de dépressions nerveuses *(nervous breakdown)* si ça continue *(go on)* comme ça !

6. Il n'y a pas assez d'internes *(junior hospital doctor, intern)*.

7. Il se peut qu'il y ait un meilleur service hospitalier *(hospital facilities)* dans cette ville *(town)*.

8. Il y aurait moins de cancer du poumon *(lung cancer)* si les gens fumaient *(smoke)* moins.

9. C'est une très petite ville mais il doit y avoir un dentiste *(dentist)*.

10. Après quelques jours de traitement *(a few days' treatment)* il devrait y avoir une amélioration *(a change for the better)*.

11. Il n'y a pas de danger à *(in)* prendre un comprimé d'aspirine *(an aspirin)* ou deux.

12. J'ai eu la grippe *(the flu)* il y a un mois *(month)*.

13. Il y a un problème de tension artérielle *(blood pressure)*, n'est-ce pas ?

14. Il y avait un asile d'aliénés *(lunatic asylum)* dans notre quartier *(district)* autrefois.

15. Y a-t-il un service d'urgence *(emergency ward)*? Oui.

16. Il y a dix ans qu'il a eu une attaque.

2. Have, **auxiliaire et verbe.** **Différents emplois**

A ■* I **have** not seen her, she **has** gone to town.
Je ne l'ai pas vue, elle est partie en ville.

▷ **Have** a plusieurs formes (conjugaison complète p. 170-171)
— deux au présent : I, you, we, they **have** ; he, she, it **has**
— une seule au prétérit : I, you, he, she, it, we, you, they **had**
— **had** au participe passé, **having** au participe présent.

— **Have** sert d'auxiliaire au present perfect (p. 32), au passé récent (have just + participe passé d'un verbe (p. 44), et au pluperfect (p. 34) :
She **has** (just) gone / She **had** gone. *Elle était partie.*
N.B. : c'est bien **have** et non **be** qui est utilisé, même pour les verbes intransitifs, à moins qu'on ne veuille insister sur le résultat de l'action :
She **has** gone. *Elle est partie* (action).
She **is** gone. *Elle a disparu* (état résultant de l'action).
N.B. : avec **have** auxiliaire on a simplement dans les phrases interrogatives et négatives :
She has gone → **Has she** gone? **She has not** gone.

— **Have**, verbe ordinaire, a les sens suivants :
1. *posséder, avoir*
Do you **have** a house? No I **don't have** a house.
Ou Have you got...? I **haven't got** (avec have auxiliaire).
2. *prendre*
(un repas, une boisson, du bon temps = fun)...
Did you **have** breakfast? No I **didn't have** breakfast.
3. *faire faire* (p. 62) : **have** + participe passé d'un autre verbe
Did you **have** that dress specially made for you?
Est-ce que tu t'es fait faire cette robe spécialement pour toi ?
4. *devoir, falloir* : **have** (**to**) : obligation, contrainte extérieure (p. 22)
Do we **have to** be there at five o'clock?
Faut-il que nous y soyons à cinq heures ?

N.B. : avec **have**, verbe ordinaire, il faut utiliser **do, does, did** dans les phrases interrogatives et négatives (ce n'est pas le cas avec **to be**, verbe ordinaire [p. 12]).

A' ■* I **have** not seen her, she **has** gone to town.

VOCABULAIRE - **Cars,** *les voitures.*

Traduisez les phrases suivantes (liste des verbes irréguliers p. 179):

1. Il a acheté une voiture d'occasion *(second-hand).*

2. Je viens de mettre la valise *(suitcase)* dans le coffre *(boot).*

3. Mr. Leadbeater avait perdu *(lose)* sa clef de contact *(ignition key).*

4. Avez-vous de bons pneus? *(tyre)* Non.

5. Il venait de faire changer *(change)* les bougies *(sparking plug).*

6. Avez-vous jamais *(ever)* conduit un break? *(estate car).*

7. Il n'a pas changé de vitesse *(change gear).*

8. Le prix *(price)* de l'essence *(petrol)* vient d'augmenter *(go up).*

9. Le pompiste a-t-il vérifié *(check)* la pression *(pressure)*?

10. Nous avons roulé *(drive)* pare-chocs contre pare-chocs *(bumper to bumper)* pendant des heures.

11. Ils s'étaient arrêtés *(stop)* à une station service *(filling-station).*

12. Nous avons fait réparer *(repair)* le moteur *(engine)* dans un garage *(garage)* du quartier *(local).*

13. Il ne prend pas de boissons alcoolisées *(alcoholic drink)* quand il doit se mettre au volant *(take the wheel).*

14. Sa voiture vient de tomber en panne *(breakdown),* elle a pris *(take)* un taxi.

15. Avez-vous remarqué *(notice)* que votre voiture consomme *(consume)* beaucoup d'essence?

16. Un automobiliste *(motorist)* prudent *(careful)* fait réviser *(service)* sa voiture régulièrement.

3. Do (does, did), **auxiliaire et verbe.** **Différents emplois**

A ■* Do you speak English? No I **don't** (speak English).

▷ **Do** sert d'auxiliaire au verbe ordinaire ou principal, porteur du sens (speak) dans les phrases interrogatives et négatives, au présent simple (p. 28). A la 3ᵉ personne du singulier (he, she, it), il prend la forme **does** :

Does Mr. Durand speak English? No he **doesn't** (speak English).

Au prétérit on a **did** à toutes les personnes :

Did Mr. Durand speak English? No he **didn't** (speak English).

Remarques

1. La négation est accolée à **do (don't, doesn't, didn't)** dans les formes contractées ou réduites, presque toujours employées dans la conversation. (La forme pleine est : I do not speak.)

2. Dans les réponses courtes (« oui », « non »), il suffit de reprendre l'auxiliaire ; c'est pourquoi "speak English" est entre parenthèses (cf. phrases elliptiques p. 46).

3. Il ne peut y avoir qu'une seule marque de temps ou de personne ; elle est portée par l'auxiliaire **do** ou par le verbe à la forme déclarative ou affirmative :

Doe**s** he work? / He doe**s** not work / He work**s**.

Did he work? / He **did** not work / He work**ed** (si le verbe est régulier ; s'il est irrégulier, on emploie la forme donnée dans la 2ᵉ colonne de la liste des verbes irréguliers (p. 179) : he **spoke** English....

▷ **Do (does, did)** s'emploie comme auxiliaire dans une phrase affirmative pour marquer l'insistance *(forme emphatique)* :

I do remember it. *Mais si, je m'en souviens.*

Do sert enfin d'auxiliaire de l'impératif négatif (p. 16) : **Don't** say that. *Ne dites pas cela.*

Do *(faire)* est aussi un verbe ordinaire, irrégulier (do, did, done) :

What shall we do tomorrow? *Que ferons-nous demain ?*

Did you do your work yesterday? *As-tu fait ton travail hier ?*

A' ■* **Do** you speak English?
No, I **don't** (speak English).

VOCABULAIRE - **Activities of the mind,** *les activités de l'esprit.*

Mettez les phrases suivantes à la forme interrogative puis à la forme négative (formes réduites et formes pleines) (cf. liste des verbes irréguliers p. 179):

1. You understand *(comprendre)* it.

2. She realized it *(se rendre compte de).*

3. Peter notices *(remarquer)* everything *(tout).*

4. Mr. Campbell mistook *(prendre quelque chose pour quelque chose d'autre)* one word for another.

5. Old Mr. Jones tended *(avoir tendance)* to mix things up *(tout mélanger).*

6. Mrs. O'Neil ignores *(feindre de ne pas connaître)* her neighbour *(voisins)* in the street.

7. Jackie misunderstood *(mal comprendre)* what I said.

8. David remembers *(se souvenir de)* it very well.

9. The student *(étudiant)* grasped *(saisir pleinement)* everything the teacher explained *(expliquer).*

10. The boss *(patron)* took it into account *(tenir compte de qqch.).*

11. Your old aunt *(tante)* gets mixed up *(mélanger tout).*

12. Mrs. MacDonald gathered that *(conclure que)* her friend would not come.

13. Mr. Leigh supposed you were right *(avoir raison).*

14. You suspect *(se douter)* something will go wrong *(ne pas aller comme il faut).*

15. Robert made up his mind *(se décider)* yesterday.

16. John forgot *(oublier)* to learn *(apprendre)* his lesson.

17. His grandfather missed the point *(ne pas voir où on veut en venir).*

4. Les auxiliaires modaux :
can, may, must...

A ■* Mr. Brown **can** play tennis. Mr. Smith **cannot (can't)** play. **Can you** play?

Mr. Brown sait jouer au tennis. Mr. Smith ne sait pas jouer. Savez-vous jouer ?

▷ Il n'y a *pas de s* à **can** à la 3ᵉ personne du singulier (he, she, it) : **can** a la même forme à toutes les personnes.

— **Can** est suivi de la base verbale, sans to (play)

— Aux formes négatives **(cannot, can't)** et interrogative **(can you?)**, can, auxiliaire modal, exclut tout autre auxiliaire (do, does, did, will et shall, would et should) : à la forme négative **not** vient simplement après l'auxiliaire modal ; il est accolé à **can** mais pas aux autres auxiliaires à la forme pleine **(can, cannot, can't** mais **must, must not, mustn't)** ; à la forme interrogative, on a une simple inversion du sujet et de l'auxiliaire : **you can → can you?**

— Les auxiliaires modaux qui suivent les règles énoncées ci-dessus permettent de manifester son attitude par rapport à ce qu'on dit. Sans auxiliaire modal on rapporte seulement les faits tels qu'ils sont. On est dans le domaine de la neutralité.

> I work hard but I **must** work harder still. *Je travaille dur* (c'est un fait) *mais je dois travailler plus dur encore.*
> I came yesterday but I **may** not come tomorrow.
> *Je suis venu hier* (c'est un fait) *mais il se peut que je ne vienne pas demain.*

Avec les auxiliaires modaux on est dans le domaine de la capacité **(can)**, de la permission **(may)** et de l'obligation **(must, ought to)**. On peut aussi évaluer les chances de réalisation des faits ; il s'agit alors de probabilité **(might, may)** et de quasi-certitude **(must)**.

— Les auxiliaires modaux ont la même forme à toutes les personnes au prétérit comme au présent (conjugaison complète p. 169-170) :

Présent	can	may	must	shall	will	ought to
Prétérit	could	might	(1)	should	would	(2)

(1) Cf. p. 22. (2) Cf. p. 24.

A' ■* Mr. Brown **can** play tennis.
Mr. Smith **cannot (can't)** play. **Can** you play ?

VOCABULAIRE - **Weekend activities,** *activités de week-end.*

Transformez les phrases suivantes selon les modèles :

{ I am practically certain the Browns are out for a picnic.
The Browns must be out for a picnic *(quasi-certitude).*

{ Perhaps *(peut-être)* I will go to the cinema.
I may go to the cinema *(probabilité).*

1. I am practically certain he is at the football match.

2. Perhaps Mr. Smith will go to the concert.

3. We are almost *(presque)* sure *(sûr)* she is at the theatre.

4. You will probably go to the restaurant tomorrow.

5. We will probably visit our friends over the weekend.

6. Mr. Jones is practically certain his children *(enfants)* are at the disco *(discothèque)* every evening.

7. The Smiths will probably go hiking *(faire une randonnée à pied)* next *(prochain)* weekend.

8. I am almost sure John is out rock climbing *(faire de la varappe)* again.

9. Perhaps Mr. and Mrs. Davies will go for a walk *(aller faire une promenade)* in the forest *(forêt)* during the weekend.

10. I am practically certain they are spending *(passer)* the long weekend *(weekend prolongé)* in their second home *(maison secondaire).*

11. Maybe *(peut-être)* Jackie will go to the museum *(musée)* on Sunday.

12. I am almost sure they are at the skating-rink *(patinoire)* with the children.

13. Perhaps Mr. and Mrs. Lancaster will go sailing *(faire de la voile)* with their friends this coming *(prochain)* weekend.

B ■* Les diverses significations des modaux, leurs substituts ou équivalents

▷ **Can** (prétérit **could**) exprime la capacité physique ou intellectuelle :

I **can** stand on my hands. *Je peux (je sais) tenir sur les mains.*

I **can** speak Russian. *Je sais parler le russe, je parle russe.*

Substitut dans ce sens : **be able to**, *être capable de :*

She will **be able to** walk again in a few days.

Elle pourra marcher de nouveau dans quelques jours.

Can sert aussi à demander la permission (style plus familier que may) et à la forme négative **cannot (can't)** exprime l'interdiction : Can I go out tonight? No, you can't. *Puis-je sortir ce soir ? Non.* **Could**, outre son sens passé, peut avoir un sens conditionnel (p. 42) : I **could** stand on my hands when I was twenty years old. I **could** not stand on my hands now! *(Je ne pourrais pas... maintenant).*

▷ **May** (prétérit **might**) sert à demander la permission (style très poli) :

May I borrow your pen? *Puis-je emprunter votre stylo ?*

Substitut dans ce sens : **be allowed to**, *être autorisé à :*

He told us he would not **be allowed to** go out.

Il nous a dit qu'il ne serait pas autorisé à sortir.

May sert aussi à exprimer une probabilité, **might** une probabilité réduite :

He **may** come. *Il se peut qu'il vienne.*

He **might** come. *Il se pourrait qu'il vienne.*

▷ **Must** (une seule forme, guère utilisée au passé) exprime l'obligation et, à la forme négative, **must not (mustn't)** exprime l'interdiction :

You **must** arrive at six. *Il faut que tu arrives à six heures.*

You **must** not say that. *Il ne faut pas dire cela.*

Substitut de **must** : **have to** (contrainte extérieure généralement) :

You will **have to** arrive at six. *Il te faudra arriver à six heures.*

Must exprime aussi une forte probabilité, une quasi-certitude :

He has not come to work, he **must** be very ill.

Il n'est pas venu au travail, il doit être très malade.

B' ■* Mr. Brown **can** play tennis.
Mr. Smith **cannot (can't)** play. **Can you** play?

Complétez les phrases suivantes à l'aide des auxiliaires modaux **can, may, must** *ou de leur substitut :*

1. You ...... practise sports *(faire du sport)*, it is good for your health *(santé)*.

2. I ...... ride a bicycle *(faire de la bicyclette)* but I ...... ride a horse *(faire du cheval)*.

3. You ...... mow the lawn *(tondre la pelouse)*, it is bad for your back *(dos)*.

4. The doctor says you ...... play tennis again *(de nouveau)* in a month's time *(dans un mois)* but not before.

5. "... I go to the swimming pool *(piscine)*?" he asked his father. "No you .... You have not finished your homework *(devoir)*."

6. I ...... do any jogging next *(prochain)* weekend, I have sprained my ankle *(se fouler la cheville)*.

7. We ...... go to the country *(campagne)* but I am not sure *(sûr)* we will.

8. John ...... go skiing during the weekend if he does not work hard *(travailler dur)* during the week.

9. My brother ...... play chess *(jouer aux échecs)* but my sister ....

10. He has stopped doing odd jobs about the house *(bricoler)* he ...... be very tired *(fatigué)*.

11. I ...... do some decorating *(refaire les peintures)* next *(prochain)* weekend or my wife *(femme)* won't leave me in peace *(paix)*.

12. We ...... go cycling *(aller faire une promenade à bicyclette)* if the weather *(temps)* is fine *(beau)*.

13. You ...... gamble *(jouer pour de l'argent)*, it is strictly forbidden *(interdit)*.

14. We ...... go to the seaside *(bord de la mer)*. God knows! *(Dieu sait !)*

C ■* ▷ **Shall**, auxiliaire du futur à la 1ʳᵉ personne (cf. p. 38) sert
aussi à
— suggérer, à proposer (à la forme interrogative)
   Shall we go to the cinema? *Et si nous allions au cinéma ?*
   Shall I help you? *Veux-tu que je t'aide ?*

▷ **Will**, auxiliaire du futur à toutes les personnes (cf. p. 38) sert
aussi à
— proposer (à la forme interrogative) :
   Will you have some tea? *Voulez-vous du thé ?*
— exprimer la volonté (la forme réduite 'll est alors exclue) :
   I **will** see to it. *Je m'en occuperai (sans faute).*
— exprimer l'habitude dans le présent ou une vérité éternelle
   (p. 56) :
   I **will** do some jogging every day. *Je fais du jogging tous les
   jours.*
   Boys **will** be boys. *Les enfants seront toujours les enfants.*

▷ **Should**, auxiliaire du conditionnel à la 1ʳᵉ personne (p. 42)
sert aussi à
— donner un conseil (2ᵉ personne) ou exprimer l'obligation
   morale (à toutes les personnes) :
   You **should** work harder. *Tu devrais travailler davantage.*
   We **should** help the poor. *Nous devrions aider les pauvres.*
— exprimer la probabilité (à toutes les personnes) :
   He **should** pass his exam. *Il devrait être reçu à son examen.*

▷ **Would**, auxiliaire du conditionnel à toutes les personnes
(p. 42), sert aussi à exprimer l'habitude dans le passé (p. 56) :
I **would** do some jogging every day. *Je faisais du jogging tous les
jours.*

▷ **Ought** (une seule forme, suivie, contrairement à tous les
modaux, de l'infinitif avec to) sert à
— donner un conseil (2ᵉ personne) ou exprimer l'obligation
   morale (à toutes les personnes) :
   You **ought to** work = you should work harder (cf. plus haut).
— exprimer une probabilité (à toutes les personnes) :
   He **ought to** pass his exam = he should pass his exam.

C' ■* Mr. Brown **can** play tennis.
Mr. Smith **cannot (can't)** play. **Can you** play?

Complétez les phrases suivantes à l'aide des auxiliaires modaux **shall, will, would** *ou* **ought to** *:*

1. ...... we have a game of cards? *(faire une partie de cartes).*

2. He is good with his hands *(être bricoleur)*. He ...... spend hours *(passer des heures)* every weekend pottering *(bricoler)* about the house.

3. We ...... go to the fun fair *(fête foraine)* quite often *(très souvent)*. We loved it.

4. We ...... adopt a child *(enfant)* rather than *(plutôt que)* buy a weekend cottage *(maison de campagne).*

5. ...... I help you to do some repairs *(réparations)* in your holiday home? *(maison de vacances).*

6. ...... you come and have dinner with us next Saturday?

7. Mr. Parhill ...... go fishing *(aller à la pêche)* every Sunday. He loved *(adorer)* it.

8. We ...... ask him to dinner *(inviter à dîner)*, he feels a little depressed *(déprimé)* these days.

9. You ...... get some fresh air *(prendre l'air)* after working so hard *(travailler si dur)* at the office *(bureau).*

10. ...... we go to the jazz club on Saturday night?

11. Car accidents ...... happen *(avoir lieu)* every weekend.

12. We ...... entertain *(recevoir)* friends every evening when we were on holiday *(en vacances).*

13. You ...... go boating *(aller faire une partie de canot)*, it will do you good *(faire du bien).*

14. ...... we listen to some music?

15. We ...... help the homeless *(les sans-abris)* instead of *(au lieu de)* building *(bâtir)* second homes *(maison secondaire).*

D ■* ▷ **Need** *(avoir besoin)* est un semi-modal c'est-à-dire qu'il fonctionne tantôt comme auxiliaire modal (p. 20), tantôt comme verbe ordinaire (prétérit **needed**).

En tant qu'auxiliaire modal, il ne s'emploie qu'à la forme négative (**need not** ou **needn't**) ou interrogative du présent ; il exprime alors :

— l'absence d'obligation :
   You **needn't** come. *Ce n'est pas la peine que tu viennes.*

— une question sur une obligation possible :
   Need I come with you? *Faut-il que je vienne avec vous ?*

N.B. : à la forme affirmative **need** ne peut s'utiliser que comme verbe ordinaire :
He **needs to** hurry. *Il a besoin de se dépêcher.*

▷ **Dare** *(oser, avoir le courage de* ; prétérit **dared**) est aussi un semi-modal (cf. les règles ci-dessus) :
She **dare not** (**daren't**) say it. *Elle n'ose pas le dire.*

Il s'emploie plus souvent comme verbe ordinaire.

E ■** *Quelques problèmes de traduction relatifs au modaux*

1. Des phrases comme *Il a pu venir* ou *Il a dû venir* contiennent des participes passés (pu, dû) ; or les auxiliaires modaux n'ont pas de participe passé. On a dans ce cas :
   He **may** (ou **might**) have come. He **must** have come.

   A savoir : le présent ou le prétérit de l'auxiliaire modal + l'infinitif passé du verbe (**have come**), composé de **have** et du participe passé de ce verbe (**come**).

2. **Des expressions impersonnelles comme** *Il se peut que, Il faut que...* sont rendues par des auxiliaires modaux qui ont pour sujet le sujet réel de la phrase (Mr. Goodall) :
   Il se peut que Mr. Goodall arrive demain.
   Mr. Goodall **may** arrive tomorrow.
   Il faut que Mr. Goodall vienne. Mr. Goodall **must** come.

D' ■** Mr. Brown **can** play tennis.
Mr. Smith **cannot (can't)** play. **Can you** play?

Traduisez les phrases suivantes :

1. Ce n'est pas la peine que vous fassiez des courses *(go shopping)* ce week-end.

2. «Faut-il que j'aille au musée?» demanda-t-il *(ask)* à son père.

3. Elle n'ose pas refuser *(refuse)* l'invitation.

4. Ce n'est pas la peine que tu prennes un week-end prolongé *(long weekend)*.

5. Les Brown n'osent pas inviter les Smith à dîner *(ask to dinner)*.

6. Mrs. Page a besoin de prendre l'air *(take some fresh air)*.

7. Elle avait besoin d'écouter *(listen to)* un peu de musique pour se calmer *(calm down)*.

8. Vous n'aurez pas besoin de tondre la pelouse *(mow the lawn)*.

9. Comment osez-vous dire pareille chose? *(such a thing)*.

E' ■** *Traduisez les phrases suivantes :*

1. Jean a dû aller danser *(go dancing)*.

2. Il se peut que nous allions à la soirée *(party)*.

3. Il faut que je fasse un peu de jardinage *(do some gardening)*.

4. Mr. Salmon a dû prendre trois jours de congé *(take three days off)*. Il a dû les passer *(spend)* dans sa maison secondaire *(second home)*.

5. Il se peut qu'il ait profité *(take advantage of)* du week-end pour laver *(wash)* sa voiture.

6. Il se peut qu'elle soit allée au restaurant pour changer *(for a change)*.

7. Il se pourrait que les enfants soient allés au centre de jeunes *(youth club)*.

8. Il faut que tu mettes de l'ordre dans ta chambre *(tidy up one's room)* ce week-end.

5. La forme progressive et la forme simple

A ■* **I am going** to the town-centre, **I go** there quite
often. *Je vais au centre ville, j'y vais assez souvent.*

▷ Les verbes anglais se conjuguent soit à la forme progressive
(I am going) soit à la forme simple **(I go)**.

La forme progressive est composée de l'auxiliaire **be** + **ing**
accolé au verbe **(go-ing)** (Voir la conjugaison complète
p. 172-173) :

présent : I am going / Am I going? / I am not going.
prétérit : I was going / Was I going? / I was not going.
futur : I will be going / Will I be going? / I won't be going.
conditionnel : I would be going / Would I be going? / I
would not be going.

La *forme simple* se présente ainsi :

	Forme affirmative	Forme interrogative	Forme négative
Présent	I (you, we, they) **work** He (she, it) **works**	**Do** (you, we, they) work? **Does** he (she, it) work?	I (you, we, they) **do** not work He (she, it) **does** not work
Prétérit	I **worked** *(v. régulier)* I **went** *(v. irrégulier* go, went, liste p. 179)	**Did** I work?	I **did** not work
Futur	I **will** work	**Shall** (I, we) work? **will** (you, he, we, it, they) work?	I **will** not work
Conditionnel	I **would** work	**would** I work?	I **would** not work

— Le **s** (3e pers. sing. au présent) se prononce : he work**s**.
— Attention aux modifications orthographiques possibles au
  présent et au prétérit à la forme affirmative : he **cries** (cry),
  he **stopped** (stop) (p. 177).
— **Do, does, did** ne s'emploient pas :
  1. avec **never** : I **never** go there, *je n'y vais jamais.*
  2. avec **neither ... nor** *(ni ... ni).*
     I work **neither** on Saturdays **nor** on Sundays.
     Je ne travaille ni le samedi ni le dimanche.
  3. avec l'interrogatif **who** sujet du verbe qui suit :
     who works on Saturdays?

A' ■* **I am going** to the town-centre, **I go** there quite
often. **I love** shopping.

VOCABULAIRE - **Shopping,** *faire les courses.*

*Complétez par la forme progressive ou la forme simple à
l'aide des verbes entre parenthèses. Consultez p. 28 et p. 30, et
la liste des verbes irréguliers (p. 179) :*

1. I (shop, *faire ses courses*) yesterday when I (see, *voir*) her.

2. He only (sell retail, *vendre au détail*) not wholesale *(en
   gros).*

3. He never (pay cash, *payer en espèces*).

4. She (window-shop, *faire du lèche-vitrine*) the other day
   when her friend (call, *appeler*) her.

5. I (linger, *traîner*) in a bookshop *(librairie)* yesterday.
   Intellectuals (love) lingering in bookshops.

6. We generally (buy) our Christmas presents *(cadeaux de
   Noël)* long in advance to avoid queueing *(éviter de faire la
   queue).*

7. We (wait, *attendre*) in the car while *(pendant que)* they
   (make some purchases, *faire quelques achats*). It was not
   great fun *(ce n'était pas très amusant).*

8. She (use, *utiliser*) neither credit cards nor cheques.

9. Many people (prefer) small shops to supermarkets.

10. Who (forget) to take his cheque-book *(carnet de chèques)*
    last week *(la semaine dernière)?*

11. He was fed up *(il en avait marre),* he (stand) in the queue.
    It (rain).

12. How much (pay for that)? I (pay) £ 10 *(dix livres)* a year ago
    (il y a un an).

13. A mail-order business *(une maison de vente par correspon-
    dance)* (send, *envoyer*) goods *(marchandises)* by post.

14. My grandmother (order, *commander*) what she (need,
    avoir besoin) from the local grocer *(l'épicier du coin).* She
    (order) vegetables *(légumes)* on the phone the other day
    when I *(arrive).*

B ■* **I am going** to the town-centre...

Cette phrase, selon le contexte, pourrait être dite :

1. par quelqu'un qui se rend effectivement au centre-ville, répondant à la question d'un ami rencontré en route : "**where are you going?**"

▷ La *forme progressive* exprime une action en cours, non encore achevée au moment où on parle ou dont on parle (au passé) ; elle implique une certaine durée de l'action, souvent par opposition à une autre action dont la durée est sans importance :

I **was going** to the town-centre when I met him.
J'allais au centre-ville quand je l'ai rencontré.

La forme progressive s'emploie couramment avec les *verbes d'attitude* (qui impliquent une certaine durée) : lie, *être allongé ;* sit, *être assis ;* stand, *être debout... :* he was **lying** on his bed.

La première phrase : "**I am going** to the town-centre" pourrait être dite :

2. par quelqu'un qui s'apprête à aller en ville : le présent progressif, souvent alors accompagné d'un complément de temps, sert à parler de projets, d'intentions ; il exprime le futur :

I am going to the town centre in a minute (tomorrow...)
Je vais au centre ville dans une minute (demain...)

— **I go** there quite often, I **love** shopping.

▷ La *forme simple* exprime des *actions habituelles* ou *répétées* qui ne se déroulent pas nécessairement au moment où on en parle (quite often, *assez souvent*), des réactions indépendantes de la volonté (love, *adorer ;* like, *aimer ;* hate, *détester ;* prefer, *préférer...*) ou des actions instinctives (see, *voir ;* hear, *entendre*), des états de fait auxquels on ne peut rien (be tall..., *être grand... ;* look, *sembler, avoir l'air ;* look like, *ressembler à ;* have money..., *posséder de l'argent...*), des notions qui n'ont pas de développement dans le temps (want, *vouloir ;* think that, believe that, *penser que, croire que ;* feel that, *avoir le sentiment que ;* know that, *savoir que ;* remember that, *se souvenir que...*).

B' ■* **I am going** to the town-centre, **I go** there quite often. **I love** shopping.

Complétez par la forme progressive ou la forme simple à l'aide des verbes entre parenthèses. Consultez p. 28 et p. 30, et la liste des verbes irréguliers (p. 179) :

1. Look! Mrs Smith (do one's shopping, *faire ses courses*). She (do one's shopping) every morning.

2. He (buy, *acheter*) that car because he could not afford *(se le permettre)* it. It was far too expensive.

3. You (buy) it on credit? No I (buy) it on credit, I (give, *donner*) 5,000 francs on the nail (cash) and I (send, *envoyer*) a cheque for 10,000 francs.

4. She always (make good bargains, *faire de bonnes affaires*). Why (make good bargains)? Because she (look round the shops, *faire le tour des magasins*) and (take one's time, *prendre son temps*).

5. People who (have much money, *avoir beaucoup d'argent*) (prefer) to pay in monthly instalments *(par mensualités).*

6. I (queue, *faire la queue*) at the butcher's *(chez le boucher)* while she (queue) at the baker's *(chez le boulanger).*

7. I (go) to the hairdresser's *(chez le coiffeur)* tomorrow, I (go) to the hairdresser's every month *(mois).*

8. She (think that) it is a mistake to go shopping locally *(dans le quartier),* she always (go) to department stores *(grands magasins).*

9. He was swindled *(roulé)* he (get one's money's worth, *en avoir pour son argent*).

10. The shop-assistants *(vendeurs)* were busy *(affairés),* the customers *(clients)* (hunt for sales, *être en quête de soldes*).

11. He (hate) queuing. Who (like) it?...

12. It was ten o'clock, Mr Marrow (drive, *emmener en voiture*) his wife to the shopping centre *(centre commercial).* He (drive) her there every Tuesday. He (like) it at all!

6. Le prétérit et le present perfect.
For, since, ago

A ■* We **arrived** in New York in May 1979, yes we **came** here ten years **ago**...

> *Nous sommes arrivés à New York au mois de mai, en 1979, oui, nous sommes venus ici il y a dix ans...*

▷ arriv**ed** est le *prétérit* de arrive, forme utilisée pour le passé, à toutes les personnes à la forme affirmative. Le prétérit est composé par addition de **ed** à la base verbale si le verbe est régulier ; aux bases verbales terminées par **e** (comme arrive) on ajoute seulement **d** ; il y a ainsi d'autres modifications orthographiques (p. 177).

Si le verbe est irrégulier, le prétérit (came) se trouve dans la 2e colonne de la liste des verbes irréguliers (p. 179) :

come, **came**, come, *venir*.

Aux formes interrogative et négative, **did** sert d'auxiliaire au prétérit, à toutes les personnes :

Did we come? We **did** not come (conjugaison complète p. 170).

— ... We **have lived** here for ten years now, since 1979, since our father's death.

> *Nous vivons ici depuis dix ans maintenant, depuis 1979, depuis la mort de notre père.*

▷ **have lived** est le present perfect : il est composé du présent de l'auxiliaire have (has à la 3e personne du singulier) et du participe passé du verbe (lived). Ce dernier peut être régulier (également en **ed**, ou irrégulier ; on le trouve alors dans la 3e colonne de la liste des verbes irréguliers (p. 179)

spend, spent, **spent** *(passer du temps)*.

I have spent ten years in New York.

J'ai passé dix ans à New York.

N.B. : Le *prétérit* et le *present perfect* s'emploient aussi à la forme progressive dans différents cas déjà évoqués ou exposés plus loin (p. 34). S'agissant de leur emploi, disons tout de suite que, comme les mots l'indiquent, le present perfect implique souvent la notion de présent ; il n'en est pas de même du prétérit, forme utilisée pour le temps passé.

A' ■* We **arrived** in New York in May 1979, yes we **came** here ten years **ago**. We **have lived** here **for** ten years now, **since** 1979, **since** our father's death.

VOCABULAIRE - **Tourism,** *le tourisme.*

Faites des phrases à l'aide des verbes proposés, au prétérit ou au present perfect, en utilisant éventuellement **for, since** *ou* **ago.** *Consultez p. 32 et 34 et la liste des verbes irréguliers p. 179:*

1. I (go) to the travel agency *(agence de voyage)* three days ...... I (spend) three hours *(heures)* there!

2. I (visit) that old town three years *(années)* .... I (take) lots of photographs.

3. Which hotel (stay, *séjourner*) in last year? We (stay) at the Red Lion. It (be) a wonderful stay *(séjour)*.

4. Yesterday the guide (show round the city, *faire faire un tour de ville*). We (be) delighted *(enchanté)*. It (be) such a sight! *(spectacle)*.

5. I (enjoy, *aimer*) that guided tour *(voyage organisé)* very much yesterday. There (be) too many ruins to visit.

6. The poor tourists (be sitting, *être assis*) on that coach (autocar)... hours and jours! They are tired out! *(épuisé)*.

7. How long (work, *travailler*) in the tourist-office *(syndicat d'initiative)*? I (work) there ...... three years, ... the day I (leave, *quitter*) school.

8. This (be) a tourist trap *(attrape-touristes)* ...... years and years. Nobody complains! *(se plaindre)*.

9. Mr. Law (be responsible for) the tourist trade *(tourisme)* in the town-council *(conseil municipal)* ...... many years, ... 1945, ... the end of the war *(fin de la guerre)*.

10. We (buy, *acheter*) a good map of the town *(plan de la ville)* yesterday, before we (go sightseeing, *visiter la ville*).

11. Unfortunately *(malheureusement)* the package tour *(voyage organisé)* include the Lake District, *(comprendre la région des Lacs)* last year *(l'année dernière)*. We (be) disappointed.

B ■* We **arrived** in New York in May, in 1979, yes, we **came** here ten years **ago**...

▷ *Le prétérit* fait souvent référence à un moment précis du passé : in May, in 1979, last week (la semaine dernière), ten years ago... Utilisé avec **ago**, le prétérit exprime combien de temps (ici dix ans) s'est écoulé depuis la fin de l'action. On peut dire aussi, pour insister sur cette durée :

It is ten years **since** we came here (since = *depuis que*). *Il y a dix ans que nous sommes arrivés ici.*

Le *prétérit* exprime des actions passées, complètement terminées (on a fini d'« arriver », de « venir »). Il y a *rupture* entre le présent et le passé :

I **lived** in New York, *j'ai vécu à New York* (je n'y vis plus).

— We **have lived** here **for** ten years, **since** 1979, **since** our father's death *(nous vivons ici depuis dix ans, depuis 1979, depuis la mort de notre père).*

▷ *Le present perfect* plonge à la fois dans le présent (nous y vivons encore en ce moment même) et dans le passé (des années se sont écoulées pendant lesquelles nous y avons déjà vécu). Il n'y a pas rupture entre présent et passé. **For** indique la durée écoulée (dix ans) depuis le début de la période de temps, **since** le point de départ (1979) de cette période (date, jour, heure..., mais aussi événement quelconque : "since our father's death", since the war [*guerre*], etc.).

Dans un récit au passé, on aurait le *pluperfect* (prétérit de have + participe passé du verbe) :

We **had lived** here for ten years since 1979 when they visited us. *Nous vivions ici depuis dix ans, depuis 1979 quand ils nous ont rendu visite* (nous y **étions** encore quand ils sont venus nous voir).

Le **present perfect** met davantage en valeur le résultat présent d'une action passée plutôt que cette action elle-même :

Look! I have bought a book! *Regarde ! J'ai acheté un livre !* (c'est sur le livre qu'on veut attirer l'attention, non sur le fait qu'il ait été acheté).

Le **present perfect** s'emploie pour des actions qui se sont passées pendant une période de temps qui n'est pas encore terminée, ou dont le moment n'est pas précisé :

I have seen her twice this week. *Je l'ai (déjà) vue deux fois cette semaine* (et c'est seulement mercredi par exemple).

B' ■* We **arrived** in New York in May, in 1979, yes we **came** here ten years **ago**. We **have lived** here **for** ten years now, **since** 1979, **since** our father's death.

*Faites des phrases à l'aide des verbes proposés, au prétérit, au present perfect ou au pluperfect, en utilisant éventuellement for, **since** ou **ago**. Consultez p. 32 et 34 et la liste des verbes irréguliers p. 179 :*

1. They (go on a tour, *aller en voyage organisé*) to Italy six months *(mois)* .... They (enjoy, *aimer*) it very much. It (be) a wonderful journey *(voyage)*.

2. I (work) as a tour operator *(organisateur de voyages)* in this town ...... many years now, ... 1970, ... I (get married, *se marier*).

3. It (be) a long time ...... I (travel abroad, *voyager à l'étranger*). The last time *(dernière fois)* I (travel abroad), it (be) in Germany.

4. When (leave, *quitter*) home for England? They (leave) a fortnight *(une quinzaine)* .... They (be) there a fortnight now.

5. When (buy, *acheter*) your ticket? I (buy) it a couple of days *(deux jours)* ....

6. I (have) my old camera *(appareil photos)* ...... ten years now. I (get) another one the other day. It (cost) me a lot of money.

7. We (go on a cycling tour, *faire une randonnée à bicyclette*) in Wales *(Pays de Galles)* a year ....

8. I (travel, *voyager*) to distant places *(pays lointains)* ...... the last *(dernier)* twenty years. I (fly, *aller en avion*) to Alaska six months ....

9. We (tour, *visiter*) Scotland ...... three weeks *(semaines)*, ... July 1st, when our father (telephone) and (ask, *demander*) us to come back urgently. Our mother (be) dangerously ill *(malade)* ...... two days. In fact she (die, *mourir*) a week after our return *(retour)*.

C ■**

Comme tous les temps grammaticaux, le present perfect et le prétérit s'emploient aussi à la forme progressive (p. 28). Notez les nuances suivantes :

1. *Le present perfect simple*, nous l'avons vu (p. 34), insiste sur le résultat d'une activité :
   Look! I have bought a book (there it is).
   Regarde! J'ai acheté un livre (le voilà).
   Look! I have washed the car (it is clean now).
   Regarde! J'ai lavé la voiture (elle est propre maintenant).
   Il s'agit de constats objectifs, neutres (livres achetés, voiture lavée...).

2. *Le present perfect progressif* met au contraire l'accent sur l'activité elle-même. C'est cette forme et non le present perfect simple qui sera employée si l'interlocuteur porte un jugement favorable ou défavorable sur cette activité.
   "You've been drinking". « *Tu as bu* » dira, par exemple, une femme en colère contre son époux ivrogne.
   Alors que le present perfect simple fait un bilan objectif, le present perfect progressif indique souvent une certaine dose d'affectivité (colère, approbation, désapprobation...).

3. *Le prétérit progressif* sert à décrire une action en cours à un moment du passé ; il s'emploie souvent par contraste avec le prétérit simple qui exprime une action plus rapide, survenue au même moment :
   I was reading when he knocked at the door.
   Je lisais quand il a frappé à la porte.

C' ■** We **arrived** in New York in May, in 1979, yes we **came** here ten years **ago**. We **have lived** here **for** ten years now, **since** 1979, **since** our father's death.

Traduisez les phrases suivantes (consultez la liste des verbes irréguliers p. 179):

1. J'essaie *(try)* d'apprendre *(learn)* cela depuis des jours mais je n'ai pas encore réussi *(succeed).*

2. J'en ai assez! *(be fed up).* Je fais la queue *(queue)* depuis deux heures.

3. J'écrivais *(write)* une lettre quand il est entré *(come in).*

4. Tu ne sais pas cela et tu apprends l'anglais depuis quatre ans! Bravo! *(congratulations).*

5. Je suis fatiguée *(tired).* Je fais la cuisine *(cook)* depuis des heures.

6. Regarde! Quel gaspillage! Cette lampe *(lamp)* a brûlé *(burn)* toute la nuit *(all night).*

7. Nous regardions la télévision *(watch television)* quand le téléphone a sonné *(ring).*

8. Tu as cassé *(break)* le vase *(vase).* Il est inutilisable *(useless)* maintenant.

9. Il essaie *(try)* de me convaincre *(convince)* depuis un quart d'heure. Il perd *(waste)* son temps!

10. Je ne peux pas aller faire du ski *(go skiing)* parce que je me suis cassé la jambe *(break one's leg).*

11. Elle lit *(read)* depuis des heures et des heures. Elle ne fait rien d'autre! *(else).*

7. Le futur
l'avenir, les projets

A ■* I will go to the USA...
J'irai aux USA...

▷ **will** (ou **'ll**, forme réduite, presque toujours employée dans la conversation) est l'auxiliaire du futur à toutes les personnes (conjugaison complète p. 171).

forme affirmative : **I will go** to the USA
forme négative : **I will not go** ou **I won't go** to the USA
forme interrogative : **will you go** to the USA?

N.B. : **Will**, **forme pleine**, est obligatoire seulement à la forme interrogative et dans les réponses affirmatives courtes :
Will you go to the USA? Yes I **will**.

L'auxiliaire **shall** remplace will surtout à la forme interrogative, à la première personne du singulier (**I**) et du pluriel (**we**) ; il sert alors à proposer, à suggérer :
Shall I come with you? *Veux-tu que je vienne avec toi ?*
Shall we go to the theatre? *Et si nous allions au théâtre ?*

— ... **When I have** enough money.
... *Quand j'aurai assez d'argent.*
▷ *Les conjonctions de temps* when, *quand,* while, *pendant que, tandis que,* as soon as, *dès que,* as long as, *tant que,* till ou until, *jusqu'à ce que,* after, *après que,* before, *avant que...* sont suivies du présent et non pas du futur.

N.B. : Il n'en est pas de même de **when**, adverbe interrogatif :
When **will** you go to the USA? When I **have** enough money.

A' ■* **I will ('ll) go** to the USA **when I have** enough money.

VOCABULAIRE - **Turning-points in life,** *les moments décisifs de la vie.*

Traduisez les phrases suivantes :

1. Il se mariera *(get married)* dès qu'il aura fini *(finish)* ses études *(studies)*.

2. Dieu *(God)* sait combien de temps *(how long)* ils resteront *(remain)* mari et femme *(man and wife)*.

3. Il dit qu'il aura une famille nombreuse *(a large family)* s'il gagne *(earn)* assez d'argent pour y subvenir *(support them)*.

4. Dès que mon bébé sera né *(be born)* j'abandonnerai *(give up)* mon métier *(job)*.

5. Se marieront-ils à l'église ? *(have a church wedding)*.

6. Elle divorcera d'avec son mari *(divorce one's husband)* dès qu'elle apprendra *(learn)* cela.

7. Quand elle sera mariée *(be married)* et qu'elle aura des enfants *(child, children)* elle les élèvera *(bring up)* elle-même.

8. Ce sera un coup *(blow)* terrible pour lui quand il apprendra *(hear about)* leur séparation *(separation)*.

9. Il deviendra fou *(go mad)* le jour où *(when)* sa femme mourra *(die)*.

10. Elle ne l'épousera pas *(marry somebody)*.

11. Je suis sûr *(sure)* que leur mariage *(marriage)* sera un échec *(failure)*.

12. Tu ne comprendras pas ça tant que tu ne seras pas tombée amoureuse *(fall in love with someone)*.

13. Quand quelque temps aura passé *(elapse)*, il oubliera *(forget about)* cette mort *(death)* tragique *(tragic)*. Il s'occupera *(look after)* de ses petits-enfants *(grandchild, grandchildren)*.

B ■**

Autres façons d'exprimer le futur, de parler d'avenir, de projets :

1. *Le présent progressif,* souvent avec un adverbe exprimant le futur :
   I **am going** to the USA tomorrow.
   Je pars aux USA demain.

2. *Le présent simple* accompagné d'un adverbe exprimant le futur :
   Our train leaves at four o'clock tomorrow.
   Notre train part à quatre heures demain.
   N.B. : Le français emploie aussi le présent dans ces cas.

3. **be going to** + verbe : pour marquer l'intention du sujet ou exprimer une prédiction *(futur proche,* p. 44*)* :
   I am going to work hard.
   Je vais travailler dur.
   I think it's going to snow.
   Je crois qu'il va neiger.

4. **be about to** + verbe : pour exprimer un *futur imminent* (p. 44) :
   I have just put on my coat, I am about to go out.
   Je viens de mettre mon pardessus, je suis sur le point de sortir.

5. **be to** + verbe : *futur de projet* (plan établi à l'avance) :
   We are to meet outside the restaurant.
   Nous devons nous rencontrer devant le restaurant.

B' ■** I will ('ll) go to the USA **when I have** enough money.

Traduisez les phrases suivantes :

1. Je crois *(think)* que ça va se terminer par *(end up in)* un mariage *(marriage)*.

2. Ils sont toujours en train de se chamailler *(quarrel)*. Ils sont sur le point de se séparer *(split up)*.

3. Ils doivent partir pour l'Écosse en voyage de noces *(on one's honeymoon)* dimanche prochain.

4. Ils vont se marier *(get married)* la semaine prochaine.

5. Il dit qu'il va rester célibataire *(remain single)*.

6. Nous partons de la maison *(leave the house)* à neuf heures demain matin. L'enterrement *(funeral)* doit commencer *(begin)* à dix heures.

7. Elle espère *(hope)* qu'elle va obtenir le divorce *(get a divorce)*.

8. Elle est enceinte *(pregnant)* depuis près de *(nearly)* neuf mois. Elle est sur le point d'accoucher *(give birth to)* d'une petite fille *(baby girl)*.

9. J'espère qu'il ne va pas demander le divorce *(start divorce proceedings)*.

10. Mes parents célèbrent *(celebrate)* leurs noces d'argent *(silver wedding anniversary)* la semaine prochaine *(next week)*.

8. Le conditionnel : hypothèses, souhaits

A ■* He said **he would go** to the USA...
Il a dit qu'il irait aux USA...

▷ **would** (**'d**, forme réduite, presque toujours employée dans la conversation) est l'auxiliaire du conditionnel à toutes les personnes (conjugaison complète p. 171) :
forme affirmative : he would go
forme négative : he would not go *ou* he wouldn't go
forme interrogative : would he go to the USA?

N.B. : **1. Would, forme pleine,** est obligatoire seulement à la forme interrogative et dans les réponses affirmatives courtes :
Would you go to the USA? **Yes I would.**
Iriez-vous aux USA ? Oui.

2. Should sert aussi parfois d'auxiliaire du conditionnel à la première personne du singulier et du pluriel (I, *je*; we, *nous*).

... **when he had** enough money.
... quand il aurait assez d'argent.
▷ *Les conjonctions de temps* **when**, *quand*, **while**, *pendant que, tandis que*, **as soon as**, *dès que*, **as long as**, *tant que*, **till** ou **until**, *jusqu'à ce que*, **after**, *après que*, **before**, *avant que...* sont suivies du prétérit et non du conditionnel.

N.B. : Il n'en est pas de même de **when, adverbe interrogatif :**
When **would** he come? When he **had** enough money.

B ■** Voici d'autres *phrases conditionnelles* qui servent à exprimer des hypothèses. Notez que dans ces phrases, le prétérit n'a pas une valeur de passé :

— **If I had** enough money I **could** go to the USA.
Si j'avais assez d'argent je pourrais aller aux USA.

— **I wish I had** enough money to go to the USA.
Je voudrais bien avoir assez d'argent pour aller aux USA.

— **If only I had** enough money I **would go** to the USA.
Si seulement j'avais assez d'argent j'irais aux USA.

— **It's time I went** to the USA.
Il serait temps que j'aille aux USA.

A' ■ He said **he would ('d) go** to the USA **when** he **had** enough money.

VOCABULAIRE - **Social behaviour,** *le comportement social.*

Traduisez les phrases suivantes :

1. Nous accepterions *(accept)* votre aimable invitation *(kind invitation)* si nous étions libres *(free).*

2. Je ne me lierais pas d'amitié avec *(make friends with)* cet homme-là !

3. Dès qu'il aurait davantage de temps il recevrait *(entertain)* tous ses amis intimes *(close).*

4. Il a dit qu'il nous rendrait visite *(call on)* quand il serait en meilleure santé *(health).*

5. Elle ne s'entendrait *(get along with)* jamais avec de tels voisins *(neighbour).*

6. Ils me le présenteraient *(introduce)* dès que nous nous reverrions *(see again).*

7. Vous sentiriez-vous si seule *(lonely)* si vos amis vous rendaient visite *(to visit)* un peu plus souvent ?

8. Ils sont en si mauvais termes *(be on bad terms)* que s'ils se rencontraient *(meet)* ils ne se serreraient même pas la main *(shake hands).* Ils affecteraient de ne pas se connaître *(ignore each other).*

B' ■** *Traduisez les phrases suivantes :*

1. Je souhaite qu'il vienne à notre soirée *(party).*

2. Si seulement ils étaient en bons termes *(be on good terms)* je les inviterais *(invite)* ensemble.

3. J'aimerais qu'il se mêle *(mix with)* un peu plus aux autres.

4. Il serait temps que nous les invitions à dîner *(ask to dinner).*

5. Je souhaite qu'il devienne *(become)* plus sociable *(sociable),* qu'il ne s'isole pas *(keep oneself to oneself).*

6. Il serait grand temps qu'ils cessent *(stop)* de se détester *(hate each other).*

9. Le passé récent et le futur proche

A ■* I have just got up...
Je viens de me lever...

▷ *Le passé récent*, comme les mots l'indiquent, sert à parler d'une action qui vient de s'accomplir.

Just se place entre l'auxiliaire have et le participe passé (**got up**).

Au passé, on aurait :
I **had** just got up, *je venais de me lever*.
Et à la forme interrogative :
Have you just got up? **Had** you just got up?

Rappelons que

1. Have a deux formes au présent (I, you, we, they **have** ; he, she, it **has**), une seule forme au prétérit **(had)**. Voir la conjugaison de have à partir du present perfect et du pluperfect (p. 170-171).

2. *Le participe passé des verbes réguliers* se forme en **ed** ajouté à la base verbale (work, work**ed**) [attention aux modifications orthographiques cf. p. 177] ; celui des verbes irréguliers (get, got, **got**) est à apprendre dans la troisième colonne de la liste (p. 179).

... I am going to wash, *je vais me laver*.
▷ *Le futur proche*, composé de **be going to** + base verbale (wash) indique une action qui va s'accomplir, une intention de la part de celui qui parle.

Si l'action est sur le point de s'accomplir, on emploie le *futur imminent* : be about to + base verbale :
I have just put on my coat, **I am about to go out**
Je viens de mettre mon pardessus, je suis sur le point de sortir.

Au passé, on aurait : I **was** going to wash, I **was** about to go out.

Rappelons que l'auxiliaire **be** *(être)* a trois formes au présent (I **am** ; you, we, you, they **are** ; he, she, it **is**) et deux formes au prétérit (voir la conjugaison de **be** aux différents temps, à partir de la forme continue) [p. 172].

A' ■* I have just got up. I am going to wash

VOCABULAIRE - **Daily actions**, *Actions journalières*.

En utilisant les couples de verbes suivants dites ce que vous venez de faire et ce que vous allez faire. Consultez la liste des verbes irréguliers si besoin est p. 179 :

Wash *(se laver)*, shave *(se raser)*

→ **I have just washed, I am going to shave**

1. Shave, comb one's hair *(se peigner)*.
2. Comb one's hair, dress *(s'habiller)*.
3. Dress, have breakfast *(prendre le petit déjeuner)*.
4. Have breakfast, get my things ready *(préparer mes affaires)*.
5. Get my things ready, put on my overcoat *(mettre mon pardessus)*.
6. Put on my overcoat, go out.
7. Go out, lock the door *(fermer la porte à clef)*.
8. Lock the door, rush for the bus *(se précipiter vers l'autobus)*.
9. Rush for the bus, board *(monter dans)* it.
10. Get off the bus *(descendre de l'autobus)*, enter the office *(entrer dans le bureau)*.
11. Walk out of the office *(sortir du bureau)*, get back home *(rentrer chez soi)*.
12. Get back home, have a bath *(prendre un bain)*.
13. Have a bath, have tea *(prendre le thé, le repas de 5, 6 h)*.
14. Have tea, listen to a record *(écouter un disque)*.
15. Listen to a record, read the newspaper *(lire le journal)*.
16. Read the newspaper, phone a friend *(téléphoner à un ami)*.
17. Phone a friend, watch the telly.
18. Watch the telly, take a cup of tea.
19. Take a cup of tea, undress *(se déshabiller)*.
20. Undress, put on one's pyjamas *(mettre son pyjama)*.
21. Put on one's pyjamas, clean one's teeth *(se laver les dents)*.
22. Clean one's teeth, go to bed *(aller se coucher)*.
23. Go to bed, have a little read *(lire un peu)*.
24. Have a little read, go to sleep *(s'endormir)*.
25. Switch off the light.

10. Question-tags
(hein ? non ? si ? n'est-ce pas ?)
et autres tournures elliptiques

A ■* It looks like rain, **doesn't it?** You can't see any drops yet, **can you?**

Le temps est à la pluie, n'est-ce pas ? Tu ne vois pas encore de gouttes, si ?

▷ Les question-tags sont des questions posées en fin de phrases. Tantôt ce sont de *simples demandes de confirmation* de ce qu'on dit (celui qui parle sait autant que l'autre si le temps est à la pluie ou non) ; l'intonation est alors descendante. Tantôt ce sont de *vraies questions* (celui qui parle veut savoir si l'autre voit réellement des gouttes de pluie ou non) ; dans ce deuxième cas l'intonation est montante.

— Contrairement aux tournures figées employées en français dans les mêmes situations (hein ? non ? si ? n'est-ce pas ?), les question-tags dont les Anglais usent (et abusent !) varient avec chaque phrase, sur trois plans :

1. *La négation*
Il y en a une seule au total, elle est incorporée au tag si la phrase est affirmative ou déclarative :
It **looks** like rain, does**n't** it?
You ca**n't** see any drops, **can** you?

2. *L'auxiliaire*
Il est différent selon la nature du groupe verbal (verbe ordinaire, auxiliaire modal, temps) :
It **looks** like rain, **does**n't it ?
It look**ed** like rain, **did**n't it ?
You **can't** see any drops, **can** you ?
You **couldn't** see any drops, **could** you ?

3. *Le pronom personnel*
Betty is English, isn't **she**? **John** is American, isn't **he**?

— Quelques tags particuliers : I am right, **aren't I**? *(J'ai raison, n'est-ce pas?).* He will come, **won't** he? Let's go, **shall we**? *(on y va, oui?).* **Everybody** went, didn't **they**? **There** is an Englishman in the room, isn't **there**?

A' ■* It looks like rain, **doesn't it?** You can't see any drops yet, **can you?**

VOCABULAIRE - **The weather,** *le temps qu'il fait.*

Complétez les phrases suivantes par des tags :

1. It's going to rain, …….
2. The sky *(ciel)* grows dark *(s'obscurcir)* before a storm *(orage)*, …….
3. It never snows *(neiger)* in this part of the country *(région)*, …….
4. It was getting cold *(commencer à faire froid)*, …….
5. There was a storm brewing *(se préparer)*, …….
6. It will soon *(bientôt)* clear up *(s'éclaircir)*, …….
7. It started *(commencer)* pouring *(pleuvoir à verse)*, …….
8. They would not go out on a rainy *(pluvieux)* day, …….
9. The sun *(soleil)* won't shine bright *(briller de tout son éclat)* until July, …….
10. There were not many bright intervals *(éclaircies)*, …….
11. We'll go out when the wind *(vent)* dies away *(commencer à baisser)*, …….
12. You can feel *(sentir)* the atmosphere is damp *(humide)*, …….
13. You must be soaked to the skin *(trempé jusqu'aux os)*, …….
14. I am very sensitive to cold *(frileux)*, …….
15. It will be stifling hot *(faire une chaleur accablante)* again *(à nouveau)*, …….
16. Let's go for a picnic, ……. Weather permitting *(si le temps le permet).*
17. You should not go out when it is freezing cold *(faire un froid glacial)*, …….
18. Everybody prefers sunny days *(jours de soleil)* to wet days *(jours de pluie)*, …….
19. You don't listen to the weather forecast *(bulletin météorologique)* every day, …….

B ■** It looks like rain, doesn't it? (look like rain?)

▷ Pour éviter une répétition qui serait lourde et inutile à la compréhension, on sous-entend "look like rain" : le question-tag est une tournure elliptique, c'est-à-dire une tournure dont il manque des éléments (sous-entendus). Ces derniers, exprimés à la suite d'un question-tag interro-négatif (avec **not**), **donnent une** *phrase interro-négative* :

Doesn't it look like rain?
Ne dirait-on pas qu'il va pleuvoir ?

Ces phrases interro-négatives attendent ou espèrent le plus souvent des réponses positives (comme les tags qui sont de simples demandes de confirmation (cf. p. 46). Elles ont pratiquement valeur d'affirmation. Elles servent notamment à exprimer *la surprise, l'étonnement, l'admiration;* le français emploie dans ce cas des phrases exclamatives :

Is**n't** it a glorious day? *Quelle journée splendide !*
Was**n't** that wonderful? *Ce fut merveilleux !*

C ■** *Autres tournures elliptiques courantes :*

1. correspondant à « *moi aussi* », « *toi aussi* » : **so** + auxiliaire + sujet.
   He is English **so am I**. She spoke English **so did John**.
2. correspondant à « *moi non plus* »... : **neither** (ou **nor**) + auxiliaire + sujet : I will not go to America, **neither will Peter**.
3. correspondant aux réponses courtes « *oui* », « *non* » :
   Would Alex come? **Yes, he would. No, he wouldn't.**

N.B : Aux tournures françaises figées, correspondent, comme pour les question-tags, des tournures anglaises qui varient avec chaque phrase. Il importe d'y veiller.

4. Des tournures elliptiques sont également courantes dans des phrases conditionnelles et comparatives :
   I'll come **if I can** (come), *je viendrai si je peux.*
   John can run faster **than I can** (run), *Jean court plus vite que moi.*

B' ■** It looks like rain, **doesn't it?** You can't see any drops yet, **can you?**

Mettez à la forme interro-négative:

1. It's a wonderful climate.

2. They went out although it was raining cats and dogs *(pleuvoir des cordes)*.

3. The barometer was rising *(monter)*.

4. You will stay *(rester)* at home if the roads *(routes)* are slippery *(glissante)*.

5. You could go out on a dry *(sec)* day like this.

6. We had lovely *(magnifique)* weather *(temps)*.

7. It would be too hot *(faire trop chaud)* for us.

8. The fog *(brouillard)* should lift *(se lever)* before midday *(midi)*.

9. It was a chilly *(frisquet)* day.

10. You think we'll be chilled to the bone *(transi de froid)*.

11. There will be a nice spell *(une période de beau temps)* before the end of the summer.

C' ■** *Complétez les phrases suivantes à l'aide de* **so, neither** *ou* **nor** *en utilisant les derniers éléments donnés entre parenthèses:*

1. My mother hates *(déteste)* thunder *(tonnerre)* (my sister).

2. Fog *(brouillard)* is unpleasant *(désagréable)* (black ice, *verglas*).

3. My uncle did not like sultry *(lourd)* weather (my aunt, *ma tante*).

4. You won't go out in such foul *(affreux)* weather (your friends).

5. Poor people dread *(redouter)* severe winters *(hivers rigoureux)* (old people).

6. They went out because the weather was fine (their parents).

11. Le passif

A ■* This young artist was encouraged by the local authorities...

Ce jeune artiste était encouragé par les autorités locales...

▷ Le passif, très employé en anglais, se forme comme en français : **sujet** (avec tout ce qui l'accompagne (the young artist) + **be** *(être)* aux différents temps (cf. p. 172-173) + **participe passé** (régulier en **ed** comme encourag**ed** ou irrégulier (cf. p. 179) + **by** *(par)* et complément d'agent désignant celui qui accomplit l'action (the local authorities).

Le complément d'agent introduit par **by** est fréquemment omis, en particulier s'il n'apporte qu'une précision évidente donc plus ou moins inutile ; en français on a souvent « on » dans ces cas :

English is spoken in some parts of Canada (by men and women).

On parle l'anglais dans certaines parties du Canada.

Mais on a : **The artist was encouraged by** the local authorities (not by his parents, par exemple).

— Le passif peut être associé à un auxiliaire modal (**can, may, must...**, p. 20) :

This artist must be encouraged.

Il faut encourager cet artiste.

— A l'exception des verbes de mouvement (**come from**, *venir de* ; **go to**, *aller à*...), les *verbes prépositionnels* en général (**listen to**, *écouter* ; **look at**, *regarder* ; **pay for**, *payer* ; **wait for**, *attendre*...) peuvent s'employer au passif (ce n'est pas le cas en français des verbes intransitifs à préposition, comme penser à qqn.) :

Such a concert would be listened to by thousands of fans.

Des milliers de fans écouteraient un tel concert.

— S'emploient également au passif les *verbes à particules adverbiales* (particules intégrées aux verbes dits verbes composés et qui modifient le sens du verbe de départ) :

tell, *dire, raconter* ; **tell off**, *gronder* :

John will be told off by his teacher.

Jean va être grondé par son professeur.

N.B. : Au passif, la préposition et la particule adverbiale suivent immédiatement le verbe.

A' ■* This young artist was encouraged by the local authorities. He was given a prize by the city council.

VOCABULAIRE - **The fine arts,** *les beaux arts.*

Mettez au passif les phrases suivantes. Employez le complément introduit par by seulement s'il ajoute une précision utile. Veillez aux temps:

1. Michael Angelo decorated that church *(église).*

2. They built *(construire)* lots of cathedrals in those days.

3. Everybody without exception praises *(louer)* this painter *(peintre).*

4. Real *(vrai)* connoisseurs will appreciate this type of painting *(peinture).*

5. They must look after *(soigner)* old paintings *(tableaux)* very carefully *(attentivement).*

6. People *(les gens)* thought highly of *(tenir en haute estime)* this young sculptor.

7. A foreign *(étranger)* architect designed *(faire les plans de)* our local museum.

8. Thousands of *(des milliers de)* tourists visit this art gallery *(musée de peinture)* every year *(année).*

9. The guide told the children off *(gronder)* because they were talking *(parler)* during the visit.

10. People look upon *(considérer)* this work of art *(œuvre d'art)* as a masterpiece *(chef-d'œuvre).*

11. They should devote *(consacrer)* more time to drawing *(dessin)* in schools.

12. A painter *(peintre)* uses *(utilise)* a brush *(pinceau)* and a palette.

13. They will exhibit *(exposer)* his sculptures next year *(l'année prochaine).*

14. Governments should encourage the fine arts *(les beaux arts)* much more.

15. They refer to him as a *(parler de lui comme d'un)* forerunner *(précurseur).*

B ■**

Le passif peut s'employer à la *forme progressive*. Observez les transformations :

Mr. Brown is repairing my car just now (phrase active)

My car is being repaired by Mr. Brown just now (phrase passive)

Mr. Brown répare ma voiture en ce moment même.

Le passif à la forme progressive est formé de :
forme progressive de be (is being) + participe passé (repaired).

— **The young artist was given a prize** by the city council.
   Le conseil municipal a donné un prix au jeune artiste.

▷ Les **verbes** qui peuvent être **doublement transitifs**, c'est-à-dire employés sans prépositions (give somebody something ; offer, *offrir* ; buy, *acheter* ; sell, *vendre* ; teach, *enseigner* ; tell, *dire* ; ask, *demander* ; show, *montrer* ; send, *envoyer*...) se construisent très souvent ainsi au passif : la personne à qui on donne... devient sujet de la phrase. Notez encore :

The children were taught English by a young lady.
Une jeune femme enseignait l'anglais aux enfants.

— La matière enseignée, l'objet donné... peuvent aussi être sujets de la phrase passive :

English was taught to the children by a young lady.
A prize was given to the young artist by the city council.

A ces deux possibilités au passif correspondent deux constructions à la voix active pour ces verbes qui peuvent aussi être prépositionnels (give something **to** somebody) :

The city council gave a prize **to** the young artist.
The city council gave the young artist a prize.

— Remarquez que ces verbes expriment souvent l'idée d'échange ou la notion contraire (refuse, *refuser*...) :

He was refused permission to go out.
On lui a refusé la permission de sortir.

B' ■** **This young artist was encouraged by the local authorities. He was given a prize** by the city council.

Mettez les phrases suivantes au passif progressif :

1. They are building *(construire)* a museum here.

2. They are cleaning up *(ravaler)* the column *(colonne)*.

3. Modern sculptors use new materials like plastics these days *(de nos jours)*.

4. They were setting up *(ériger)* a new statue in this square *(place)* last week *(la semaine dernière)*.

Transformez les phrases suivantes selon le modèle :

My parents bought *(acheter)* me that water-colour *(aquarelle)*.
I was bought that watercolour by my parents.

1. The government gave her a scholarship *(bourse)* to go to the art school *(école des beaux arts)*.

2. The examiners *(examinateurs)* unanimously awarded *(accorder)* the art student *(étudiant des beaux arts)* the first prize.

3. The policeman told them that the famous *(célèbre)* artist's studio *(atelier)* was not very far *(loin)* from there.

4. An old guide showed us round *(faire visiter)* the exhibition *(exposition)*.

5. A famous *(célèbre)* professor will teach *(enseigner)* him architecture.

6. My friend asked *(demander)* me if I had been to the British Museum in London.

7. My brother sent me a few sketches *(esquisses)*.

8. They offered her a job as a model; they told her she could start *(commencer)* in a week's time *(dans une semaine)*.

9. They have offered us £ 700 *(700 livres sterling)* for this picture *(tableau)*.

12. La proposition infinitive
avec expect *(s'attendre à)*,
(would) like, love *(aimer)*,
prefer *(préférer)*, want *(vouloir)*

A ■ ****I want** the pupils **to work,**
   I want **them** to work hard.
   Je veux que les élèves travaillent,
   je veux qu'ils travaillent dur.

▷ Le verbe de la proposition infinitive est à l'infinitif **(to work)**. Remarquez que si le sujet de la proposition infinitive est un pronom, celui-ci doit être à la forme complément **(them, me, him, her, us...)** [cf. p. 120].

Sont suivis de la proposition infinitive les verbes suivants : **want, like** et **love** (surtout avec would), **prefer** *(préférer)*, **hate** *(détester)*, **expect** *(s'attendre à)*, **wish** *(souhaiter)*... Ce sont des verbes qui expriment une volonté, un ordre, un désir... qu'on impose à quelqu'un d'autre.

— La proposition infinitive est dans certains cas introduite par **for** :

  1. après **wait** *(attendre)* :
     John is waiting for them to come.
     Jean attend qu'ils viennent.

  2. après **enough** *(assez)* et **too** *(trop)* :
     It was too late for them to do it.
     Il était trop tard pour qu'ils le fassent.

  3. après **certains adjectifs** ou **certains noms** (hard, *dur,* difficult, *difficile,* impossible, important, vital, [un]necessary...) :
     It's **vital** for him to arrive on time.
     Il est vital qu'il arrive à l'heure.

— On a aussi des propositions infinitives avec un *infinitif négatif* ; remarquez la place de **not** :
  I prefer him **not to** do it at once.
  Je préfère qu'il ne le fasse pas tout de suite.

A' ■** I **want** the pupils **to work**,
I want **them** to work hard.

VOCABULAIRE - **At school**, *à l'école*.

Traduisez les phrases suivantes:

1. Le professeur *(teacher)* voulait qu'ils se taisent *(keep quiet)*.

2. Elle aimerait que nous fassions des progrès *(make progress)*.

3. Le professeur s'attend-il à ce que je lise *(read)* tous ces livres? *(book)*.

4. J'entends *(expect)* que vous appreniez *(learn)* ce poème *(poem)* par cœur *(by heart)*.

5. Je déteste que les élèves répondent à mes questions *(answer questions)* tous ensemble. Je veux qu'ils lèvent le doigt *(put up one's hand)*.

6. Il est vital qu'il ne se surmène pas *(overwork oneself)*.

7. Il a commencé à travailler mais c'est trop tard pour qu'il réussisse à son examen *(pass one's exam)*.

8. Veux-tu que je t'aide *(help)* à faire ton devoir? *(do homework)*. Oui j'aimerais que tu m'aides à traduire ce passage en anglais *(translate into English)*.

9. Je m'attendais à ce qu'ils fassent cette faute *(make a mistake)* dans la dictée *(dictation)*.

10. Il voulait que nous ne nous écartions pas du sujet *(wander from the subject)*.

11. Il est important qu'elle apprenne *(learn)* deux langues étrangères *(foreign language)*.

12. Il préfère que nous ne traduisions pas mot à mot *(translate word for word)*.

13. L'expression des penchants naturels, des habitudes : will, would

A ■** When the cat is away the mice **will** play.
Quand le chat n'est pas là, les souris dansent.

▷ Il en est ainsi et il en sera toujours ainsi ; c'est dans la nature des choses. Plus qu'une habitude, **will** exprime une *tendance naturelle* (parfois impérieuse) chez les êtres, un *comportement prévisible*, caractéristique de ceux-ci. S'agissant des événements, **will** exprime une *vérité à caractère inévitable ou éternel* :

People **will** die on the roads every weekend.
Des gens meurent sur les routes chaque week-end.

N.B. : **Will** (forme pleine seulement) ne s'emploie dans ce sens que dans les phrases déclaratives (ou affirmatives). Il ne faut pas confondre ce will avec le will du futur (p. 38). **Will** a ici une *valeur de présent*.

— **Would**, avec une *valeur de passé*, a le même sens que **will** ; il est alors *accentué* dans la phrase :

He **would** read his paper every morning.
Il fallait (à tout prix) qu'il lise son journal chaque matin.

I have lost my key. — You **would**!
J'ai perdu ma clef. — Il fallait s'y attendre (de ta part).

— *Non accentué*, **would** exprime une *action répétée dans le passé* (surtout en anglais écrit, en forme pleine) :

He **would** read every morning, he **would** walk every afternoon.
Il lisait tous les matins, il marchait tous les après-midi.

N.B. : **Would**, dans ces deux sens, ne doit pas se confondre avec le **would** du conditionnel (p. 42).

A' ■** When the cat is away the mice will play.

VOCABULAIRE - **Parents and children,** *parents et enfants.*

Traduisez les phrases suivantes en utilisant **will** *ou* **would.**
La traduction des adverbes de fréquence est superflue :

1. Les parents répètent *(repeat)* toujours les mêmes choses à leurs enfants *(children)*.

2. Comme disait *(say)* souvent mon père : « Les enfants *(boy)* sont toujours les enfants *(boy)*. »

3. Les mêmes questions *(subject)* revenaient *(crop up)* toujours entre mon père et mon frère.

4. Ma mère insiste pour que nous rentrions *(come back home)* à l'heure *(in time)* pour les repas *(meal)*.

5. Ce père critique *(criticize)* toujours tout ce que *(whatever)* fait *(do)* son fils *(son)*.

6. Il se levait *(get up)* toujours tard *(late)*.

7. Il n'éteignait *(switch off)* jamais les lumières *(light)*, ce qui agaçait *(annoy)* sa mère.

8. « Il passe *(spend)* des heures *(hour)* à lire *(read)*, au lieu de *(instead of)* faire ses devoirs *(do one's homework)* », répétait toujours sa mère.

9. Les parents donnent *(give)* toujours des conseils *(advice)* à leurs enfants qui, de toute façon *(in any case)* agissent à leur guise *(have their own way)*.

10. « Elle se comporte *(behave)* de façon idiote *(foolishly)*. Elle n'y peut rien *(she can't help it)* », répétaient toujours ses parents.

11. Leur fille *(daughter)* rentre toujours en retard *(late)*, quoi qu'en *(whatever)* disent les parents.

14. Le passé révolu :
used to

A ■** When grandfather was young he **used to smoke** twenty cigarettes a day
(quand grand-père était jeune, il fumait vingt cigarettes par jour).

▷ **used to**, employé à toutes les personnes, sert à exprimer la rupture entre le passé et le présent, à opposer ce qui était vrai autrefois à ce qui ne l'est plus maintenant (ce grand-père n'est plus jeune et ne fume plus vingt cigarettes par jour).

— **Used to** est assez souvent employé avec un adverbe ou une locution adverbiale qui exprime la répétition :
When grandfather was young he used to go fishing every Sunday.
Quand grand-père était jeune il allait à la pêche tous les dimanches.

— Aux *formes interrogative et négative*, on a :

Did grandfather **use**(d) **to** go fishing?
Grandfather **didn't use**(d) **to** go fishing.

— Ne pas confondre **used to** (qui est toujours au passé) avec **be used to** suivi d'un *gérondif* (en ing, p. 148) ou d'un *nom*, conjugué à tous les temps :

He is used to doing it, *il a l'habitude de le faire.*
You'll soon **be used to** the climate, *vous vous habituerez vite au climat.*

N.B. : Il y a aussi le verbe **use** (prétérit **used**), verbe transitif (sans préposition) qui signifie se servir de, utiliser :

I used a dictionary to do that translation.
Je me suis servi d'un dictionnaire pour faire cette traduction.

A' ■** When grandfather was young he **used to smoke** twenty cigarettes a day

VOCABULAIRE - **Young men's activities,** *les activités des jeunes gens.*

Utilisez **used to** *avec les verbes soulignés dans les phrases suivantes (cf. liste des verbes irréguliers p. 179) :*

1. When he was a young man he **had** quite a few girlfriends.

2. You **went** out quite a lot *(beaucoup)* in those days *(en ce temps-là).*

3. They **went** dancing every Saturday night.

4. I have changed now but I **was** an idealist.

5. He **collected** stamps at the time *(à l'époque).*

6. You **cycled** *(faire de la bicyclette)* a lot when you were in your teens *(entre 13 et 19 ans).*

7. He **went** to the cinema quite often.

8. I **sang** *(chanter)* in the choir *(chorale)* every Sunday.

9. He **did** a lot of sports; he **practised** tennis, badminton...

10. They **worked** hard *(travailler)* at their studies *(études).*

11. John **had** a terrific *(formidable)* energy.

12. We **spent** hours *(passer des heures)* with our friends at the pub.

13. Peter **read** *(lire)* like mad *(comme un fou).*

14. Jack and I **went** to the youth club *(foyer de jeunes)* regularly.

15. We **played** golf in Scotland every summer *(été).*

16. He **discussed** politics with passion, he **was** a militant at one time *(à une certaine époque).*

17. We **went** to discos *(discothèques)*, we **loved** dancing.

15. Les verbes de perception :
see *(voir)*, hear *(entendre)*, feel *(sentir)*

A ■* I could **see** him walk**ing** down the street. It was
six o'clock.

Je le voyais marcher le long de la rue. Il était six heures.

▷ Les verbes de perception, **see** *(voir)*, **hear** *(entendre)*, **feel**
(sentir)... employés souvent avec can (qui ne se traduit pas),
peu utilisés à la forme continue ou progressive, sont *suivis du
participe présent : verbe + ing (walking)* quand l'action (walk)
implique une certaine durée et qu'on a affaire à une situation
particulière (qui se déroule sous nos yeux, à un moment
précis).

Si l'action n'est pas nécessairement en cours au moment où
l'on parle (on attire seulement l'attention sur la notion de
« marcher ») ou si elle est *brève*, on emploie la *base verbale
(walk)* :

I (can) see him **walk** down the street every evening.
Je le vois descendre la rue tous les soirs.

I heard her **fall** off her bicycle (action brève).
Je l'ai entendue tomber de sa bicyclette.

N.B. :

1. On ne trouve donc en aucun cas l'infinitif **(to walk)** avec les
verbes de perception, au moins à la forme active.

2. **Look at** *(regarder)*, **listen to** *(écouter)* admettent une seule
construction : **verbe + ing** ; at et to ne s'emploient que s'il y
a un complément :
Look! Look **at** him! Look at him runn**ing** across the field.
*Regardez ! Regardez-le ! Regardez-le traverser le champ en
courant.*

A' ■* I could **see** him walk**ing** down the street.

VOCABULAIRE - **Bodily activity, movement,** *l'activité physique, le mouvement.*

Complétez les phrases suivantes en utilisant les verbes entre parenthèses :

1. Did you see the baby ......? (go on all fours, *marcher à quatre pattes*).

2. We could hear the old man ...... (shuffle along, *traîner les pieds*).

3. Did you see the hare *(lièvre)* ......? (jump off, *partir d'un bond*).

4. Look at him ...... along the street (stride, *marcher à grandes enjambées*).

5. You often see little old women ...... across the street. How dangerous! (take short steps, *marcher à petits pas*).

6. We could hear the rain *(pluie)* ...... (fall, *tomber*).

7. Did you hear him ......? (fall off the ladder, *tomber de l'échelle*).

8. I could feel the insect ...... (run on my hand).

9. We saw the thief *(voleur)* ...... (steal into the room and disappear in no time, *entrer furtivement dans la pièce et disparaître en un rien de temps*).

10. Watch *(observer)* him ...... (reel like a drunken man, *tituber comme un homme ivre*).

11. You should have seen her ...... when she heard the news *(nouvelle)* (leap from her chair, *bondir de sa chaise*).

12. It makes me laugh *(rire)* to see people ...... (slip on a banana skin, *glisser sur une peau de banane*).

13. I saw her ...... (lean out of the window), ... (fling an object, *jeter violemment un objet*) and ...... (rush out of the room, *se précipiter hors de la pièce*). It did not take long!

14. Look at John ...... (bend, *se pencher*) over his bicycle and ...... (try to repair it, *essayer de la réparer*).

16. Make, let, etc., suivis de la base verbale (infinitif sans to)

A ■* I **make** them **work,**
I don't **let** them **talk**...
Je les fais travailler, je ne les laisse pas parler.

▷ **make** dans le sens de faire agir quelqu'un d'autre (« faire faire »), **let** (laisser, permettre) sont suivis de la base verbale ou infinitif incomplet, **sans to** (work, talk).

Il en est de même de **had better, had rather** et des auxiliaires modaux **can, may, must** (p. 20) :
I had better **work** but I had rather **play.**
Je ferais mieux de travailler mais j'aimerais mieux jouer.

Par contre **like** *(aimer)*, **love** *(adorer)*, **prefer** *(préférer)*, **want** *(vouloir)* ne sont jamais suivis de la simple base verbale :
I like (love, prefer) to work/working.
I want to work (seule possibilité).

— **Make**, dans le même sens, a pour équivalents :

● **have**, avec une structure active ou passive :
I'll have him **paint** the kitchen.
I'll have the kitchen **painted** (by him).
Je lui ferai peindre la cuisine.

● **get** suivi de l'infinitif complet **avec to** :
I'll get him **to** paint the kitchen *(je l'en persuaderai)*.

— **Let** est également suivi de la base verbale quand il sert d'auxiliaire *à l'impératif.* Ceci est le cas à toutes les personnes sauf à la deuxième :
Let him do it (qu'il le fasse) ≠ Don't **let** him do it *(qu'il ne le fasse pas).*

A la première personne du pluriel (nous) **let's** est plus courant que **let us** :
Let's go (let us go), *allons* ≠ don't **let's** go (familier), *n'allons pas,* **let's** not go (plus recherché).

A la deuxième personne (vous, tu), on a :
Come *(venez, viens)* ≠ don't **come** *(ne venez pas, ne viens pas).*

A' ■* I **make** them **work**,
I don't **let** them **talk** and **do** nothing.

VOCABULAIRE - **Do-it-yourself**, *le bricolage*.

Complétez si besoin est. Utilisez éventuellement le verbe entre parenthèses :

1. He is no handy man *(bricoleur)*. You won't ...... him ...... drive in a nail! *(enfoncer un clou)*. He had rather ...... read a book than ...... mend a cupboard *(réparer un placard)*.

2. Don't ...... the baby ...... play with the hammer *(marteau)*.

3. She had the living-room ...... by the painters (decorate, *peindre, tapisser*).

4. You had better ...... a new screwdriver *(tournevis)* (buy, *acheter*).

5. You must take your time unless *(à moins que ...ne)* you want ...... burgle it *(tout bousiller)*.

6. I don't want ...... watch T.V. this afternoon, I would prefer ...... tinker about the house *(bricoler autour de la maison)*.

7. I had the lawn mower *(tondeuse à gazon)* ...... in case you wanted ...... mow the lawn *(tondre le gazon)* (repair).

8. She made me ...... fix some shelves *(poser des étagères)*, she wanted ...... do some tidying up *(faire du rangement)*.

9. We had all the plugs *(prises)* ...... (change), we preferred ...... *(prendre toutes les précautions)* be on the safe side.

10. I'll have him ...... do some odd jobs *(faire quelques bricolages)* about the house. I won't ...... him stay *(rester)* there doing nothing.

11. We need *(avoir besoin de)* some screws *(vis)*, ... go to the do-it-yourself department *(rayon bricolage)*, ... see if they have what we need.

12. ...... me give you a hand *(donner un coup de main)* with the gardening *(jardinage)*, I want ...... be useful *(utile)*.

17. Passage du style direct au style indirect

A ■** He said to me: "**I will** come with **my** friend **tomorrow**". → He told me **(that) he would** come with **his** friend **the following day**.

▷ Le passage du style direct (avec les guillemets) au style indirect (qui sert à rapporter ce qui a été dit ou écrit) entraîne diverses transformations, entre autres, dans le cas présent :

1. *l'introduction de* **that**, *que,* très souvent omis, notamment en anglais parlé.
2. *un changement de pronoms* (**I → he**) et de possessifs (**my → his**).
3. *le passage d'un temps à un autre,* ici du futur (**will**) au conditionnel (**would**).
4. *un changement dans le complément de temps :* tomorrow → the following (next) day, *le lendemain* (yesterday → the day before, *la veille,* etc.)

    Autres changements de temps usuels (concordance des temps) :

    a) "I **go** every day" → he said to me, he told me he **went**... : présent → prétérit (p. 32-34).

    b) "I **saw** her" → he said to me, he told me he **had seen**... : prétérit → pluperfect (p. 34).

    c) "I **have seen** her" → he said to me, he told me he **had seen**... : present perfect (p. 32-34) → pluperfect (p. 34).

    N.B. Cette concordance des temps s'applique aussi à la forme progressive (p. 28).

Le passage du style direct au style indirect peut entraîner *aussi les modifications suivantes* :

1. "**Do you like it?**": he asked me → he asked me **if I liked it**:
    — phrase interrogative (**do you like?**) → phrase affirmative (**I liked**) ;
    — introduction de **if**, *si*, ou **whether** et suppression des guillemets.
2. "**Come, please**" he said to me → he told me **to come**.
    Impératif (ordre, requête) → infinitif complet avec **to** (**to come**).
    He said to me "**Don't come**" → he told me **not to come**.
    Impératif négatif (défense, interdiction) → infinitif négatif (**not to come**).

A' ■** He said to me: **"I will** come with **my** friend **tomorrow"** → He told me **(that) he would** come with **his** friend **the following day.**

VOCABULAIRE - **A road accident,** *un accident de la route.*

Mettez les phrases suivantes au style indirect :

1. "I'll note down *(noter)* your car number *(numéro d'immatriculation)*" he said to me.
2. "Did your car come from the right?" *(la droite)* the policeman asked *(demander)* him.
3. "You'll have a car accident, driving *(conduire)* so fast" *(vite)* she told me.
4. "Is there any witness?" *(témoin)* the policeman asked.
5. "You have knocked in *(enfoncer)* my wing *(aile)*" he said to me.
6. "Did you use *(utiliser)* your brakes?" *(freins)* she asked him.
7. "Pull over *(se ranger)* to the side *(côté)* of the road *(route)*" he said to the lorry driver *(chauffeur de camion)*.
8. "You are in the wrong *(dans votre tort)*" he told us.
9. He said to me "You jumped the lights!" *(brûler le feu)*.
10. He said to the other driver "We'll find *(trouver)* the cheapest way *(le moyen le moins onéreux)* to settle this" *(régler)*.
11. "Don't get excited like that!" the traffic warden *(contractuel [le])* said to the cyclist.
12. "You came from the left" *(la gauche)*, the policewoman said to the cyclist.
13. "There was a terrible clash" *(collision)* he said.
14. "The responsibility is yours" the insurance agent said to us.
15. He said to her: "It will cost *(coûter)* you a fortune to put it right!" *(redresser l'aile..., etc.)*.
16. "Did you have the right of way?" *(la priorité)* the policeman asked the motorist *(automobiliste)*.
17. "I have a clean record" *(n'avoir jamais eu de contravention)* he said proudly *(fièrement)*.
18. "You have made a mess *(bousiller)* of my bumper *(pare-chocs)*" he said to me.

18. L'article indéfini a, an

A ■* Mr. Brown is **a** cook. What **a** good cook! I have never had such **an** excellent meal!

L'article indéfini a deux formes :
— **a** + consonne : **a b**ottle of whisky
— **a** + u prononcé [ju:] : **a u**niversity
— **an** + voyelle : **an e**normous piece of cheese *(fromage)*
— **an** + h muet en début de mot (très rare) : **an h**our *(une heure)*, **an h**onourable man, **an h**onest woman.

a, an s'emploie devant un nom *comptable* ou *dénombrable* (désignant ce qui peut se compter), concret, singulier.
Comparez :
I eat **a** big piece of cheese every day. I love Ø cheese.
He is **a** patient man. He never loses Ø patience *(il ne perd jamais patience).*

B ■** Mr. Brown is **a** cook. *Mr. Brown est Ø cuisinier*

▷ L'article indéfini **a, an** s'emploie devant un *nom attribut*.

Il en est de même avec un *nom en apposition* :
Mr. Davies, **a** grocer in Cardiff, sells very good pickles.
Mr. Davies, Ø épicier à Cardiff, vend de très bonnes conserves au vinaigre.

— **What a** good cook! *Quel Ø bon cuisinier !*
I have never had **such an** excellent meal!
Je n'ai jamais mangé un si bon repas !

▷ **What** (exclamatif), **such** + **a, an** + nom comptable ou dénombrable, concret, singulier.

Exceptions : What **a** pity! *(quel dommage !)* What **a** relief! *(quel soulagement !)* What **a** shame! *(quel dommage !)* : notions abstraites, noms indénombrables ou non comptables.

— I can't cook a meal **without a** gas cooker or **without an** electric cooker! *(Je ne peux pas faire un repas sans Ø cuisinière à gaz ou sans Ø cuisinière électrique !)*

▷ **Without** (aussi **with**) + **a, an** + nom dénombrable, concret, singulier.

A' ■ Mr. Brown is **a** cook. What **a** good cook! I have never had such **an** excellent meal!

VOCABULAIRE - **Food**, *la nourriture.*

Complétez par l'article indéfini a, an, *si nécessaire:*

1. ...... vegetarian never eats ...... meat *(viande)*.
2. Drink ...... cup of tea, ... tea will do you good.
3. He is ...... admirable man. He is full of ...... energy.
4. Buy ...... greens *(légumes verts)* not ...... frozen foods *(surgelés)*.
5. I'll just have ...... piece of toast, ... toast is all right.
6. The English people prefer ...... tea to ...... coffee.
7. You should eat ...... vegetables *(légumes)* not ...... sweets *(desserts)*.
8. I had ...... mutton chop *(côtelette)* for lunch. I like ...... mutton, I prefer it to ...... pork *(du porc)*.
9. Take ...... umbrella *(parapluie)*, it's going to rain.
10. I wouldn't say he's ...... humble man. I wouldn't call *(appeler)* that ...... humility!

B' ■** *Complétez par l'article indéfini* a, an *si nécessaire:*

1. I couldn't do without *(je ne pourrais me passer de)* ...... mustard *(moutarde)*.
2. What ...... delicious meal! *(repas)*.
3. That was such ...... good marmalade! *(confiture d'oranges)*.
4. Monsieur Dupont, ... French chef *(chef cuisinier)* is very popular in our town.
5. What ...... shame you can't eat such ...... wonderful kippers! *(harengs fumés)*.
6. Mrs. Jones is ...... grocer *(épicier)*, not ...... butcher.
7. What ...... big piece of cake! *(gâteau)*.
8. It's such ...... pity you can't touch such ...... delicious jam! *(confiture)*.
9. You'll have to do without ...... crackers *(biscuits salés)*.
10. He always has his coffee without ...... sugar *(sucre)* and without ...... milk *(lait)*.
11. What ...... bad luck! *(malchance)*. The steak is overdone *(trop cuit)* again!
12. He is ...... teetotaller (He never drinks ...... alcohol).

C ■**

— Remarquez la place de **a, an** quand un adjectif est précédé de **as** (*aussi... que*, as... as), **so** (*tant, tellement, si*), **too** (*trop*).

It's too big **a** meal (*c'est un trop gros repas*).

Notez l'emploi de **a, an**, dans ces expressions :

● The shopkeeper (*commerçant*) works twelve hours **a** day (*par jour*).

That cider costs £ 1 **a** bottle (*1 livre sterling la bouteille*).

Sixty miles **an** hour (*60 miles à l'heure*).

— Distinguez **a, an** de **one**, nombre cardinal :

I have **a** brother who keeps a delicatessen (*épicerie fine*).
I have **one** brother not two!

— Traduction de **· en tant que, en qualité de ·** :

I know him **as a** shopkeeper, that is all.
As + a, an + nom dénombrable, singulier.

— Notez l'emploi et la position de **a, an** dans : a quarter of **an** hour (*un quart d'heure*), Ø half **an** hour (*une demi-heure*), an hour and **a** half (*une heure et demie*).

— **An** est attaché à **other** dans **another** (*un autre*).

C' ■** Mr. Brown is **a** cook. What **a** good cook! I have never had such **an** excellent meal!

Traduisez :

1. Il boit deux pintes *(pint)* de lait par jour.

2. Il y a une seule épicerie fine dans notre petite ville.

3. Le boulanger *(baker)* passe *(come)* deux fois *(twice)* par semaine *(week)*.

4. Le connaissez-vous en tant qu'homme ou seulement en tant que commerçant *(shopkeeper)*?

5. Je reviendrai un autre jour.

6. Combien est-ce ? Trente francs le litre.

7. Il lui a fallu un quart d'heure pour le faire. Non pas une demi-heure.

8. Sois raisonnable *(reasonable)*, prends un verre de cognac *(brandy)* pas deux !

9. C'est une bière trop forte pour moi.

10. Ce marchand de vins *(wine-merchant)* vend plus de *(over)* cent bouteilles de whisky par mois.

19. L'article défini the

A ■* ... The big cities I visited were fascinating.

▷ **The** article défini *(le, la, les)* a *une seule forme*.

Il peut précéder n'importe quel type de nom (de personnes, d'animaux, de choses) concret ou abstrait, singulier ou pluriel : the boy(s), the girl(s), the cat(s), the horse(s).

— **The** *se prononce de deux manières :*

[ðə] devant une consonne : the burglar *(le cambrioleur)*, the dormitory town *(la ville dortoir)*.

[ði] devant une voyelle (a, e, i, o, u, y) et devant l'h initial non aspiré des mots hour *(heure)*, honest *(honnête)*, honour *(honneur)*, heir *(héritier)*... et de leurs dérivés : the outskirts *(les quartiers périphériques)*, the honest man, the heiress *(l'héritière)*.

B ■** I like Ø big cities in general.
The big cities I visited were fascinating.

L'article défini **the** ne s'emploie pas quand on exprime une *généralité* ; il s'emploie quand une précision est apportée :

a) par un *relatif* sous-entendu (**which** ou **that, whom**) ou exprimé : dans la 2ᵉ phrase il ne s'agit plus des grandes villes en général mais de « celles que j'ai visitées » ;

b) par un *complément de nom* introduit par une préposition (**of, with, in...**) : **The** United States of America ;

c) par le fait que l'objet désigné est unique en son espèce : **the sun** *(le soleil)*, **the** moon *(la lune)*, **the wind** *(le vent)* ;

d) par le *contexte* : "**The** children have been unbearable" said Mrs. Brown to her husband as he came back from work.
« *Les enfants ont été insupportables* », *dit Mrs. Brown à son mari alors qu'il rentrait du travail.*
(Il est évident que Mrs. Brown parle de ses enfants et non pas des enfants en général.)

A' ■* I like **0** big cities in general.
   The big cities I visited were fascinating.

VOCABULAIRE - **Life in a big town,** *la vie dans une grande ville.*

*Complétez les phrases suivantes à l'aide de l'article défini.
Lisez-les à haute voix en vous rappelant que la prononciation
de* **the** *est liée au mot qui le suit :*

1. ...... council flats *(H.L.M.)* were not very comfortable.
2. He lives near ...... industrial estate *(zone industrielle).*
3. ...... townplanner *(urbaniste)* was speaking about green areas *(espaces verts).*
4. They live in ...... blind alley *(impasse).*
5. He is no longer *(ne... plus)* ...... honorable man he used to be.
6. ...... ringroad *(boulevard périphérique)* is always crowded *(encombré).*
7. ...... garden city *(cité jardin)* is very pleasant to live in.
8. We listened to ...... hourly news bulletin *(bulletin de nouvelles)* during ...... war *(guerre).*

B' ■**

Ajoutez l'article défini si nécessaire :

1. ...... shopwindows *(devantures)* are full of toys *(jouets)* at Christmas time.
2. ...... districts we visited were full of semi-detached houses *(maisons jumelles).*
3. We could hardly *(à peine)* see ...... sun for *(à cause de)* ...... highrises *(tours d'habitation)* in that American city.
4. ...... people sit and relax *(se détendent)* in ...... public gardens of the town.
5. ...... pedestrians should use ...... pedestrian crossings.
6. Always be very careful *(prudent)* at ...... crossroads *(carrefour)*, ... car-drivers tend to ignore ...... traffic-lights *(feux de signalisation).*
7. ...... housing estates *(lotissements)* I was telling you about are located in ...... suburbs *(faubourgs)* of our town.
8. Oh please, John, tell ...... kids *(gosses)* to be quiet *(se taire).*

C ■**

Quelques emplois particuliers :

a) Adjectifs convertis en noms (**the rich, the poor**...) [p. 110] :
bien qu'ils désignent une généralité, l'ensemble d'une
catégorie, ils sont **précédés de the**.

b) Noms propres précédés d'un titre ou d'une appellation
familière : **Ø President George Bush, Old Smith** *(le père
Smith, le vieux Smith)*, **Ø Little John** *(le petit Jean)*.

c) Noms de repas pris dans leur sens général :
Ø Breakfast is my favourite meal.

d) Noms désignant des institutions et non pas tel établissement
particulier : **schoolboys go to Ø school, students go to Ø
university / Some people go to Ø church** *(église)* **on Sundays
/ When you are dangerously ill** *(malade)* **you go to Ø
hospital**.

e) Noms d'instruments de musique : **I don't play the oboe**
(hautbois) **but the clarinet**.

f) Noms de pays singulier : sans article pour la plupart : **Ø
Germany, Ø Italy, Ø France**...

g) Expressions de temps avec next *(prochain)* et last *(dernier)* :
Come Ø next week / He arrived Ø last month.

h) Ne pas confondre la langue avec ceux qui la parlent : **The
English speak Ø English. The French speak Ø French**.

C' ■** I like **∅** big cities in general.
The big cities I visited were fascinating.

Traduisez les phrases suivantes :

1. Un homme assis sur le trottoir *(pavement)* jouait de l'accordéon *(accordion)*.

2. Edimbourg *(Edinburgh)* est la capitale de l'Écosse *(Scotland)*.

3. Les jeunes doivent aller à l'école jusqu'à l'âge de seize ans.

4. Le prince Charles est venu en France le mois dernier.

5. Les Français pensent que le russe *(Russian)* est une langue difficile.

6. Que pensez-vous du petit déjeuner anglais ?

7. Où irez-vous l'année prochaine *(next)* ? Je visiterai la Pologne *(Poland)*.

8. Les vieilles *(elderly)* personnes refusent souvent d'aller à l'hôpital.

9. J'ai pitié *(to pity)* des pauvres et je n'envie pas les riches *(to envy)*.

10. Le président Roosevelt était assez populaire auprès *(popular with)* des Français, je crois.

11. Quelle langue préférez-vous, l'allemand ou l'espagnol ?

12. Les aveugles sont souvent musiciens *(musical)*.

20. Les démonstratifs this et that

A ■* Take **this** plate (here) not **that one** (there).
Prenez cette assiette-ci, pas celle-là.

▷ En principe, on emploie **this** quand l'objet est plus *rapproché*, **that** quand il est plus *éloigné*. Cette distinction est peut-être plus nette dans le domaine du temps (I am not going to London **this** week. I didn't go to London **that** week). En fait **this** et **that** servent souvent à *contraster deux éléments en présence* (sans qu'il y ait toujours notion d'éloignement).

— Les démonstratifs **this** et **that** s'accordent en nombre mais pas en genre ; le pluriel de **this** est **these**, celui de **that** est **those** :
Take **these** plates not **those** plates.

— **This** (**these**), **that** (**those**) s'emploient comme *adjectifs* (avec un nom) ou seuls, comme *pronoms* :
Give me **these** knives not **those**.
Donnez-moi ces couteaux-ci, pas ceux-là.

Ils s'emploient aussi *avec one(s)* pour éviter la répétition d'un nom déjà exprimé :
Take **this** plate, not **that one**.
Which fork *(fourchette)* do you want? **This one** or **that one**?

— En tant que pronoms, this (these), that (those) servent à *présenter choses et gens* :
This *(ceci)* is a fork, **that** *(cela)* is a spoon *(cuiller)*.
This is Mr. Jones — Delighted to meet you.
Je vous présente Mr. Jones — Enchanté de faire votre connaissance.

A' ■ Take **this** plate (here) not **that one** (there).

VOCABULAIRE - **At table,** *à table.* **The cutlery,** *les couverts.*

Complétez les phrases suivantes par **this, that, these** *ou* **those** :

1. Take ...... knives *(couteaux)*, not ....

2. Put ...... serviette *(serviette de table)* in the serviette-ring *(rond de serviette).*

3. ...... is a soup-plate *(assiette creuse)*, ... is a dinner-plate *(assiette plate).*

4. Will you put ...... tablecloth *(nappe)* in ...... sideboard *(buffet)* over there *(là-bas).*

5. ...... is Mr. Law. Very pleased to meet you *(très heureux de faire votre connaissance).*

6. Can you pass me ...... dishes *(plats)* over there?

7. Come and get ...... teaspoons *(cuillers à café)*, put them in ...... drawer *(tiroir)* over there.

8. I'll never forget ...... days in the USA in 1950.

9. What's ...... here? And what's ......?

10. Come and wash ...... cups and saucers *(soucoupes).*

11. Do you remember ...... glasses they gave us as a wedding present? *(cadeau de mariage).*

12. Which glass is yours? ...... or ......? It's ...... over there.

13. ...... is a teapot *(théière)*, ... is a coffee-pot.

14. I can't forget ...... terrible day we spent in ...... storm *(orage)* years ago.

21. Les quantificateurs some, any, no

A ■* Is there **any** milk in the fridge?
Yes there is **some** (milk). No there is**n't any**
(milk). No, no, there is **no** milk.

Les quantificateurs **some, any, no** servent à exprimer une
quantité *indéterminée*. Ils s'emploient devant des noms singuliers *indénombrables* (désignant les choses vues globalement,
ce qui ne peut se compter, du lait, du sucre...) *et* devant des
noms *dénombrables* pluriels (des litres de lait, des morceaux
de sucre...).

— Is there **any** milk in the fridge? Is there **any** (milk)?
(Y a-t-il du lait dans le réfrigérateur ? Y en a-t-il ?)

▷ **Any** s'emploie dans des phrases *interrogatives*.

— Yes there is **some** (milk).

▷ **Some** s'emploie dans des phrases *affirmatives* ou *déclaratives*.

— No there is**n't any** (milk). No, there's **no** milk.

→ Dans les phrases *négatives* on a **not... any**, ou **no** si on
veut insister (le verbe est alors à la forme affirmative
puisqu'on ne peut avoir deux négations en anglais).

N.B. : Des mots déjà employés (milk) sont *souvent sous-
entendus* après some et any. Par contre no est nécessairement
suivi d'un nom. On a :

There are **no sweets** *(il n'y a pas de bonbons)*
ou There are **none** *(il n'y en a pas, il n'y en a aucun)*.

A' ■* Is there **any** milk in the fridge?
   Yes there is **some** (milk). No there isn't **any**
   (milk). No, no, there is **no** milk.

VOCABULAIRE - **Food,** *la nourriture.*

Complétez par **some, any** *ou* **no** :

1. Is there ...... water in the jug? *(carafe).* No there isn't ......

2. He bought ...... sausages *(saucisses)* at the butcher's.

3. Let's have ...... porridge *(bouillie d'avoine)* for breakfast.

4. He didn't have ...... cereals *(flocons de céréales)* this
   morning. Did you have ...... ?

5. Drink ...... orange juice, it'll do you good *(faire du bien).*

6. There were ...... eggs *(œufs)* in the fridge, ... at all
   (absolument aucun).

7. Have ...... cream *(crème)* with your coffee.

8. She didn't have ...... soup, she never has ......
   N.B. : never, *ne... jamais,* est une négation.

9. He always eats ...... fruit at the end of the meal *(repas).*

10. ...... sweets for you! You are too greedy! *(gourmand).*
    Leave ...... for your brother!

11. There wasn't ...... tea in the teapot *(théière).*

12. You may drink ...... whisky but not too much. So the doctor
    said *(c'est ce qu'a dit le docteur).*

B ■**

— **Some** *s'emploie aussi :*

a) dans une question dont on attend une réponse affirmative : May I have **some** salt? *Puis-je avoir du sel ?*

b) dans une question qui a valeur d'affirmation ; par exemple quand on propose quelque chose à quelqu'un ou quand on lui donne un ordre :

Would you like **some** chips? *Voulez-vous des frites ?*

Could you bring me **some** butter?
Pourriez-vous m'apporter du beurre ?

— **Any** *s'emploie aussi :*

a) dans une phrase affirmative dans le sens de « *n'importe* » :

Any child knows that. *N'importe quel enfant sait cela.*

b) avec **if** *(si)* pour exprimer une supposition, un doute :

If you have **any** spare fish, just tell us.
S'il vous reste du poisson, dites-le-nous.

C ■**

— **Some, any, no** peuvent se combiner à :

a) **more** pour exprimer une quantité supplémentaire indéterminée :

I'd like **some more** ham please.
J'aimerais encore du jambon, s'il vous plaît.

Sorry you can't have **any more**.
Désolé, vous ne pouvez pas en avoir d'autre.

b) **left** (participe passé de leave, laisser) pour dire ce qu'il vous reste sans préciser la quantité ou le nombre :

Have you got **any** potatoes **left**? Yes I've **some left**.
Vous reste-t-il des pommes de terre ? Oui il m'en reste.

— **Some, any, no** ont des composés : **somebody** ou **someone** *(quelqu'un)*, **something** *(quelque chose)*, **somewhere** *(quelque part)* : Do you know **anybody** here? No I don't know **anybody**. I know absolutely **nobody**.

B' ■** Is there **any** milk in the fridge?
   Yes there is **some** (milk). No there isn't **any**
   (milk). No, no, there is **no** milk.

Complétez les phrases suivantes:

1. Can you buy ...... pepper *(poivre)*?

2. ...... doctor will tell you that you that must drink a lot of
   (beaucoup de) water.

3. If there are ...... tomatoes, they will be welcome *(bien-venu)*.

4. Would you like ...... lemonade? No thanks, I won't have
   ...... for lunch today.

5. Will you bring me ...... beans *(haricots)* and ...... peas
   (petits pois)? We'll have ...... for lunch today.

6. Take ...... ham *(jambon)* if you can find ......

7. ...... grocer *(épicier)* will sell *(vendre)* you that.

8. You will find *(trouver)* that in ...... little village.

9. Can I have ...... lettuce *(laitue)* please?

10. If you have ...... objections, please tell us.

C' ■**

Traduisez les phrases suivantes:

1. Il ne reste pas de café dans la cafetière *(coffee pot)*. Il n'en
   reste pas.

2. Voulez-vous encore des beignets *(doughnut)*?

3. Je vais prendre encore du cacao *(cocoa)*.

4. Il n'a vu personne dans la rue, absolument personne.

5. Il nous reste de la bière blonde *(ale)* et de la bière brune
   (stout).

6. Je n'irai nulle part cet été. Nulle part.

7. N'importe qui vous dira cela!

8. Il ne dit jamais rien. D'autres disent n'importe quoi.

9. Elle ne veut plus de jus d'orange.

10. Il voudrait encore du lait et du sucre.

22. Les quantificateurs
much, many, (a) little, (a) few

A ■* He does not drink **much water**!... Ah!... Does he
drink **much wine**?... Yes quite **a few glasses**
every day... and **many** more at the weekend...

▷ **much**, *beaucoup de,* (**a**) **little,** *(un) peu de* s'emploient seuls
ou avec des noms indénombrables, singuliers, désignant quel-
que chose de global, qui ne se compte pas, concret (du vin, du
lait, de la farine...) ou abstrait (la patience, le courage...).

Our cat drinks **a little milk** every day.
Notre chat boit un peu de lait tous les jours.

He showed **little tolerance**.
Il a fait preuve de peu de tolérance.

▷ **many**, *beaucoup de,* **a few**, *quelques,* **few**, *peu de,* s'emploient seuls ou avec des noms dénombrables, pluriels,
désignant ce qui peut se compter (un verre de vin, un kilo de
farine, un, deux... hommes patients...) :

He does not eat **many sweets** *(bonbon).*
I gave him **a few biscuits**.

Remarque : **much** et **many** s'emploient surtout dans les
phrases négatives et interrogatives. Dans les phrases affirmatives
ou déclaratives, on utilise de préférence **a lot of, lots of** (plus
familier), **plenty of**, indifféremment devant les dénombrables
(appelés aussi comptables) et les indénombrables (non comptables).

A' ■* He does not drink **much water!**... Ah!... Does he drink **much wine?**... Yes, quite **a few glasses** every day... and **many** more at the weekend...

VOCABULAIRE - **In the street,** *dans la rue.*

Complétez à l'aide de **much, many, (a) little, (a) few, a lot of ou lots of, plenty of:**

1. There are not ...... pedestrian crossings *(passages pour piétons)* in this street *(rue).*

2. Motorists *(automobilistes)* often show ...... patience, yes, very ...... indeed.

3. Are there ...... traffic lights *(feux de circulation)* in this town? Not ......

4. There is ...... traffic *(circulation)* at twelve o'clock.

5. You see very ...... vehicles at four in the morning.

6. The careless driver *(chauffeur imprudent)* did not pay ...... attention at the cross-roads *(carrefour).*

7. There are not ...... streetlamps *(lampadaires)* in these alleys *(ruelles).*

8. There is very ...... noise *(bruit)* in this sidestreet *(rue secondaire)* and not ...... traffic.

9. ...... cars were running *(rouler)* round the roundabout *(rond-point).*

10. You won't see ...... bicycles in this thoroughfare *(artère)* at six o'clock in the evening.

11. If you don't drive at rush hours *(aux heures de pointe),* there is not ...... danger.

12. Foreign visitors *(touristes étrangers)* do not take ...... interest in this metropolis *(grand centre urbain).*

B ■**

Much, many, little, few *s'emploient avec :*

1. **too** *(trop)*

   He drinks **too much** whisky.
   He eats **too little** meat *(viande)*.

2. **so** *(tant, tellement)*

   She drank **so many** glasses of champagne.
   He gave me **so few** details.

3. **as... as** *(autant que)*

   I don't know **as much** Spanish as John.
   I know **as few** people here as Peter does.

4. **how** exclamatif ou interrogatif
   How many books did you read?
   How few books you read! You are an ignoramus! *(un ignare)*.

   N.B. :

a) Les mots **too, so, as, how** s'emploient seuls (sans much, many...) uniquement avec un adjectif et un adverbe :

   He is **so** clever *(intelligent)*, he reads **so** fast *(vite)*.

b) Modifiant un verbe, **too, so, as, how** sont obligatoirement suivis de much :

   You work **too** much.
   Tu travailles trop.

B' ■** He does not drink **much** water!... Ah!... Does he drink **much** wine?... Yes, quite **a few** glasses every day... and **many** more at the weekend...

Complétez à l'aide de **much, many, little, few** *si nécessaire:*

1. There are not as ...... street sweepers *(balayeurs des rues)* as before.

2. Dustmen *(éboueurs)* have so ...... work in a big city!

3. The town is too ...... quiet *(calme)* in summer. So ...... people are away on holiday.

4. You drive either *(ou)* too ...... fast *(vite)* or too ...... carelessly *(imprudemment)*.

5. How ...... foreign cars *(voitures étrangères)* did you count *(compter)?* Not as ...... as yesterday.

6. You should not drive for so ...... long *(longtemps)*. Driving too ...... long is dangerous. Too ...... motorists forget this. It isn't as ...... easy as all that to remember!

7. Town-dwellers *(citadins)* are so ...... irritable! They show so ...... patience!

8. I didn't arrive in time. There was too ...... traffic *(circulation)*.

9. You sleep too ...... You don't work as ...... as you should. I wish you spent as ...... time at your desk *(bureau)* as you do in your bed!

C ■★★

Notez les emplois des *comparatifs* respectifs de **much, many,** de **little,** de **few.**

a) I eat **more bread** and **more cakes** now.
Je mange davantage de pain et davantage de gâteaux en ce moment.

▷ **more** + noms indénombrables *et* dénombrables.

b) I drink **less coffee.**
Je bois moins de café.

▷ **less** + noms indénombrables, le plus souvent.

c) She eats **fewer cakes**
Elle mange moins de gâteaux.

▷ **fewer** + noms dénombrables seulement.

— Remarquez les combinaisons possibles :

a) He reads **much more** during the holidays.
Il lit beaucoup plus pendant les vacances.

b) He reads **much more poetry.**
Il lit beaucoup plus de poésie.

c) He reads **much less** poetry.
Il lit beaucoup moins de poésie.

d) He reads **many more** novels.
Il lit beaucoup plus de romans.

C' ■** He does not drink **much water**!... Ah!... Does he drink **much wine**?... Yes, quite **a few glasses** every day... and **many more** at the weekend...

Traduisez :

1. Il y a moins de circulation *(traffic)*, il y a moins de camions *(lorry)*.

2. Il y a plus de taxis autour de la gare *(station)*, plus d'animation *(bustle)* aussi.

3. Une camionnette *(van)* fait moins de bruit qu'un gros camion *(lorry)*.

4. Il y a moins de trams *(tramcar)* et moins de vacarme *(din)*.

5. On voit moins d'autobus à double étage *(double decker)* ces temps-ci.

6. Il y a beaucoup plus de policiers dans ce quartier *(district)*.

7. Il y a beaucoup moins de bruit dans cette impasse *(cul-de-sac)*.

8. On voit beaucoup plus de revendeurs de drogue *(drug-dealer)* dans ces rues transversales *(side street)*.

9. Il y a beaucoup plus d'embouteillages *(traffic jam)* à ce carrefour *(crossroads)*.

23. Les nombres cardinaux et ordinaux (pour compter et classer)

A ■*

Les nombres cardinaux servent à compter :

a) **zero** (pour les températures), **0** (au téléphone), **nought** (le terme le plus généralement employé).

b) one, two, three, four, five, six, seven, eight, nine, ten, eleven, twelve *(douze)* (attention à l'orthographe de two et de eight).

c) thir**teen**, four**teen**, fif**teen**, six**teen**, seven**teen**, eigh**teen**, nine**teen** *(dix-neuf)*.

d) twen**ty**, twenty-one, twenty-two...
thir**ty** *(trente)*, for**ty**, fif**ty**, six**ty**, seven**ty**, eigh**ty**, nine**ty**.

N.B. : Ne pas confondre les chiffres en **"teen"** (syllabe accentuée) avec les chiffres des dizaines en **"ty"** (syllabe non accentuée).

e) a hundred ou one hundred *(cent)*, a thousand ou one thousand (1,000), a million ou one million (1,000,000).

B ■*

Les *nombres ordinaux* servent à *classer* :

a) fir**st**, 1st *(premier, 1er)* ; seco**nd**, 2nd *(deuxième, 2e)* ; thi**rd**, 3rd *(troisième, 3e)*.

b) four**th**, 4th *(quatrième, 4e)* ; fif**th**, 5th ; six**th**, 6th ; seven**th**, 7th ; eigh**th**, 8th ; nin**th**, 9th... ; eleven**th**, 11 th ; twelf**th**, 12th...

→ sauf pour les trois premiers, les nombres ordinaux sont formés par addition de **th** aux nombres ordinaux.

Remarquez les *modifications orthographiques* dans fif**th**, nin**th**, twelf**th** et dans twenti**eth** (20th, *vingtième*), thirti**eth**, forti**eth**, fifti**eth**...

Remarquez aussi qu'entre les dizaines on a :

twenty-first *(vingt et unième)*, twenty second... ; thirty first...

A' ■* There were hundreds of flowers, **six hundred** perhaps.

VOCABULAIRE - **Flowers,** *les fleurs.*

Complétez :

1. Two minus *(moins)* two is ......

2. Four multiplied by three is ......

3. Twelve plus one is ......

4. ...... divided by ten is four.

5. Seventy minus one hundred is ......, not ......!

6. How many inhabitants *(habitants)* are there in France? There are ...... inhabitants *(55,000,000)*.

7. There are ...... minutes in an hour *(heure)*, not ......!

8. It is 25 (......) minutes past 8 (......) by my watch *(à ma montre)*.

9. He is an old man, he is eighty, not ......!

10. He gave me 75 p (...... pence).

N.B. : Notez l'emploi de **is, are** (verbe be, *être*) dans toutes ces phrases.

B' ■* There were hundreds of flowers, **six hundred** perhaps.

Lisez en anglais et écrivez en toutes lettres les nombres ordinaux correspondant à :

29	9
33	3.000
81	200
42	3.891
80	703
8	12
90	30

C ■** There were hundreds of flowers, **six hundred** perhaps.

Il y avait des centaines de fleurs, six cents peut-être.

Dans le premier cas hundred est un ***nom*** ; il prend le **s** du pluriel ; il est suivi de **of** ; il exprime une ***approximation*** : des centaines de...

Dans le deuxième cas, hundred précédé d'un nombre précis (de a **few**, *quelques*, **several**, *plusieurs*, **many**) est un ***adjectif*** numéral, donc ***invariable*** comme les adjectifs qualificatifs.

Il en va de même de **dozen** *(douzaine)*, **thousand** *(mille)*, **million** et de **billion** (*million* en G.-B., *milliard* aux U.S.A.).

There are thousand of daisies *(pâquerettes)*, several thousand, five thousand perhaps.

D ■** Emploi (ou non) de **and** avec **hundred** et **thousand**.

a) **and** est *obligatoire après **hundred*** :

five hundred **and** two, five hundred **and** twenty-two, three hundred **and** fifty thousand.

b) **and** est obligatoire ***après*** thousand ***seulement si le nombre qui suit*** thousand ***n'est pas une centaine***, on a :
three thousand **and** five *mais* three thousand five hundred.

C' ■** There were hundreds of flowers, **six hundred perhaps.**

Traduisez :

1. Des millions de fleurs *(flower)* se vendent chaque année, plusieurs millions.

2. J'ai acheté deux douzaines de roses *(rose)* hier matin.

3. Il y avait des milliers de jonquilles *(daffodil)* dans les champs *(field)*.

4. Cet horticulteur *(horticulturist)* a vendu des centaines de jacinthes *(hyacinth)* le mois dernier, cinq cents, six cents peut-être.

5. Ils ont cueilli *(pick)* quelques douzaines de boutons d'or *(buttercup)*.

6. Toutes ces tulipes *(tulip)* ont coûté *(cost)* plus de trois cents francs.

D' ■** There were hundreds of flowers, **six hundred perhaps.**

Lisez en anglais et écrivez en toutes lettres :

803	6.757
233	82.088
2.009	306
542	7.435
4.076	12.027

E ■** Les nombres ordinaux s'emploient :

a) pour les **dates** :
December 12th (se lit December the twelfth ou the twelfth of December)

N.B. : Les **années** se lisent généralement ainsi : nineteen sixty (1960, 19/60).

b) avec les **noms de souverains, de papes** :
Elizsabeth II (on dit : Elizabeth the second)

— Les adjectifs **first** *(premier)*, **last** *(dernier)*, **next** *(suivant, prochain)*, **other** *(autre)* **précèdent les nombres cardinaux** :
the first two days *(les deux premiers jours* ; l'ordre est inversé en français)*.

F ■**

Notez les mots suivants :

a) **once** *(une fois)*, **twi e** *(deux fois)*, puis **three times** *(trois fois)*, **four times**..., etc.

b) **Both** traduit la notion de « deux » ; il donne lieu à diverses constructions :

— en position de sujet :
both Jackie and Mary came = **both** came = they **both** came = **both of them** came (on a aussi **both of us**, *nous deux*, **both of you**, *vous deux)*

— en position de complément :
I expected **them both** ou I expected **both of them** *(je les attendais tous les deux)*

— Yves Montand is **both** a singer and an actor *(à la fois, les deux à la fois)*

— **both** se construit aussi comme un adjectif :
he speaks **both languages**
(il parle les deux langues)

E' ■** There were hundreds of flowers, **six hundred** perhaps.

Traduisez :

1. Je n'aime pas ses deux derniers romans *(novel)*.

2. Le 14 février c'est la Saint-Valentin *(Saint Valentine's Day)*.

3. Les Forces Alliées *(The Allied Forces)* ont débarqué *(land)* en Normandie le 6 juin 1944.

4. Comment avez-vous trouvé *(like)* les deux premiers actes *(act)*?

5. Le 23 février c'est mardi-gras *(Shrove Tuesday)*.

6. Henri VIII, Louis XIV sont des rois *(king)* très célèbres *(famous)*.

7. Le muguet *(lily of the valley)* est associé au 1er mai.

F' ■** There were hundreds of flowers, **six hundred** perhaps.

Traduisez :

1. Je les ai vus tous les deux hier matin *(deux possibilités)*.

2. Il viendra une fois, pas deux.

3. Il est à la fois poète *(poet)* et romancier *(novelist)*.

4. Nous sommes allés quatre fois aux U.S.A.

5. Elle apprend l'anglais et l'allemand *(German)*.

6. Tous les deux sont américains *(trois possibilités)*.

7. Il nous a parlé à tous les deux.

8. Les deux langues sont très difficiles.

9. Elle écrit à la fois des nouvelles *(short story)* et des romans *(novel)*.

24. Le pluriel des noms

A ■* Boys and girls...

▷ La plupart des noms forment leur *pluriel* par addition de **s** au singulier. Ce **s** *se prononce*.
a car → car**s**

— Observez les modifications orthographiques :

    — des noms terminés par **s**, **x**, **z**, **ch**, **sh** :
    bus → bus**es** (pluriel en **es**)

    — des noms communs terminés par **y** *précédé d'une consonne* :
    body *(corps)* → bod**ies** (pluriel en **ies** ; mais on a boy**s**)

    — de certains noms terminés par **f** ou **fe** :
    a knife *(couteau)* → knives ; de même a half *(moitié)* → halves, a loaf *(miche de pain)* → loaves, a thief *(voleur)* → thieves ; a wife *(épouse)* → wives... ; on a par contre a chief *(chef)* → chiefs, a cliff *(falaise)* → cliffs, a proof *(preuve)* → proofs, a safe *(coffre-fort)* → safes...

    — de certains noms terminés par **o** :
    a potato → potato**es**, a tomato → tomato**es** (pluriel en **oes**)... ; on a par contre photos, pianos.

A' ■* Boys and **girls** (child**ren**) keep white **mice**.

Traduisez :

1. Il y a beaucoup de pommes de terre cette année *(year)*.

2. Les voleurs ont été arrêtés *(arrest)* hier.

3. Avez-vous vu les falaises de Douvres? *(Dover)*.

4. Les ménagères *(housewife)* ont beaucoup de travail chaque jour.

5. Avez-vous visité les églises *(church)* de notre ville *(town)*?

6. N'oubliez pas de fermer *(lock)* vos coffres-forts !

7. J'aime les pianos blancs *(white)*.

8. J'ai acheté une douzaine de couteaux et de fourchettes *(fork)*.

9. Il y avait des tas de *(lots of)* voitures et de camions *(lorry)*.

10. J'ai pris ces photos l'été dernier *(last summer)*.

11. Mettez ces images *(picture)* dans ces boîtes *(box)*.

12. Posez *(lay)* les plats *(dish)* sur la table.

13. Ses passe-temps favoris *(hobby)* sont la musique et la peinture *(painting)*.

14. Où sont les clefs *(key)*?

15. C'est l'automne *(Autumn)*. Les feuilles *(leaf)* sont jaunes *(yellow)*.

B ■**

— La marque **s** du pluriel est utilisée aussi pour les *noms propres* et les *abréviations* :

The Browns, The Wilsons.
The MP's ou the MPs (the Members of Parliament, *les Députés à la Chambre des Communes*).

— Dans les *noms composés*, seul le deuxième élément prend en général la marque du pluriel, le premier jouant un rôle d'adjectif qualificatif (donc invariable) :

a taxi-driver → taxi-drivers

N.B. : Si le deuxième élément d'un nom composé est une préposition, c'est le premier qui porte la marque du pluriel :
a passer-by *(passant)* → **passers-by**.

— Avec un possessif pluriel (our, your, their), le nom doit être au pluriel *s'il désigne un objet qui n'appartient pas en commun aux différents possesseurs* :

The junior executives came in their cars.
Les jeunes cadres sont venus en voiture
(chacun dans sa voiture ; s'ils étaient venus dans une seule et même voiture, on aurait eu : **in their car**)

Jane and Jacqueline put on their hats and went out.
Jane et Jacqueline ont mis leur chapeau et sont sorties.

B' ■** Boys and girls (children) keep white **mice.**

Traduisez :

1. Il y a beaucoup de chauffeurs de taxi dans cette ville.

2. La rue était pleine de passants.

3. Je préfère les Smith aux Jackson.

4. J'aime les tartes aux cerises *(cherry tart)*.

5. Peter et Bob ont rencontré leurs amies devant le cinéma.

6. Les députés *(MP)* entrèrent dans la chambre des Communes *(the House of Commons)*.

7. Que pensez-vous *(think of)* de nos compagnons de voyage *(fellow-traveller)* ?

8. Ils entrèrent la pipe à la bouche *(mouth)*.

9. Ces dames *(lady)* sont toutes des mères-poules *(mother-hen)*.

10. Ils ont tous perdu *(lose)* la vie dans ce terrible accident.

11. Ils vinrent tous à bicyclette *(on their...)*.

12. Êtes-vous allés au zoo hier ? Avez-vous vu les éléphanteaux *(baby elephant)* ?

13. Tous nos amis, qui étaient nombreux *(many)*, sont venus en voiture *(in their...)*.

C ■** ... children keep white mice.

Pluriels irréguliers et problèmes d'accord du verbe:

1. Pluriel en **en**
   child → children, man → men, woman → women
   ox *(bœuf)* → oxen

2. Pluriel vocalique (changement de voyelle)
   foot *(pied)* → feet, goose *(oie)* → geese, tooth *(dent)* → teeth
   mouse *(souris)* → mice

3. Double pluriel
   penny → pennies *(pièces de un penny)*
   penny → pence *(pour exprimer la valeur)*

4. People *(les gens)* est un *nom pluriel*
   These people **are** very rich.

5. Sheep *(mouton)* a la même forme au singulier (sixty sheep);
   il en est de même le plus souvent de fish *(poisson)* (six fish
   ou fishes) et de fruit *(fruit)*.

6. Advice *(des conseils)*, furniture *(les meubles)*, hair *(cheveux)*,
   information *(des renseignements)*, luggage *(les bagages)*,
   news *(les nouvelles)* sont du *singulier*:
   My luggage **is** heavy *(lourd)*.
   This is the news.

   Ce sont là des noms indénombrables qui désignent des
   choses vues globalement. Si on veut parler d'un ou de
   plusieurs éléments (dénombrables, que l'on peut dénom-
   brer, compter) de l'ensemble on dit: **a piece of** advice, **two
   pieces of** furniture, **a piece of** information, **a piece of** news
   (un conseil, un meuble, etc.*)*.

C' ■** Boys and girls (childr**en**) keep white **mice.**

Traduisez :

1. Elle ne mange jamais de poisson.

2. J'ai deux dents très mauvaises *(bad).*

3. Ces hommes et ces femmes manifestaient *(demonstrate)* dans la rue.

4. Ce fermier *(farmer)* a cent moutons et cinq ou six bœufs.

5. Les nouvelles sont-elles bonnes ?

6. Combien d'enfants a-t-elle ?

7. Regarde tes pieds ! Ils sont tout sales *(dirty).*

8. Vos cheveux sont trop longs.

9. Les renseignements sont gratuits *(free).*

10. Voici un très bon renseignement.

11. Les conseils qu'elle vous donne sont tout à fait *(quite)* inutiles *(useless).*

12. Il y avait des gens dans la rue *(street).*

13. Ce petit garçon a *(keep)* deux souris blanches.

14. Vos bagages sont légers *(light).*

15. Il m'a donné un conseil. Je suis *(take)* toujours ses conseils.

16. Il mange *(eat)* des fruits tous les jours.

17. Je préfère ces gens aux Wilson.

18. Les meubles sont chers *(expensive).*

25. Le génitif (ou cas possessif)

A ■* The old manager's new suit is grey...

(le costume neuf du vieux directeur est gris...)

▷ Appelé « *cas possessif* » quand il exprime comme ici un rapport de possession, le génitif est composé de trois éléments :

1. le possesseur avec **tout** ce qui le précède (article, adjectif...) ; the old manager

2. la marque du génitif, **'s**, vestige d'une langue autrefois déclinée (cf. le s du génitif allemand)

3. l'objet possédé avec tout ce qui le précède (adjectif...) **sauf l'article** : "new suit". Le génitif étant comparable à un possessif, on comprend mieux l'effacement de cet article :

his ⎫
the old manager's ⎬ new suit

N.B. :

1. Si le possesseur n'est pas précédé d'un article, il n'y a *aucune raison d'en mettre un au génitif* :
   — **Jane's** red dress *(robe)* : prénom.
   — **Old Smith's** jacket, **President Reagan's** speech *(discours)* : appellation familière ou titre + nom propre (cf. chapitre 19, p. 72, b).

2. Si le possesseur est désigné par un nom dont le **pluriel** est **en s**, *la marque du génitif est réduite à* **'** :
   — the secretaries**'** cardigans
   — mais the people**'s** clothes *(vêtements)*
       the children**'s** sweaters *(chandail)*

3. Le génitif s'emploie *surtout avec des noms de personnes et d'animaux* ; il est obligatoire avec des noms de famille, des prénoms, des termes de parenté :
   — **Mr. Wilson's** overcoat *(pardessus)*, **Dad's** hat *(le chapeau de Papa)*.

4. Le génitif ne s'emploie pas :

   a) avec des noms d'objets concrets ; on utilise alors of ou un mot composé :
      — **the door of the house, the house door.**

   b) avec des adverbes convertis en noms (p. 110) :
      — **the arrogance of the rich.**

A' ■* **The old manager's new suit** is grey, **the young executive's** is blue.

VOCABULAIRE - **Clothes,** *les vêtements.*

Traduisez les phrases suivantes selon le modèle, en employant le génitif:

The secretary is wearing a new scarf *(la secrétaire porte une nouvelle écharpe)* → I don't like the secretary's new scarf.

1. My sister has a new bathing suit *(maillot de bains).*
2. Jane bought a blue raincoat *(imperméable).*
3. The children are wearing white shorts *(short).*
4. Old Brown has got a red dressing-gown *(robe de chambre).*
5. These workers are wearing caps *(casquettes).*
6. Mummy *(maman)* has a new blouse *(chemisier).*
7. These young ladies are wearing short skirts *(jupes).*
8. The senior executives *(cadre supérieur)* are carrying their umbrellas *(parapluies).*
9. My brother has new shoes *(souliers).*
10. Businessmen wear bowler hats *(chapeaux melons).*
11. These people are wearing red ties *(cravates).*
12. Soldiers *(soldat)* wear uniforms.

Traduisez (employez le génitif quand c'est possible):

1. Les pyjamas *(pyjamas)* des petites filles étaient trop longs.
2. Regarde la queue du chien.
3. L'ouvrier a réparé *(repair)* le toit *(roof)* de la vieille maison.
4. Avez-vous remarqué *(notice)* le smoking *(dinner jacket)* du Président George Bush?
5. Les boutons *(button)* de son corsage *(blouse)* étaient blancs.
6. Ma mère a réparé *(mend)* la manche *(sleeve)* de mon imperméable *(raincoat).*
7. Je n'aime pas la couleur du survêtement *(tracksuit)* de l'oncle Jean.
8. Pensez aux *(think of)* difficultés des pauvres.
9. Que pensez-vous de la couleur de ses gants?
10. Les manteaux de fourrure *(furcoat)* des deux femmes étaient identiques *(identical).*
11. La fermeture Éclair *(zip)* de mon pantalon *(trousers)* est cassée.

B ■★★

Outre qu'il exprime un rapport de possession ou de parenté (the typist's father, *le père de la dactylo*), le génitif s'applique :

1. À des *objets... propres à une catégorie d'individus* par opposition à tels objets précis appartenant à telles personnes en particulier : **a** junior executive's attaché case *(un attaché-case **de** jeune cadre*, comme on en voit aux jeunes cadres), **a** worker's cap *(une casquette **d'**ouvrier)*, **a** dog's life *(une vie **de** chien...)*. C'est le *génitif générique*.

2. À des notions de *durée* et à des *divisions du temps* : a month's holiday *(un congé d'un mois)*, yesterday's newspaper *(le journal d'hier)*.

3. À des notions de *distance* :
   a mile's walk *(une marche d'un mile)*.

4. À des *groupes de personnes*, partis, gouvernements... : the committee's decision, the government's attitude.

5. À des *villes*, à des *pays* :
   Britain's entry into the Common Market *(l'entrée de la Grande-Bretagne dans le Marché Commun)*.

B' ■★★ **The old manager's new suit** is grey, **the young executive's** is blue.

Exprimez la même idée à l'aide du génitif et des éventuelles suggestions entre parenthèses :

1. We walked for three hours (take a walk).

2. We visited England for a week (have a holiday).

3. I'll buy the newspaper tomorrow.

4. What do you think of what the party decided (decision)?

5. The crisis in Poland *(Pologne)* is given front page coverage *(est à la une).*

6. The visit lasted *(durer)* a fortnight *(quinzaine de jours).*

7. Let us rest *(se reposer)* for a moment *(have a rest).*

8. It's a job *(travail)* for a man, not for a woman.

9. What do you think of Turkey *(la Turquie)* entering the Common Market *(entry)*?

10. The schoolboys are having their break *(récréation)* (ten minutes).

11. Did you listen to the weather forecast *(bulletin météorologique)* last night *(hier soir)*?

12. How long does it take to become *(devenir)* a doctor (get a degree, *obtenir un diplôme)*?

C ■** The old manager's new suit is grey, the young executive's is blue.

— The old manager's new suit is grey, the young executive's is blue (*celui... du* jeune cadre est bleu).

▷ Il est courant d'*éviter* ainsi *la répétition* d'un mot déjà exprimé (ici "suit"), par effacement du troisième élément du génitif ; notez encore :

Mr Smith's briefcase is black, **Mr. Law's** is brown.
Le porte-documents de Mr. Smith est noir, celui de Mr. Law est marron.

— Sont également *sous-entendus* les mots **house, shop** *(boutique)*, **church** *(église)* :

I went to the baker**'s** near St Martin**'s**, then I went to my aunt**'s**. *Je suis allé* chez *le boulanger près de l'église St-Martin, puis je suis allé* chez *ma tante.*

— Remarquez la différence entre ces deux phrases :
Mr. Wall's and Mr. Wolf's offices.
Mr. Wall and Mr Wolf's office.

Dans le premier cas les deux hommes ont *chacun un bureau*, dans le deuxième ils partagent *un seul et même bureau*.

C' ■** The old manager's new suit is grey, the young executive's is blue.

À l'aide des éventuelles suggestions entre parenthèses, transformez ou complétez les phrases suivantes en utilisant le génitif:

1. Aunt Mary has a big handbag *(sac à main)*. Aunt Helen has a very small one.

2. She bought some meat *(viande)* *(go/ butcher)*.

3. Jane is wearing black tights *(collants)*, Betty is wearing brown ones.

4. Shall we visit our old friends? *(go)*.

5. We go to church every Sunday, we *(go/ St Peter)*.

6. This man has very old slippers *(pantoufles)*, that man has brand new *(flambant neufs)* ones.

7. Robert and Jack sleep *(dormir)* in the same *(même)* bedroom *(it is very large)*.

8. What do you think of their new aprons *(tabliers)* *(Margaret/Joan)*?

9. These young ladies have red suits *(tailleurs)*, those old ladies have green ones.

10. Let us stay *(séjourner)* for a week... *(at/our uncle)*.

26. Les possessifs

A ■*

Le tableau ci-dessous classe les *adjectifs* possessifs **(mon, ma...)** et les *pronoms* possessifs **(le mien, la mienne...)** correspondant aux pronoms personnels sujets (je, tu...), singulier et pluriel.

	Pronoms personnels sujets	Adjectifs possessifs	Pronoms possessifs
Singulier 1re personne 2e personne 3e personne	I you { he she it	my your { his her its	**mine** yours { his hers its own
Pluriel 1re personne 2e personne 3e personne	we you they	our your their	ours yours theirs

Remarques

— My **brother** went skiing with **his** instructor *(moniteur)*, my **sister** went with **her** friends.

▷ À la 3e personne du singulier l'adjectif possessif est **his** si l'antécédent (le nom qui précède) représente une personne de *sexe masculin* (frère), **her** s'il représente une personne de *sexe féminin* (sœur).

Si l'antécédent représente quelque chose d'*inanimé* on emploie **its** :
Look at this mammoth hotel! Look at **its** height!
Regarde cet hôtel gigantesque ! Regarde sa hauteur !

— I put on **my** anorak, **my** ski suit (ma *combinaison*) and **my** boots (mes *chaussures*)

▷ Contrairement au français la forme du possessif ne dépend pas du nom qui suit.

A' ■* My **brother** went skiing with **his** instructor, my **sister** went with **her** friends.

VOCABULAIRE - **Sports**, *les sports.*

Complétez par un adjectif ou un pronom possessif :

1. This anorak belongs to *(appartenir à)* me, it is ...... anorak, it is ......

2. Mary takes great care *(prendre grand soin)* of ...... equipment. Do you take care of ......?

3. I like this instructor, I like ...... way of teaching *(sa façon d'enseigner)*.

4. Look at this motorbike *(moto)!* Look at ...... size *(taille)*.

5. This tent belongs to Peter and Paul, it is ...... tent, it is ......

6. Can you pass her ...... ski sticks? *(bâtons)*.

7. Is this Jane's racket? Yes it is ...... racket, it's ......

8. We enjoyed ...... skiing holidays. Did you enjoy ......?

9. The young boy has lost *(perdre)* ...... skates *(patins)*.

10. The poor fellow *(type)* has broken ...... fishing-rod *(canne à pêche)* again!

11. Where is ...... riding school? *(école d'équitation)*. It is near here. Is ...... far from here?

12. That gentleman is quite rich, ... sailing boat *(voilier)* is quite big ...... isn't as big! I am not as rich!

13. They always go there. It is ...... favourite winter sports resort *(station de sports d'hiver)*. It is not ......, we do not like it so much.

14. Whose gloves *(gants)* are these? They are the young lady's, they are ......

B ■**

Le possessif est obligatoire devant un nom de *partie du corps* ou de *vêtement* :

They came in with **their** on **their** heads.
Ils entrèrent le chapeau sur la tête.

Remarquez aussi l'emploi de **with** et du *pluriel* du nom avec un possessif pluriel (**our, your, their**) si le nom désigne un objet... (hat, head...) qui *n'appartient pas en commun* aux différentes personnes. Rappelez-vous la différence (p. 94) entre :

They came in their car**s** (chacun dans sa voiture)
They came in their **car** (dans une seule et même voiture)

— Avec **everybody, every one** *(tout le monde)*, **every** + nom, on emploie le plus souvent le possessif pluriel :
  Everybody brought **their** umbrella**s**, didn't **they**?
  Tout le monde a apporté son parapluie, n'est-ce pas ?

— Le possessif est parfois renforcé par **own** *(propre, personnel, à soi)* :
  I did it with my **own** hands.
  Je l'ai fait de mes propres mains.

N.B. C'est **its own** et jamais its seul qui correspond à it en guise de pronom (cf. tableau p. 104).
This house has a charm of **its own**.
Cette maison a un charme particulier (propre).

— Emploi particulier, courant, du pronom possessif :
  She is **a friend of mine** *(c'est une de mes amies)*.

— Traductions du pronom possessif :
  It's his bicycle, it's **his** (... *c'est la sienne,* mais aussi « *elle est* à **lui** »).

— Au pronom indéfini **one** (« on », dans le sens général) correspond le possessif **one's** :
  One generally looks after **one's** interests first.
  On s'occupe généralement d'abord de ses intérêts.

B' ■** My **brother** went skiing with **his** instructor, my
sister went with **her** friend.

Traduisez les phrases suivantes :

1. Les deux scouts *(scouts)* s'en allèrent le sac *(rucksack)* sur le dos.

2. Regardez les Wilson dans leur bateau à moteur *(motor boat)*. Ils l'ont acheté, il est à eux.

3. Le jeune homme se tenait sur le terrain de golf *(golf links)*. Il avait la canne de golf *(golf club)* à la main.

4. Les jeunes filles sont venues à bicyclette *(on... bicycle)*.

5. Tout le monde est venu en voiture.

6. Tous les chasseurs *(hunters)* durent montrer leur permis *(hunting permit)*.

7. Je l'ai vu de mes propres yeux.

8. Il va se baigner *(go swimming)* avec un de ses amis tous les après-midi.

9. Tous ces riches passent des heures sur leur yacht *(yacht)* à ne rien faire.

10. Occupez-vous de *(mind)* vos affaires, je m'occuperai *(see to)* des miennes.

11. On devrait toujours porter *(wear)* son gilet de sauvetage *(life jacket)* sur son bateau.

12. Elle est allée skier *(go skiing)* avec une de ses sœurs.

13. Elle va à l'école d'équitation *(riding school)* mais c'est son cheval à elle.

14. C'est son ballon *(ball)*, il est à lui.

15. Il a battu *(break)* son propre record *(record)*. Battre son propre record est un événement *(quite an event)*.

16. Nous jouons au tennis avec deux de nos amis.

17. Skier avec ses amis est un grand plaisir *(great fun)*.

27. Les adjectifs qualificatifs

A ■*

L'adjectif qualificatif est *invariable* en genre et en nombre :

This man (woman, house...) is **wonderful.**
These men (women, houses...) are **wonderful**.

N.B. : **Other** est donc également *invariable s'il est adjectif* ; il n'en est pas de même s'il est pronom :

There are no **other** houses, there are no other**s**.
Il n'y a aucune autre maison, il n'y en a aucune autre.

Un adjectif peut être attribut ou épithète :

— *Attribut*, il est placé *après* be *(être)*, look *(avoir l'air)*, seem *(sembler)*, become *(devenir)*... :

This bedroom is very large.
Cette chambre est très grande.

— *Épithète*, l'adjectif est placé *avant* le nom :

John has a very comfortable bedroom.
Jean a une chambre très confortable.

Exceptions :

1. L'adjectif épithète *avec un complément* :
a full glass, mais a glass **full** of beer *(plein de bière)*

2. L'adjectif épithète *avec les composés* de some, any, no (cf. p. 78) :

Nothing **new** was announced.
Rien de neuf n'a été annoncé.

Par ailleurs l'adjectif (comme l'adverbe) se place *avant* enough *(assez)* :

This house is big enough for us.
Cette maison est assez grande pour nous.

A' ■* He is **blind**, he is **a blind man**; like all **the blind** he is very musical.

VOCABULAIRE - **The house,** *la maison.*

Traduisez :

1. Les salons *(sitting-room)* sont très grands dans les maisons modernes.

2. Nous avons une salle de bain *(bathroom)* très petite.

3. Une maison n'est jamais assez grande.

4. Nos enfants *(child)* ont une salle de jeux *(rumpus-room)* très agréable.

5. Les autres étaient assis *(sitting)* devant la belle cheminée *(fireplace).*

6. Y a-t-il quelque chose d'intéressant *(interesting)* à la télé? *(on the telly).*

7. Il y avait des verres pleins de whisky sur la table ronde *(round).*

8. Que pensez-vous *(think of)* de ces cuisines *(kitchen)* modernes?

9. Ils ont un grenier *(attic)* plein de meubles *(furniture)* poussiéreux *(dusty).*

10. Ils sont très riches. Ils ont une maison secondaire *(second home)* splendide.

11. Son bureau *(study)* est plein de très vieux livres.

12. C'est une petite chambre d'amis *(spare room)* mais elle est très utile.

13. Avez-vous visité les autres maisons secondaires? — Les autres? — Non.

B ■** He is **blind**, he is **a blind man**; like all **the blind**
he is very musical.

> *Il est aveugle, comme tous les aveugles, il est très
> musicien.*

▷ Certains *adjectifs* peuvent être *convertis en noms* quand ils
désignent *l'ensemble* d'une catégorie de personnes ; les plus
courants sont : the blind, the rich, the poor *(les pauvres)*, the
young *(les jeunes)*, the old ou the elderly *(les personnes âgées)*,
the living *(les vivants)*, the dead *(les morts)*...

Il en est de même des *adjectifs de nationalité en ch et sh* :
the English (les Anglais en général, tous les Anglais), the French.

Remarques

1. L'adjectif converti en nom est précédé de **the** bien qu'il
   désigne une généralité (cf. p. 72). Ne pas confondre : **the**
   English et English *(l'anglais, la langue anglaise)*...

2. Même converti en nom et malgré son sens pluriel, l'adjectif
   demeure invariable :

   The rich are not always happy.
   Les riches ne sont pas toujours heureux.

3. L'adjectif converti en nom ne s'emploie *pas au génitif ou cas
   possessif* :

   The humility of the poor.

4. Pour désigner une catégorie entière d'individus on a également : **English people, rich people, poor people**...

— He is blind, he is **a blind man**... (*il est aveugle, c'est* un
aveugle)

▷ *S'il désigne seulement un ou plusieurs éléments* mais non la
catégorie entière, l'adjectif ne peut être converti en nom ; il doit
être alors *suivi d'un nom ou du pronom* one(s) : two blind
children (boys, girls), *deux petit(e)s aveugles*; two rich men
(women) ; the red book(s), not the blue one(s), *le(s) livre(s)
rouge(s), pas le(s) bleu(s)*...

B' ■** He is **blind**, he is **a blind man**; like all **the blind** he is very musical.

Complétez en utilisant les adjectifs entre parenthèses ou les pronoms **one, ones**:

1. Not all ...... play musical instruments, but I know many ...... who do (blind).
2. You shouldn't envy ...... (rich).
3. There are a lot of *(beaucoup de)* ...... in Britain ...... receive unemployment benefits *(allocations de chômage)* (unemployed, *chômeur)*.
4. ...... have a world-wide *(mondial)* reputation for their cuisine (French).
5. I visited an ...... (elderly, *âgé)* yesterday. She said she often felt lonely *(se sentir seul)*.
6. This ...... plays the piano very well. She is only nine years old (blind).
7. Some ...... are very optimistic (handicapped).
8. I pity *(avoir pitié de)* ......, but I don't do much for them (poor).
9. Take the big box *(boîte)* not the small ......
10. ...... drink tea all day (British).
11. I saw a ...... in the street; she was begging *(mendier)* (poor).
12. Which dress *(robe)* do you prefer, the long ...... or the short ......?
13. Mrs Shaw is very devoted *(dévoué)* to ...... (elderly).
14. The tall girls are English, the small ...... are French.
15. I like ......, I like ...... too, it is a beautiful language (English).
16. How many ...... are there in the room? (English).
17. ...... are fond of music *(aimer beaucoup)* (Welsh, *Gallois)*.
18. The ...... crossed *(traverser)* the street. He was accompanied by his father (blind).
19. Wasn't it terrible to see those ...... playing in the slums *(quartiers pauvres)*? We should think of ...... a little more (poor).
20. Who is Mr. Brown? The tall man or the small ......?

C ■**

S'il y en a plusieurs, *l'ordre des adjectifs épithètes* (avant le nom) pose des problèmes délicats ; on peut seulement proposer quelques principes, à partir d'exemples :

1. a **beautiful** old house : vient *en tête* l'adjectif correspondant à *l'appréciation subjective* de celui qui parle (wonderful, marvellous, nice, good...).

2. a **large** square house (*une grande maison carrée*) : *la taille* vient *avant la forme*.

3. a **large** old house : *la taille* vient *avant l'âge*.

4. a **square** old house : *la forme* vient *avant l'âge*.

5. an **old** grey house (*une vieille maison grise*) : *l'âge* vient *avant la couleur*.

    N.B. : Notez l'absence de **and** et de virgules (le plus souvent).

D ■** Les *adjectifs composés* sont formés de deux éléments dont *le premier précise le sens du second* :

green, vert → apple-green, *vert pomme*.

Les combinaisons suivantes sont les plus courantes :

a) Le *second élément* est un *adjectif*.

    A navy-blue uniform. *Un uniforme bleu marine.*

b) Le *second élément* est un *participe présent* (à sens actif) :

    A hard-working student.
    Un étudiant travailleur (who works hard).

    An oil-producing country. *Un pays producteur de pétrole (which produces petrol).*

c) Le *second élément* est un *participe passé* (à sens passif) :

    A hand-knitted pullover. *Un pull-over tricoté à la main.*

    A horse-drawn carriage. *Une voiture à cheval* (tirée, *drawn*, par un cheval ou des chevaux — pas de s à *horse* !).

d) Le *second élément* est un nom auquel on ajoute **ed** (« faux participe passé ») :

    A fair-haired boy. *Un garçon aux cheveux blonds.*

    A blue-uniformed officer. *Un officier à l'uniforme bleu.*

    A narrow-minded specialist. *Un spécialiste à l'esprit étroit.*

C' ■** He is **blind**, he is **a blind man**; like all **the blind**
he is very musical.

Traduisez (bien placer les adjectifs épithètes) :

1. C'est un vieil homme extraordinaire *(extraordinary)*.
2. Il y avait un immense *(immense)* champ *(field)* vert *(green)*.
3. C'est un jeune *(young)* chat *(cat)* gris *(grey)*.
4. Il portait *(wear)* un nouveau *(new)* costume *(suit)* bleu *(blue)*.
5. C'est une vieille femme *(woman)* charmante *(charming)*.
6. Nous avons une vieille voiture *(car)* rouge *(red)*.
7. C'était une grande *(large)* table ronde *(round)*.
8. C'était une femme jeune et grande *(tall)*.
9. Prenez la grande *(large)* boîte *(box)* ovale *(oval)*.
10. C'est une grande et vieille ville.

D' ■** *Formez des adjectifs composés à l'aide des mots en
gras :*

1. A bungalow *(pavillon)* with a red roof *(toit)*.
2. A kitchen *(cuisine)* that looks *(avoir l'air)* dirty *(sale)*.
3. A cake you made at home.
4. A lamp with a green *(vert)* shade (abat-jour).
5. A cottage *(maisonnette)* covered with snow *(neige)*.
6. A cart *(charrette)* drawn *(tiré)* by horses.
7. A house with three storeys *(étages)*.
8. A sailor *(marin)* who is sick *(malade)* at sea *(en mer)*.
9. A gentleman *(monsieur)* in a black hat *(chapeau)*.
10. A rumpus-room *(salle de jeux)* with many colours.
11. A drawing-room *(salon)* which looks comfortable.
12. A table with three legs *(pieds)*.
13. A lady with a long nose *(nez)*,
14. An exile *(exilé)* who is sick for his home *(qui a le mal du
pays)*.
15. Bob writes *(écrire)* with his left *(gauche)* hand.
16. A rabbit *(lapin)* is an animal with long ears *(oreilles)*.
17. A second home *(maison secondaire)* with white walls
(murs).

28. Le comparatif (plus que..., moins que...) et le superlatif (le plus..., le moins...)

A ■*

La supériorité (plus que, le plus)

C'est ici seulement qu'il faut distinguer entre :

a) Adjectifs courts, d'une ou de deux syllabes terminées en y :
This settee *(canapé)* is long**er** than mine *(plus long que le mien)*.

An armchair *(fauteuil)* is heav**ier** than a chair *(plus lourd qu'une chaise)*.

Au superlatif (le plus) on a :
The longest *(le plus long)*, **the heaviest** *(le plus lourd)*.

N.B. : Attention aux modifications orthographiques (p. 177)

b) Adjectifs longs, de plus de deux syllabes :
An armchair is **more comfortable than** a chair.
Au superlatif on a : **the most comfortable**.

Comparatifs et superlatifs irréguliers :

— Good, well *(bien)* → better *(meilleur, mieux)* → the best *(le meilleur, le mieux)*.
— Bad *(mauvais)*, ill *(malade)* → worse *(pire, plus malade)* → the worst *(le pire, le plus malade)*.
— Far *(loin)* → farther ou further *(plus loin)* → the farthest, the furthest, *le plus loin.*

L'infériorité (moins que, le moins)

— Comparatif : less + adjectif
This settee is **less big** and it is **less expensive than** the other one.
Ce canapé est moins grand et il est moins cher que l'autre.
— Superlatif : the least + adjectif
This settee is **the least expensive** of them all.

L'égalité (aussi... que)

This settee is not **as** big **as** the red one but it is **as** expensive **as** the other one.

N.B. : Pour exprimer la même idée on dit surtout this settee is not as big as the red one, plutôt que this settee is less big... (beaucoup moins courant).

A' ■* Genuine antiques are **more and more expensive**. They are **all the more expensive as** they are rare. **The rarer** they are **the more expensive** they are.

VOCABULAIRE - **Furniture, domestic appliances,** *les meubles, les appareils ménagers.*

Traduisez :

1. Cette lampe de chevet *(bedside lamp)* est plus moderne que la mienne.

2. Votre lampadaire *(standard-lamp)* est plus joli *(nice)* que le rouge.

3. Cette horloge rustique *(grandfather clock)* est-elle plus vieille que celle que nous avons achetée ?

4. Ce magnétoscope *(video tape recorder)* est le plus cher et le plus sophistiqué *(sophisticated)* de tous.

5. Ce magnétophone *(record player)* est pire que les autres.

6. Ce poste de télévision *(television set)* est-il meilleur que le vôtre ? Non, il est pire.

7. Un lave-vaisselle *(dishwasher)* est aussi utile qu'une machine à laver *(washing machine)*.

8. Cette commode *(chest of drawers)* est la plus grosse des trois.

9. Ce bureau *(writing-table)* est le moins commode *(convenient)* de tous ; il n'est pas aussi commode que le vôtre.

10. Trouvez-vous ce convertible *(bed-settee)* plus confortable ou moins confortable que l'autre ?

11. C'est l'armoire *(wardrobe)* la plus grande *(large)* que j'aie jamais *(ever)* achetée.

12. Vous ne trouverez pas de coussins *(cushion)* plus gros que celui-ci ; c'est vraiment *(really)* le plus gros que j'ai trouvée.

13. Ces tableaux *(painting)* ne sont pas aussi rares que les vôtres.

14. Je pense que les meubles *(furniture)* des Brown sont plus simples *(plain)* que ceux des Smith ; mais ils sont aussi chers.

B ■**★★**

Genuine antiques are **more and more expensive.**
Les antiquités authentiques sont de plus en plus chères...
▷ Avec un adjectif long l'accroissement progressif (de plus en plus) s'exprime à l'aide de **more and more** ; si l'adjectif est court on a :
Modern furniture tends to be **lighter and lighter.**
Les meubles modernes tendent à être de plus en plus légers.

L'idée contraire (de moins en moins) s'exprime à l'aide de **less and less** + adjectif (court et long) :
Genuine antiques are **less and less** easy to find.
Les antiquités authentiques sont de moins en moins faciles à trouver.

— ... They are **all the more** expensive **as** they are rare.
... Elles sont d'autant plus chères qu'elles sont rares.
▷ Le comparatif est précédé de **all the** ou **the**, adverbe ; **as** (comme, étant donné que) est parfois remplacé par **because** (parce que) ou **since** (puisque).

Si l'adjectif est court on a :

Prices are **all the higher as** antiques are rare.
Les prix sont d'autant plus élevés que les antiquités sont rares.

L'idée contraire (d'autant moins) s'exprime à l'aide de **all the less** + adjectif (court et long) :

These chests are **all the less expensive as** you see them everywhere.
Ces bahuts sont d'autant moins chers qu'on les voit partout.

— **The rarer** antiques are **the more expensive** they are.
Plus les antiquités sont rares plus elles sont chères.
▷ Chaque proposition commence par le comparatif précédé de **the**, adverbe dans ce cas *(d'autant)*. Il en est de même quand on exprime l'idée contraire (moins... moins).

The less rare antiques are **the less expensive** they are.

B' ■** Genuine antiques are **more and more expensive**. They are **all the more expensive as** they are rare. **The rarer** they are **the more expensive** they are.

Traduisez :

1. Il est de plus en plus difficile de trouver de vieux meubles.

2. Il était d'autant plus heureux d'avoir un répondeur téléphonique *(answering machine)* qu'il était souvent absent.

3. Les annuaires de téléphone *(telephone book)* sont de moins en moins disponibles *(available)*.

4. Plus nous vieillissons *(get old)* plus nous sommes attachés à *(become attached to)* notre maison.

5. Aujourd'hui la moquette est de plus en plus épaisse *(thick)*... et de plus en plus chère !

6. Une pièce paraît d'autant plus chargée *(look crowded)* qu'on y amasse des bibelots *(collect trinkets in it)*.

7. Sa machine à écrire *(typewriter)* est de plus en plus utile *(useful)* ; il est de plus en plus affairé *(busy)*.

8. Ce salon *(sitting-room)* est d'autant plus douillet qu'il y a beaucoup de rideaux *(curtain)*.

9. Il lui faut *(he needs)* des classeurs *(filing-cabinet)* de plus en plus grands *(big)* ; c'est un homme d'affaires de plus en plus important.

10. Les papiers peints *(wallpaper)* sont d'autant plus appréciés *(popular)* qu'ils sont lavables *(washable)*.

11. Plus les chaînes de télévision *(T.V. channel)* sont nombreuses *(numerous)* plus vous êtes hésitants *(hesitant)* quand vous choisissez votre programme.

12. Un bureau *(writing-desk)* est d'autant plus commode *(convenient)* qu'il a beaucoup de tiroirs *(drawer)*.

C ■**

Au lieu du superlatif ou du simple adjectif comme en français, l'anglais emploie le *comparatif* quand il n'y a que deux éléments de comparaison.

The old**er** carpet is **the more expensive** of the two.
Le vieux tapis est le plus cher des deux.

Se construisent comme des comparatifs, étant donné leur sens :

a) **Same**, même :

I bought the **same** bookcase **as** he did.
J'ai acheté la même bibliothèque que lui.

b) **Other**, autre :

I have no **other** sideboard **than** this one.
Je n'ai pas d'autre buffet que celui-ci.

C' ■** Genuine antiques are **more and more expensive**. They are **all the more expensive as** they are rare. **The rarer** they are **the more expensive** they are.

Traduisez :

1. Il y avait deux grands réfrigérateurs *(fridge)*, nous avons acheté le plus cher *(expensive)*.

2. Ils n'ont pas d'autre congélateur *(deep-freeze)* que celui-ci.

3. Nous avons la même cuisinière à gaz *(gas cooker)* que les Smith.

4. Voyez ces deux chauffe-eau *(geyser)* ; le moins efficace des deux est celui-ci.

5. Il n'y a pas d'autres casseroles *(saucepan)* que la rouge et la bleue ; prenez la plus grande des deux.

6. Nous n'avons pas ici les mêmes appareils ménagers *(household appliances)* que dans notre maison secondaire *(second home)*.

29. Les pronoms personnels

A ■*

Le tableau ci-dessous met en parallèle les pronoms personnels sujets (**je, tu, il...**) et les pronoms personnels compléments (**me, moi ; te, toi ; le, lui...**).

	Sujets	Compléments
Singulier		
1re personne	I	me
2e personne	you	you
3e personne	{ he / she / it	{ him / her / it
Pluriel		
1re personne	we	us
2e personne	you	you
3e personne	they	them

Remarques

1. **You** sert au singulier et au pluriel ; il correspond à la fois au ·**tu**· et au ·**vous**· de politesse (s'agissant d'une seule personne, selon le degré de familiarité) et au ·**vous**· (s'agissant de plusieurs personnes) :
   Oh, John, **you** are ridiculous! *(tu)*.
   Oh, Mr. Brown, **you** are ridiculous! *(vous)*.
   Oh, John and Peter, **you** are ridiculous! *(vous)*.

2. À la 3e personne du singulier **he** reprend un antécédent animé de sexe *masculin*, **she** un antécédent animé de sexe *féminin* ; **it** reprend un antécédent qui représente tout le reste (choses...) :
   John said **he** would come *(Jean a dit qu'il viendrait)*.
   Betty said **she** would come.
   My **house** is large *(grande)*, **it** is comfortable.

3. Les pronoms personnels compléments sont employés comme objet direct *et* comme objet indirect, alors qu'en français nous avons : me, moi ; te, toi ; le, lui...
   I see **her** every day, I speak to **her**.
   *Je **la** vois tous les jours, je **lui** parle.*

N.B. : Les pronoms personnels compléments se trouvent *après* le verbe dans les deux cas.

A' ■* Ian and I are cousins, we live in Scotland.

VOCABULAIRE - **The family,** *la famille*.

Remplacez par un pronom personnel sujet ou complément les groupes nominaux en gras :

1. **The little boy** was playing with **his grandparents**.
2. **My niece** was with **her husband** *(mari)*.
3. **The father and the son** *(fils)* went out together.
4. Look at **my daughter** *(fille)*, she's playing with **her doll**.
5. **My aunt** *(tante)* has been living in **that house** since 1960.
6. **The grandmother** spoils *(gâte)* **her grandson** *(petit-fils)*.
7. Have you seen **my parents**?
8. I saw **my nephew** *(neveu)* and I told him about **the problem**.
9. **My wife** *(épouse)* is jealous *(jaloux)*.
10. How old is **his father-in-law**? *(beau-père)*.
11. **Jane and Peter** went to the cinema with **their cousins**.
12. Don't speak to **your sister** *(sœur)* like that!
13. **Her grandfather** is a widower *(veuf)*.
14. **My mother** has never accepted **the loss** *(perte)* of **my brother**.
15. **Parents and children** don't always get on well *(s'entendre bien)*.
16. **Little John** is an orphan *(orphelin)*.
17. **My parents** are very interested in **their family-tree** *(arbre généalogique)*.
18. I visited **my in-laws** *(beaux-parents)* last week.
19. **Betty's house** is near **the bridge** *(pont)*.
20. **Jeff and John** are twins *(jumeaux)*.
21. **Grand-parents** enjoy **their grand-children's company**.
22. **My sister-in-law** *(belle-sœur)* is English.
23. Have you met **my stepfather**? *(beau-père, second mariage)*.

B ■** Ian and I are cousins.

Ian et moi, nous sommes cousins.

▷ En anglais c'est le pronom personnel *sujet* (I) qui s'emploie dans ce cas. On a de même :

Who broke the glass ? I did.
Qui a cassé le verre ? (C'est) moi.
You didn't break the glass, I did.
Ce n'est pas toi qui as cassé le verre, c'est moi.

(L'insistance est marquée par des pronoms en italique dans un texte imprimé ; en anglais parlé on accentue fortement ces derniers.)

Par contre, *avec un comparatif* il est courant d'employer un pronom personnel *complément* :

My brother is taller than me.
On dit aussi :
My brother is taller than I am.

— On peut dire soit : she took off her hat *(elle enleva son chapeau)*, soit : she took her hat off, mais on peut dire seulement : she took it off.

▷ Le *pronom personnel complément* se place obligatoirement *entre le verbe et la particule adverbiale* (off, on...).

— **We, you, they,** utilisés dans certains contextes, correspondent au « on » français ; un Anglais dira par exemple :

We drink a lot of tea in England.
They drink a lot of beer in Germany.

De même, vérité plus générale encore, plus universelle :

You don't do things like that for pleasure.
On ne fait pas des choses comme ça pour le plaisir.

ou One doesn't do things like that for pleasure.

▷ One est un pronom personnel indéfini qui désigne *les gens en général*, il est d'un usage beaucoup moins courant que « on » en français.

B' ■** Ian and **I** are cousins, **we** live in Scotland.

Traduisez :

1. Mon frère et moi, nous aimons beaucoup *(be fond of)* le sport.

2. Moi, je viendrai mardi, et lui, il viendra mercredi.

3. Elle est plus jeune que moi *(deux possibilités)*.

4. On ne sait jamais *(deux possibilités)*.

5. Vous et moi, nous ne sommes pas toujours d'accord.

6. Mettez *(put on)* votre imperméable *(raincoat)*, oui, mettez-le, il pleut.

7. « On boit beaucoup de vin en France », dit M. Dupont.

8. Qui l'a fait ? — Lui.

9. Sa sœur et lui sont venus jeudi matin.

10. Qui viendra demain ? — Moi.

11. Si on fait ça on cherche des histoires *(look for trouble)*.

12. Elle le fit entrer *(let in)*.

13. On dit que c'est un très bon professeur *(teacher)*.

14. Vous ne l'avez pas vue, mais elle vous a vu.

15. Ne la laisse pas tomber *(let down)*.

16. Elle conduit plus vite que lui.

17. On peut toujours essayer.

18. Qui accepterait cela ? Elle.

19. On ne saurait dire si elle est heureuse ou non.

20. On doit payer des impôts *(income taxes)*.

30. Les pronoms réfléchis et réciproques

A ■*

Le tableau ci-dessous met en parallèle les pronoms personnels sujet (**je, tu, il...**) et complément (**me, moi ; te, toi...**), les pronoms réfléchis (**moi-même, toi-même...**) et réciproques (**l'un l'autre, les uns les autres**).

Pronoms personnels sujets	Pronoms personnels compléments	Pronoms réfléchis	Pronoms réciproques
Singulier I you he she it	me you him her it	myself yourself himself herself itself	
Pluriel we you they	us you them	ourselves yourselves themselves	each other ou one another

Remarques

1. Les pronoms *réfléchis* en **self** (**selves** au pluriel) jouent deux rôles :

   a) Ils servent à *insister* sur la personne (ou la chose...) :
   I dit it **myself**, nobody helped me.
   Je l'ai fait moi-même, personne ne m'a aidé.

   b) Ils indiquent que le sujet et le complément de la phrase sont *une seule et même personne* :
   The woman was looking at **herself** in the mirror.
   La femme se regardait dans la glace.

2) Les pronoms *réciproques* **each other** et **one another**, employés indifféremment, invariables et inséparables, indiquent qu'une personne agit sur une autre et vice-versa.
   The man and the woman were looking at **each other**.
   L'homme et la femme se regardaient.
   (Point de glace ici. Il y a réciprocité, échange.)

A' ■* If only men loved each other instead of loving themselves.

VOCABULAIRE - **Feelings,** *les sentiments.*

Complétez à l'aide d'un pronom réfléchi ou réciproque :

1. Don't be selfish *(égoïste).* Don't think of ...... all the time.
2. They are enemies, they hate ...... *(détester).*
3. She blushed *(rougir).* She was ashamed of ...... *(avoir honte de).*
4. He is self-centred *(égocentrique),* he is always talking about ...... *(parler de).*
5. These two people admire ......
6. John and Peter often laugh at ...... *(se moquer).*
7. I did it, I only have ...... to blame *(s'en prendre à).*
8. Defend your interests, young men, defend ......! *(défendre).*
9. We kissed ...... and went away.
10. Did you enjoy ...... at the party, you two? *(s'amuser).*
11. We could not stand ...... *(supporter).*
12. John and Mary fell in love with ...... *(tomber amoureux).*
13. They did it ......, nobody helped them *(aider).*
14. Richard and Mary felt attracted to ...... *(éprouver de l'attirance pour).*
15. I don't like the city ......, I prefer the suburbs *(banlieue).*
16. The mother and the daughter dote on ...... *(raffoler de).*
17. We should always control ...... *(maîtriser).*
18. Mr. Brown and I were not very fond of ...... *(bien aimer).*
19. I cursed ...... *(s'en vouloir)* for being so stupid.
20. This old man talks to ......
21. They hardly *(à peine)* know ......
22. Those two girls can't bear ...... *(supporter),* they loathe ...... *(détester).*
23. Let me do it. I will do it ......

B ■** If only men loved **each other** instead of loving **themselves.**

Si seulement les hommes s'aimaient les uns les autres au lieu de s'aimer eux-mêmes

▷ Il n'est pas toujours simple d'utiliser à bon escient pronoms réciproques et pronoms réfléchis. La difficulté est accrue par le fait qu'en français le pronom « *se* » peut avoir un sens réciproque ou un sens réfléchi :

Ils s'admiraient (l'un l'autre) (they admired **each other**).
Il s'admirait (lui-même) (he admired **himself**, he was **self**-important, *suffisant, m'as-tu-vu*).

Par ailleurs certains verbes anglais qui ont un sens réfléchi s'emploient sans pronoms réfléchis ; ils expriment des actions machinales : wake up *(se réveiller)*, get up *(se lever)*, wash *(se laver)*, shave *(se raser)*, dress *(s'habiller)* :

I woke up at six. *Je me suis réveillé à six heures.*

Enfin d'autres verbes à sens réciproque s'emploient *sans each other* ou *one another* : fight *(se battre)*, gather *(se rassembler)*, meet *(se rencontrer)*, quarrel *(se quereller)*... :

We met in London. *Nous nous sommes rencontrés à Londres.*

— Quand *préposition* il y a, elle est toujours placée *avant* each other et one another :

They were speaking **to** each other. *Ils se parlaient.*

— Notez le sens du pronom réfléchi précédé de **by** :

I was by myself, I was travelling by myself.
J'étais seul, je voyageais seul.

— Au pronom personnel indéfini **one** désignant les gens (en général) correspond le réfléchi **oneself** :

One is sure to hurt oneself in doing it this way.
On est sûr de se blesser en le faisant de cette manière.

B' ■** If only men loved **each other** instead of loving **themselves.**

Traduisez :

1. Il était désespéré *(in despair)*, il s'est tué *(kill)*.

2. Ils étaient amoureux l'un de l'autre *(be in love with)*.

3. Si seulement vous pouviez vous voir ! Vous avez l'air *(look)* ridicule !

4. Respectez-vous les uns les autres.

5. Elle ne pouvait s'imaginer dans cette situation. *(imagine)*.

6. À quelle heure vous êtes-vous levé hier ?

7. Ils se sont pris de sympathie l'un pour l'autre *(take to)*.

8. Je me rase et je m'habille en dix minutes.

9. Ils sont très en colère l'un contre l'autre *(be angry with)*.

10. Ils se querellent souvent, ils ont une dent l'un contre l'autre *(bear a grudge against)*.

11. Les manifestants *(demonstrator)* se rassembleront à dix heures.

12. Mes cousins sont très proches les uns des autres *(be close to)*, ils se rencontrent souvent et parlent des heures.

13. Arrêtez de vous battre !

14. Vous êtes des égoïstes *(a selfish lot)*, vous ne pensez qu'à vous !

15. Elle s'est tuée dans un accident de voiture.

16. Ils ne s'écoutent même pas. Ils n'éprouvent aucun respect les uns pour les autres.

17. Je ne suis pas sûr de moi *(be sure of)*.

18. Nous ne pouvons pas compter sur *(rely on)* eux. Nous devons compter sur nous-mêmes. .

19. Il faut le faire soi-même.

20. Elle était seule, elle était très malheureuse *(unhappy)*.

21. On ne devrait pas penser qu'à soi.

22. Avez-vous passé la soirée seul ?

31. **Les relatifs** who **et** which, that, **etc.**

A ■* Tableau des relatifs (qui, que, dont)

Antécédent animé (surtout humain)	Antécédent non animé	Antécédent animé et non animé
Sujet **WHO**	**WHICH**	**THAT**
Complément **WHOM**	**WHICH**	**THAT**
Génitif **WHOSE** (possession) *(dont)*	**WHOSE** et **OF WHICH**	

L'observation de ce tableau montre la différence entre le français et l'anglais, illustrée dans la phrase suivante :

Did you see **the man who** took **the book which** was on the table?

*Avez-vous vu **l'homme qui** a pris **le livre qui** était sur la table ?*

▷ En anglais le relatif (sujet ou complément) n'est pas le même *selon que l'antécédent est animé (« homme ») ou non animé (« livre »).* Par contre, surtout en anglais parlé, on emploie souvent that à la place de who, whom et which.

A' ■* Did you see the man **who** took the book **which** was on the table?

VOCABULAIRE - **Trades, jobs,** *les métiers.*

Complétez par le relatif **who** *ou* **which :**

1. This man, ... is an industrialist *(un industriel),* works twelve hours a day *(par jour).*

2. He is the G.P. *(généraliste)* ...... lives next door *(qui habite à côté).*

3. Have you been to the garage ...... he recommended?

4. Is he the mechanic *(mécanicien)* ...... repaired your car?

5. He is a bookseller *(libraire)* ...... knows his onions *(connaît son affaire).*

6. It is a job ...... demands *(exiger)* a lot of patience.

7. Do you remember the vet *(vétérinaire)* ...... came for the dog?

8. The plumber *(plombier)* ...... came was not very efficient *(efficace).*

9. It is a salary ...... is hardly *(à peine)* sufficient to survive.

10. Publishing *(l'édition)* is a trade *(métier)* ...... attracts him.

11. He is a journalist ...... works for *The Financial Times.*

12. It is an area ...... does not offer many job opportunities *(débouchés).*

B ■**

— En position de *complément d'objet direct* c'est-à-dire non
précédé d'une préposition, le relatif est le plus souvent
supprimé, notamment en anglais parlé :

> The woman I met yesterday is a teacher (whom I met).
> *La femme que j'ai rencontrée hier est professeur.*

> The book I gave you wasn't new (which I gave you).
> *Le livre que je vous ai donné n'était pas neuf.*

— En position de *complément d'objet indirect*, c'est-à-dire
avec une préposition (to, with...), le relatif est aussi *supprimé*
la plupart du temps, mais alors il y a rejet de la préposition
après le verbe (intransitif).

> The man I was talking to was an engineer.
> The man to (whom) I was talking was an engineer.
> *L'homme à qui je parlais était ingérieur.*

N.B. : **That n'est *jamais précédé d'une préposition*** ; on a :

> It is the film that I was alluding to.
ou It is the film I was alluding to.
> *C'est le film auquel je faisais allusion.*

B' ■** Did you see the man **who** took the book **which** was on the table?

Transformez les phrases selon le modèle :

It is the workshop *(atelier)* in which the tailor *(tailleur)* worked.

▷ It is the workshop the tailor worked **in**.

1. Is he the butcher *(boucher)* about whom you were speaking?

2. It is the tool *(outil)* with which the technician worked.

3. The newspaperman *(journaliste)* with whom I had an argument *(se disputer)* was not sincere.

4. These are the scissors *(ciseaux)* with which the hairdresser *(coiffeur)* cut her hair.

5. The barrister *(avocat)* to whom I was speaking was quite famous *(célèbre)*.

6. This is the oven *(four)* in which the baker *(boulanger)* makes such good bread.

7. That was the dentist with whom he was so angry *(être en colère contre)*.

8. Mary is a typist *(dactylo)* with whom he is madly in love *(être follement amoureux de)*.

C ■**

It is the man **whose house** stands by the river.
*C'est l'homme **dont** la maison se tient près de la rivière.*

▷ **whose** *(dont)* exprime une relation de *possession*; la construction est identique à celle du génitif ou cas possessif; comparez :

the man's
the man whose } house (*sans* article)

Whose s'emploie aussi, notamment en anglais d'aujourd'hui, avec un antécédent *inanimé*, remplaçant la construction avec **of which**, plus lourde :

It is the house **whose shutters** are green.
It is the house **the shutters of which** are green.
C'est la maison dont les volets sont verts.

— Les constructions avec whose et of which se rencontrent surtout en anglais écrit; à l'oral on leur préfère des constructions plus simples :

It's the house **with the green shutters.**
C'est la maison aux volets verts.

— *L'homme **dont** il parlait.*
{ The man **about whom** he was speaking.
{ The man he was speaking about.

▷ Ici « **dont** » n'exprime pas une relation de possession; il signifie « au sujet de qui », « à propos de qui » (**about whom**); il ne peut donc se traduire par **whose**.

C' ■** Did you see the man who took the book which was on the table?

Traduisez les phrases suivantes :

1. C'est un dentiste *(dentist)* dont la femme est anglaise.

2. Vous souvenez-vous du pharmacien *(pharmacist)* dont je parlais ?

3. Il a été opéré *(operated on)* par un chirurgien *(surgeon)* dont la réputation *(reputation)* est mondiale *(world-wide)*.

4. Dans ce pays dont la production *(output)* est si élevée *(high)*, les ouvriers non spécialisés *(unskilled worker)* dont les salaires *(wages)* sont si bas *(low)* peuvent à peine *(hardly)* survivre *(survive)*.

5. Connaissez-vous le fleuriste *(florist)* dont il parle ?

6. C'est un homme de loi *(lawyer)* dont l'intégrité *(integrity)* est hors de doute *(unquestionable)*.

7. Mon ami Pierre dont je vous ai parlé *(tell about)* est professeur d'université *(professor)*.

8. C'est une maison à grandes *(large)* fenêtres *(window)* dont le propriétaire *(proprietor)* est un célèbre *(famous)* scientifique *(scientist)*.

9. C'est le bijoutier *(jeweller)* dont le magasin a été cambriolé *(burglarize)* la semaine dernière *(last week)*.

32. Les relatifs what et which, those who

A ■** **What** I love is playing the piano
I play the piano every day, **which** is a great joy.
*(Ce que j'aime c'est jouer du piano. Je joue du piano
tous les jours, ce qui est une grande joie)*

▷**What** (the thing which) *annonce* ce qu'on va dire alors que
which (and this), précédé d'une virgule, *reprend* ce qu'on vient
de dire.

« Ce qui », « ce que » se traduisent donc par « **what** » ou
« **which** » selon le cas mais « tout ce qui », « tout ce que » se
rendent par **all that** ou **all** ou **everything**. On a donc :

Tell me **what** you know *(dites-moi ce que vous savez)* mais
Tell me **all that** you know *(... tout ce que vous savez).*

— « *Ceux qui* », « *ceux que* », « *celles qui* », « *celles que* » se
traduisent par those who, those which ou the ones who, the
ones which :

Those who came were English.
The ones who came were English.
Ceux (celles) qui sont venu(e)s étaient anglais(es).

Au singulier on a :

The one who came was English.
Celui (celle) qui est venu(e) était anglais(se).

A' ■** **What** I love is playing the piano.
I play the piano every day, **which** is a great joy.

VOCABULAIRE - **Music,** *la musique.*

Complétez à l'aide de **what, which, all (that), those who,
the one(s) who** :

1. Tell me ...... you know, ... you know about this great
musician *(grand musicien).*

2. ...... I like best of all *(préférer de tout)* is going to the
concert.

3. He practises the violin *(il joue du violon)* every day, ...
pleases *(faire plaisir à)* his parents.

4. I envy ...... can play a musical instrument.

5. ...... is sitting on the right is a famous opera singer
(chanteur d'opéra).

6. He played out of time *(à contretemps)*, ... made the
conductor *(chef d'orchestre)* mad *(fou).*

7. ...... I can't bear *(supporter)* is people singing at the top of
their voices *(à tue-tête).*

8. He gave up the cello *(violoncelle)*, ... was a big mistake
(erreur).

9. ...... I can say is that the acoustics in that concert hall are not
very good, ... is a pity *(dommage).*

10. ...... you must have is a good ear *(l'oreille juste)*, especially
if you play a wind instrument *(un instrument à vent).*

33. Les interrogatifs who? *(qui?)* et whose *(à qui?)*, what? *(que? quoi?)* et which? *(lequel?)*, etc.

A ■*

— **What?** *(quoi? que?)* employé seul (comme pronom) se réfère à des **choses** ou, s'agissant de personnes, à la **profession** :
What are you reading? I'm reading a book.
What is Mr. Johnson? He's a doctor.

What et **which** *(quel)*, employés devant un nom (comme adjectifs) se réfèrent à des choses et des personnes ; contrairement à what, **which** (qui s'emploie aussi avec one pour éviter la répétition d'un nom déjà exprimé) **implique un nombre plus restreint** de choses ou de personnes, déjà évoquées ou connues de ceux qui parlent :
What cars do you like? (What sort of cars do you like in general? (parmi **toutes** les voitures)
mais **Which** car did you buy in the end? The Austin or the Ford? **Which one?** *Quelle voiture as-tu achetée finalement? L'Austin ou la Ford? Laquelle?*

N.B. : Si what est sujet il ne peut y avoir de structure interrogative (donc ni do, does, did) dans la question ; il en est de même avec **who?** *(qui?)* utilisé pour interroger sur *l'identité* des personnes. Comparez :
What did you say? (complément). *Qu'as-tu dit?*
What made you say it? (sujet). *Qu'est-ce qui t'a fait le dire?*
Who opened that door? (sujet). *Qui a ouvert cette porte?*

— **Whom**, forme complément de who, est rare en anglais parlé ; il est souvent remplacé par who :
Who(m) did you call on the phone? I called John.

— **Whose?** *(à qui?)* génitif ou cas possessif de who sert à interroger sur *l'appartenance* ; il se place devant le nom (sans article) :
Whose car is that? It's **Mr. Brown's**. It's **his**.
À qui est cette voiture? Elle est à Mr. Brown. C'est la sienne.

N.B. : Aux questions avec whose on répond avec un génitif (Mr. Brown's [car]) ou un pronom possessif (his). Il n'en va pas de même en français (à Mr. Brown, à lui, à moi...).

A' ■* **Who** was in that film? **Which** actor, Dustin Hoffman or Robert De Niro? **What** part *(rôle)* did he play? **Whose** husband was he in the story? Meryl Streep's.

VOCABULAIRE - **The cinema, the movies (U.S.),** *le cinéma.*

Complétez par un interrogatif :

1. ...... was that actress? Vivien Leigh.

2. ...... wife *(épouse)* was Vivien Leigh? Laurence Olivier's.

3. ...... is he? He is a film director *(metteur en scène).*

4. ...... sort of film was it? A thriller *(un film à suspense).*

5. ...... film star *(étoile du cinéma)* is your favourite, Fay Dunaway or Jane Birkins?

6. ...... do you think of the dubbing? *(doublage).*

7. ...... was on *(passer)* at the Gaumont?

8. ...... detective film *(film policier)* did you prefer, the English one or the American one?

9. ...... film made a hit *(faire un tabac)* that season? Woody Allen's.

10. ...... do you like most *(préférer)*? Documentary films.

11. ...... job *(travail)* is that? It's the scriptwriter's *(scénariste).*

12. ...... won *(gagner)* the oscar? An Italian actress.

13. ...... film won the oscar? Hitchcock's.

14. ...... is the famous actor who is also well-known as a stuntman? *(cascadeur)* Jean-Paul Belmondo.

15. ...... film was entirely shot *(tourné)* in the open *(en extérieur)*? I think it was that American producer's *(producteur).*

16. ...... cinema did you go to, the Gaumont or the Realto?

B ■**

Si *l'interrogatif* est accompagné d'une préposition (to whom?, in what?), il est placé la plupart du temps *au début de la question* ; la *préposition* se trouve alors après le verbe *en fin de phrase*. (Il en va de même des relatifs compléments d'objet indirect, p. 130.)

Who(m) did you play cards **with**?
Avec qui as-tu joué aux cartes ?

Who(m) were you talking **to**?
À qui parliez-vous ?

What is it made **of**?
De quoi est-ce fait ?

C ■*

Il y a aussi des *adverbes interrogatifs* pour interroger sur le *lieu* (where? *où ?*), la *période* (when? *quand ?*), la *cause* (why? *pourquoi ?*).

Remarquez qu'avec ces adverbes on a toujours une *structure interrogative* (avec do, does, did...) :

Where did he go? He went to Scotland.
Où est-il allé ? Il est allé en Écosse.

When will your parents visit Germany? In June.
Quand vos parents visiteront-ils l'Allemagne ? En juin.

Why would John prefer to go to Italy? Because he can speak Italian.
Pourquoi Jean préférerait-il aller en Italie ? Parce qu'il parle l'italien.

How, *adverbe interrogatif*, sert à poser de nombreuses questions sur l'*âge* (how old...), les *mesures* (how long...), les *distances* (how far...), la *fréquence* (how often...), la *durée* (how long), le *prix* (how much...)... : cf. p. 144.

B' ■** **Who** was in that film? **Which** actor, Dustin Hoffman or Robert De Niro? **What** part *(rôle)* did he play? **Whose** husband was he in the story? Meryl Streep's.

Posez des questions sur les mots en gras :

1. I was talking about **the props** *(accessoires)*.

2. He was referring to *(parler de)* **Orson Welles**.

3. I'll go to the **6 o'clock** performance *(séance)* not the ten o'clock performance.

4. The cinema was made of **brick**.

5. She is fond of **cartoons** *(dessins animés)*.

6. He looks like **a super star** *(monstre sacré)*.

7. This film reminded her of *(rappeler quelque chose à quelqu'un)* **a western**.

8. He played with **Laurence Olivier** in Hamlet.

C' ■*

Posez des questions portant sur les mots en gras :

1. She had an ice-cream *(glace)* **during the interval** *(entracte)*.

2 The shots on location *(les extérieurs)* were taken **in New York City**.

3. The film was a flop *(four)* **because the acting** *(le jeu des acteurs)* **was no good**.

4. They are showing *(passer)* that film **in a local cinema** *(du quartier)*.

5. She watched *(regarder)* that film **on Thursday**.

6. I did not enjoy *(aimer)* the film **because there were too many extras** *(figurants)*.

7. The film lasts *(durer)* **three hours**.

8. I go to the movies *(cinéma, U.S.)* **during my spare time** *(temps libre)*.

34. La place des adverbes de manière, de lieu, de temps, etc.

A ■* I like this ballerina **very much**, I saw her **again** yesterday.

J'aime beaucoup cette danseuse, je l'ai encore vue hier.

▷ La place de l'adverbe pose des problèmes délicats mais un principe demeure presque toujours valable : *ne pas le placer entre le verbe et le complément d'objet direct* (ici *ballerina,* *her*).

— Quand il y a plusieurs adverbes ou expressions adverbiales, l'ordre habituel est le suivant :
I'll examine this dossier **very carefully in my office tomorrow** :
1. *adverbes de manière* (le plus souvent en **ly** ajouté à l'adjectif : careful, *soigneux*; carefully, *soigneusement*).
2. *adverbes de lieu,* ou expressions adverbiales : in my office, *dans mon bureau*; here, *ici*; there, *là.*
3. *adverbes de temps* subdivisés en adverbes *de moment* (tomorrow, *demain*; yesterday, *hier*; now, *maintenant*; then, *alors...*) et *de fréquence* (always, *toujours*; ever, *jamais*; never, *ne... jamais*; generally, *généralement*; often, *souvent*; rarely ou seldom ; sometimes, *parfois*; usually, *habituellement...*).

N.B. : Les *adverbes de moment* se placent aussi en tête de phrase ; on pourrait donc avoir également :
Tomorrow I'll examine this dossier very carefully in my office.

— **Enough** *(assez)* se place après l'adjectif ou l'adverbe qu'il modifie mais le plus souvent avant le nom :
I had **enough** tea but it was not warm **enough**.
J'avais assez de thé mais il n'était pas assez chaud.

— **Perhaps, maybe** (surtout américain) placé en tête de phrase *n'entraîne pas*, contrairement au français, *une construction interrogative* du verbe :
Perhaps **she will come** to Paris.
Peut-être viendra-t-elle à Paris.

A' ■* I like this ballerina **very much**, I saw her **again** yesterday.

VOCABULAIRE - **Entertainments,** *les spectacles.*

Intégrez aux phrases suivantes les adverbes ou expressions adverbiales indiqués entre parenthèses :

1. I'll go to the circus *(cirque)* (tomorrow).

2. He likes conjuring tricks *(tours de prestidigitation)* (very much).

3. We are going to a show *(spectacle)* next week *(la semaine prochaine).*

4. We'll go to the fun fair *(foire d'attractions)* with them (perhaps).

5. The children liked the pantomime *(spectacle traditionnel de Noël en Grande-Bretagne* (very much).

6. She does not fancy *(aimer)* musical comedies *(comédies musicales)* (too much).

7. The interval *(entracte)* was too long, wasn't it? (enough).

8. We'll go to a disco *(discothèque)* (perhaps).

9. I could not see the jugglers *(jongleurs)* from my seat *(place)* (very well).

10. I don't like this company *(troupe)* (very much).

11. Actors should speak loud *(fort)* for everybody to hear them (enough).

12. I know this ballet dancer (very well).

13. This play *(pièce de théâtre)* is complicated for us (enough).

14. They hissed *(siffler)* the clowns the other day (very loudly, *très fort*).

15. The audience *(public)* was enthusiastic, wasn't it? (enough).

16. He read the programme (in his office, the day before, *la veille,* very conscientiously, *très consciencieusement*).

B ■** Have you **ever** seen that ballerina? No I have **never** seen her.

Avez-vous jamais vu cette danseuse? Non je ne l'ai jamais vue.

▷ **ever** (utilisé dans les phrases interrogatives et affirmatives ou déclaratives) et **never** (dans les phrases négatives) se placent entre l'auxiliaire have et le participe passé (seen). Aux autres temps ils se placent *devant le verbe* :

I **never** see her. I will **never** see her.

N.B. : Il en est ainsi pour les *adverbes de fréquence* (cf. liste dans l'unité précédente) et pour les *adverbes d'appréciation* (almost, *presque*; hardly, *à peine*; quite, *tout à fait*; nearly, *presque*: rather, *plutôt, assez...*).

Dans une réponse courte, les adverbes de fréquence et d'appréciation *précèdent l'auxiliaire* :
Do you often go to the theatre? No I **rarely** do.

Ils se placent *après be, verbe d'état* :
She **is always** there on time.
Elle est toujours là à l'heure.

— **Never** *(ne... jamais),* **not only** *(non seulement),* **hardly** *(à peine)* placés *en tête de phrase* pour marquer l'insistance, entraînent la construction interrogative du verbe :

Never **did I say** such a thing!
Jamais je n'ai dit pareille chose !

Hardly **had I finished** when he arrived (notez when).
À peine avais-je fini qu'il est arrivé.

B' ■** I like this ballerina **very much**, I saw her **again** yesterday.

Intégrez aux phrases suivantes les adverbes indiqués entre parenthèses :

1. Has the little girl been on that merry-go-round? *(manège)* No she has ...... been (never, ever).

2. We go to a show during the weekend (often).

3. They have outstanding performances *(représentations exceptionnelles)* at this theatre (usually).

4. We book stalls *(louer des fauteuils d'orchestre)*, we are not rich (rarely; enough).

5. He books his seat *(place)* long in advance (sometimes).

6. He went out of the house *(salle)* in the middle *(milieu)* of the performance. The actors were not good in his eyes (nearly; enough).

7. I have heard such a good performance *(interprétation)* of Bach (never dans les deux positions possibles).

8. The curtain *(rideau)* had hardly risen *(se lever)* when the audience *(le public)* started clapping their hands *(applaudir)* (mettre hardly en tête de phrase).

9. I liked her performance of Gisèle (rather).

10. I have been to that nightclub *(boîte de nuit)* (never).

35. How, adverbe interrogatif et exclamatif

A ■* How old **are you**? *(Quel âge avez-vous ?)*

▷ **How interrogatif** sert à poser des questions ; le verbe sera donc à la forme interrogative ; c'est **be** *(être)* qu'on emploie dans les quatre cas suivants, pour s'informer sur :

a) *L'âge*
How old **is** he? He **is** twenty (years old).

b) *Les mesures*
How long (wide, *large*; high, *haut*) is the sitting-room? It **is** seven metres long (wide, high).

c) *Les distances*
How far *(loin)* **is** it from London to Glasgow?
It **is** 400 miles.

d) *Les prix*
How much is that book?
It is £ 5.95 (5 livres 95 pence).

How sert aussi à se renseigner sur :

a) *La durée*
How long did you stay in the U.S.A.?
Combien de temps êtes-vous resté aux U.S.A. ?

b) *La fréquence*
How often *(souvent)* do you come here? Every day.

c) *La quantité, le nombre*
How much wine did you drink, **how many** glasses?
Quelle quantité de vin avez-vous bu, combien de verres ?

N.B. : **How** modifiant un adjectif (old, long, far...) ou un adverbe (often...) est suivi immédiatement de cet adjectif ou de cet adverbe ; s'il modifie un nom il ne peut s'employer qu'**avec much** ou **many** (cf. p. 80).

A' ■* "How old you are..." Sorry, I meant "How old are you?"

VOCABULAIRE - **Travelling,** *les voyages.*

En utilisant **how,** *posez les questions portant sur les mots en gras dans les phrases suivantes :*

1. The journey *(voyage)* lasted *(durer)* **two hours** *(deux questions possibles).*

2. I take the plane **twice** a month *(deux fois par mois).*

3. It is **242 miles** from London to Liverpool.

4. The railway *(chemin de fer)* ticket costs *(coûte)* **£ 2** *(deux livres sterling).*

5. That jet *(avion à réaction)* is **fifteen years old.**

6. I travel *(voyager)* from New York to Boston **every week** *(semaine).*

7. I don't have much **luggage** *(bagages).* I've only **two suitcases** *(valises) (posez deux questions).*

8. This train has **seven carriages** *(wagons).* It is **a hundred meters long** *(posez deux questions).*

9. A double-decker bus *(un autobus à double étage)* is about **six metres high.**

10. There were **forty passengers** *(voyageurs)* on the coach *(car).*

11. The track railway *(voie de chemin de fer)* is **one and a half metres wide.**

12. It took me **three hours** to pack my luggage *(posez deux questions).*

13. My car consumes **two gallons** *(gallon = 4,5 litres)* of **petrol** *(essence)* per 100 kms *(posez deux questions).*

14. I check the tyre pressure *(vérifier la pression des pneus)* **every week.**

B ■* How old you are! *(Comme vous êtes vieux!)*

▷ **How exclamatif** sert à exprimer son étonnement, sa surprise, son admiration... ; il ne s'agit plus de question mais de déclaration ; on emploiera donc une phrase déclarative ou affirmative. **How** est *suivi immédiatement de l'adjectif ou de l'adverbe* qu'il modifie :

How wonderful that actor is!
Comme cet acteur est merveilleux!

How well he played!
Comme il a bien joué!

— **How exclamatif** peut porter aussi sur un verbe :
How he laughed!
Comme il a ri!

B' ■* **"How old you are!"**... Sorry, I meant **"How old are you?"**

Transformez les phrases suivantes selon le modèle :

The Austin-mini is so convenient *(commode)* in a town.

▷ **How convenient it is!**

1. Hiking *(excursions à pied)* is so good for your health *(santé)*.

2. What an old moped *(cyclomoteur)!*

3. It was such a sturdy *(solide)* motorbike *(moto)!*

4. He was such a reckless *(imprudent)* motorist *(automobiliste)!*

5. The death toll *(le chiffre des morts)* is so high *(élevé)* every weekend!

6. The roads will be so slippery *(glissant)* in the rain!

7. What a crowded *(encombré)* motorway *(autoroute)!*

8. Hitchiking *(autostop)* was so dangerous in that country!

9. Travelling *(voyager)* is such a wonderful thing!

10. What an eventful *(mouvementé)* trip *(excursion)* we had!

36. Le gérondif ou nom verbal

A ■* I love **shopping**, I hate **cooking**.
J'adore (l'action, le fait de) faire des commissions, je déteste faire la cuisine.

▷ *Le gérondif ou nom verbal* (shopping, cooking) est formé de la base verbale (**shop, cook**) + **ing**. Il désigne une activité, un sport... (cycling, *la bicyclette, le cyclisme*, à ne pas confondre avec bicycle, l'objet). Il a toutes les fonctions du nom :

— *sujet :* shopping is one of my favourite occupations

— *complément :* I love **shopping**.

— Il s'emploie (au même titre que table, chair...) *avec tous les déterminants du nom* (articles, démonstratifs, possessifs, cas possessif...).
I couldn't bear all **that cooking** for so many people.
Je ne pouvais supporter de faire toute cette cuisine pour tant de gens.
It's **her husband's drinking** that worries her, yes it's **his drinking**.
C'est le fait que son mari boive qui l'inquiète, oui, c'est le fait qu'il boive.

— Tenant aussi du verbe, le nom verbal peut, comme un verbe, être *suivi d'un complément d'objet, d'un adverbe :*
I like **driving a sports car**, I like **driving fast**.
J'aime conduire une voiture de sport, j'aime conduire vite.

— Le nom verbal ou gérondif s'emploie *après toutes les prépositions sauf* to :
Did he do it **before coming** or **after coming**?
L'a-t-il fait avant de venir ou après être venu ?
He came in **without knocking**.
Il est entré sans frapper.

A' ■* I love **shopping,** I hate **cooking.**

VOCABULAIRE - **Housework,** *travaux de ménage.*

Complétez les phrases ci-dessous en utilisant les verbes entre parenthèses :

1. I am not interested in ...... all day (do the housework, *faire le ménage*).

2. ...... is hard work (polish the floor, *cirer le parquet*).

3. I'm fed up with ...... in this house (make the beds, *faire les lits*).

4. It's her ...... all the time that annoys *(agacer)* me! (knit, *tricoter*).

5. I'll dust *(épousseter)* the furniture *(meubles)* before ...... (sweep the floor, *balayer le parquet*).

6. ...... damages *(abîmer)* your eyesight *(la vue)* (sew, *coudre*).

7. ...... a carpet *(tapis)* is not more interesting than ......! (hoover, *passer l'aspirateur sur*, sweep, *balayer*).

8. John hates ...... his room (tidy up, *ranger*).

9. I much prefer ...... to ...... (make cakes, *faire des gâteaux*; wash up the dishes, *faire la vaisselle*).

10. I don't like the children's ...... when I am doing a room *(faire une pièce)* (play about, *jouer ici et là*).

11. You can't very well darn socks *(repriser des chaussettes)* without ...... a needle, can you? (use, *utiliser*).

B ■**

Quelques *verbes courants suivis du gérondif* ou nom verbal :

— **avoid** (smoking...), *éviter (de fumer...)*; **burst out** (laughing), *éclater de rire*; **consider** ou **envisage** (going...), *envisager (d'aller)*; **enjoy** ou **like** (dancing...), *aimer (danser...)*; **give up** (smoking), *cesser (de fumer...)*; **go on** ou **keep on** (doing...), *continuer (à faire)*; **mind** ou **object to**, *voir un inconvénient à* (do you mind my smoking?, *ça vous dérange que je fume ?*) ; **prevent from** (doing...), *empêcher (de faire...)*; **stop** (working...), *arrêter de (travailler...)*; **succeed in** (doing...), *réussir (à faire...)*

— **Like** *(aimer)*, **love** *(adorer)*, **hate** *(détester)*, **prefer** *(préférer)* sont suivis du nom verbal pour exprimer un goût... *permanent*.

I love going to the theatre (generally) ≠ I'd love to go to the theatre tomorrow.

N.B. : **like, love, hate, prefer** sont donc suivis du nom verbal ou de l'infinitif (to go), *jamais de la simple base verbale* (go).

— **Begin** ou **start** *(commencer)*, **intend** *(avoir l'intention de)* sont suivis du nom verbal ou de l'infinitif :

It started **raining** ou It started **to rain**.
Il commença à pleuvoir.

Quelques *expressions courantes suivies du gérondif* :

I am **used to** going there. *J'ai l'habitude d'y aller.*
I **can't help** laughing. *Je ne puis m'empêcher de rire.*
I **feel like** smoking a cigar. *J'ai envie de fumer un cigare.*
I **look forward to** seeing her again. *J'ai hâte de la revoir.*
It is **no good** (ou **no use**) crying. *Ça ne sert à rien de pleurer.*
It is **worth** doing it. *Ça vaut la peine de le faire.*

B' ■** I love **shopping**, I hate **cooking**.

Traduisez les phrases suivantes. Employez le gérondif ou nom verbal correspondant aux verbes entre parenthèses :

1. J'ai envie de lire *(read)*, pas de faire le ménage! *(do the housework)*.

2. Elle ne peut s'empêcher de tricoter *(knit)* quand elle regarde la télévision *(watch T.V.)*.

3. Ça ne sert à rien d'épousseter *(dust)* les meubles *(furniture)* toutes les cinq minutes.

4. Elle a hâte de regarder la télévision après avoir fait le ménage *(do the chores)*.

5. Je préfère la couture *(sew)* au tricot *(knit)*.

6. Elle m'a empêché de faire la vaisselle *(do the washing up)*.

7. J'envisage de prendre une femme de ménage *(hire a charwoman)*.

8. Elle a l'intention de repasser *(iron)* avant de faire les lits *(make a bed)*.

9. Se servir *(use)* d'une machine à coudre *(sewing machine)* n'est pas toujours si simple.

10. L'opération qui consiste à *(consist in)* à faire *(do)* toutes les pièces à fond *(thoroughly)* s'appelle *(is called)* le grand nettoyage de printemps *(spring-cleaning)*.

37. Les prépositions de lieu, (in, at, to), de temps (till, until) etc.

A ■* With this ticket you can go **from** London **to** Manchester, you can stay **in** Manchester for three days, **till** Sunday.

Avec ce billet vous pouvez aller de Londres à Manchester, vous pouvez rester à Manchester pendant trois jours, jusqu'à lundi.

▷ 1. « à », « jusqu'à », prépositions de *lieu*, se traduisent par **to** ou **in** (ou **at**) selon qu'il y a notion de déplacement, de mouvement ou non. Cette distinction n'existe pas en français. Remarquez la même différence d'emploi entre **in** *(dans, à l'intérieur de)* et **into** (vers l'intérieur de, avec déplacement) :

He read **in** the carriage and then he went **into** the corridor.
Il a lu dans le compartiment puis il est allé dans le couloir.

2. En français « jusqu'à » est à la fois préposition de lieu et de temps (« jusqu'à lundi »). En anglais **till** ou **until** est seulement préposition de *temps*. Remarquez :

I'll go **to** (**as far as**) Manchester, I'll stay there **till** Sunday.
J'irai jusqu'à Manchester, j'y resterai jusqu'à Dimanche.

3. **From** (de) indique la *provenance*.

— Il faut bien distinguer aussi entre **across**, d'un côté à l'autre de, à travers (une *étendue* : les champs, la mer, la rue...) et **through**, à travers (une *épaisseur*) :

He swam **across** the lake.
Il a traversé le lac à la nage.

The explorer was walking **through** the jungle.
L'explorateur s'enfonçait dans la jungle.

— Avec les interrogatifs (p. 138) et les relatifs, quand ils sont omis en position de complément d'objet indirect (p. 130), les prépositions sont placées *après* le verbe : c'est la pratique courante en anglais parlé :

Who did you talk **to**? (to whom did you talk?)
À qui avez-vous parlé ?

The man you spoke **about** was English (the man about whom...).
L'homme dont vous parliez était anglais.

A' ■* With this ticket you can go **from** London **to** Manchester, you can stay **in** Manchester for three days, **till** Sunday.

VOCABULAIRE - **Business and the firm,** *les affaires et la société.*

Complétez les phrases suivantes par des prépositions :

1. The businessman walked …… his office *(bureau).*

2. The firm *(société)* was prosperous …… 1982.

3. The junior executive *(jeune cadre)* travelled *(voyager)* …… London …… New York every month.

4. Who was the accountant *(comptable)* talking ……? He was talking …… the boss *(patron).* What was he talking ……? He was talking …… the company.

5. The manager *(directeur)* held a meeting *(réunion)* …… his office …… four o'clock.

6. There was a big slogan written …… the front *(façade)* of the company building.

7. Business was brisk *(marche bien)* …… 1929.

8. The head-office *(siège social)* is …… Brussels.

9. The clerk *(employé de bureau)* commuted *(faire la navette)* …… home …… work.

10. I'll be doing clerical work *(travail de bureau)* …… November.

11. The General Manager *(président-directeur général)* travels *(voyage)* …… Japan for business.

12. She is a typist *(dactylo)* …… a joint-stock company *(société par actions).*

13. Wait …… six o'clock, when I come back …… the office.

14. The paper knife *(couteau à papier)* went …… the sheet of paper *(feuille de papier).*

B ■**

Prépositions de temps ou expressions de temps: emplois particuliers, confusions à éviter :

— **for** s'emploie pour une *durée*, **during** pour une *période* :
  I was in London **for** a week. It was **during** the holidays.
  J'étais à Londres pendant une semaine. C'était pendant les vacances.

— I worked **in** the morning, never **in** the afternoon.
  Je travaillais Ø le matin, jamais Ø l'après-midi.

— What did you do Ø **last week**? (last month, last year, *mois, année*). What will you do Ø **next week?** (next month...).
  Qu'avez-vous fait la semaine dernière ? Que ferez-vous la semaine prochaine ?

— **On** s'emploie pour indiquer le jour, la date :
  I'll come **on** that day, **on** Wednesday, **on** December 12th.
  Je viendrai ce jour-là, le mercredi, le 12 décembre.

— **One** day (**one** morning, **one** afternoon, **one** evening) he went away.
  Un jour (un matin, un après-midi, un soir) il s'en alla.

  Notez l'emploi de **one** (et non pas de a).

B' ■** With this ticket you can go **from** London **to** Manchester, you can stay **in** Manchester for three years, **till** Sunday.

Complétez par des prépositions si nécessaire:

1. The Board of Directors *(conseil d'administration)* met *(se réunir)* ...... three hours ...... February 3rd.

2. Business was slack *(ralenti)* ...... the summer.

3. The staff *(personnel)* met ...... the morning, not ...... the afternoon.

4. I'll learn shorthand *(sténo)* ...... day.

5. Inflation was rampant *(faire rage)* ...... last year.

6. The secretary did not come to work ...... Thursday.

7. That senior executive *(cadre supérieur)* usually *(habituellement)* spends three weeks ...... Spain ...... his holidays.

8. I must buy a typewriter *(machine à écrire)* ...... day.

9. The executive worked ...... the City ...... a month ...... last winter *(l'hiver dernier)*.

10. I worked in that firm ...... years ...... the war *(guerre)*.

C ■**

Des problèmes délicats se posent quand les prépositions ne sont pas les mêmes dans les deux langues ; il est alors conseillé d'*apprendre en même temps que les verbes, noms, adjectifs...* nouvellement rencontrés, *les prépositions qui leur sont associées.* Il arrive aussi avec certains verbes qu'il y ait une préposition en anglais mais pas en français et vice-versa.

Voici quelques exemples parmi les plus courants :

— *avec les verbes* on a :

arrive in, at ; ask somebody for something, *demander quelque chose à quelqu'un* ; borrow something from somebody, *emprunter quelque chose à quelqu'un* ; consist in, of, *consister en* ; cover with, in, *couvrir de* ; deal with, *traiter (un problème...)* ; depend on, *dépendre de* ; enter a room, *entrer dans une pièce* ; go home, come home (pas de préposition avec home et les verbes de mouvement) ; prevent from doing, *empêcher de faire* ; remind somebody of something, *rappeler quelque chose à quelqu'un* ; suffer from, *souffrir de* ; think of, about, *penser à* ; wait for somebody..., *attendre quelqu'un...,* etc.

— *avec les qualificatifs* on a :

angry with somebody, *en colère contre quelqu'un* ; angry at something, *en colère contre quelque chose* ; disappointed at, about, in, with, *déçu de, par* ; different from ; good at (≠ bad at), *bon en (langues...)* ; interested in, *intéressé par* ; responsible for, *responsable de* ; satisfied with, *satisfait de* ; surprised at, *surpris de, par...*

— *avec la notion de but :*

(pour, afin de + verbe) on a le plus souvent to ou **in order to** (plutôt que for + ing) :

You must work (in order) to succeed.
Il vous faut travailler pour réussir.

C' ■** With this ticket you can go **from** London **to** Manchester, you can stay **in** Manchester for three days, **till** Sunday.

Complétez par des prépositions si nécessaires :

1. I am not interested ...... book-keeping *(comptabilité)*.

2. The secretary asked ...... the boss *(patron)* ...... a pay rise *(augmentation de salaire)*.

3. The manager's desk *(bureau)* was covered ...... dossiers.

4. It was not easy to deal ...... the industrial dispute *(conflit social)*. The staff *(personnel)* were very angry ...... the boss *(patron)*.

5. It depends ...... the order-books *(carnets de commandes)*.

6. Executives often go ...... home late *(tard)* ...... the evening.

7. You must not make the boss wait ...... you.

8. The manager was not satisfied ...... his employee *(employé)*.

9. Will you remind me ...... that letter I have to type? *(taper à la machine)*. If you don't, I'll never think ...... it.

10. The boss is responsible ...... the running *(organisation)* of the business *(entreprise, affaire, commerce)*. He must work hard run to it properly *(comme il faut)*.

11. A multinational *(une multinationale)* is not very different ...... another.

12. He entered ...... his office at 8 o'clock sharp *(à 8 heures tapantes)*.

13. He did not have enough money, he had to borrow some ...... a friend.

D ■**

Les prépositions et les particules adverbiales des verbes composés ont souvent la même forme : in, out, up, down, off, through..., etc. Il importe de ne pas les confondre.

a) Les *prépositions* sont nécessairement *suivies d'un complément* :

He is **in London**.

Il est donc logique que dans les verbes à *particules prépositionnelles* les prépositions soient supprimées s'il n'y a pas de complément. On dit wait **for** me *(attendez-moi)* mais wait *(attendez)*.

b) Les *particules adverbiales*, par contre, *ne peuvent être supprimées* ; elles sont liées aux verbes composés qui les précèdent ; elles en modifient le sens, parfois considérablement sinon totalement :

run, *courir* ; run in, entrer *(en courant)* ; run out, *sortir en courant*
take, *prendre* ; take over, *prendre la relève* ; take off, *décoller (avion)*

D' ■** With this ticket you can go **from** London **to** Manchester, you can stay **in** Manchester for three days, **till** Sunday.

Traduisez :

1. Écoutez. Écoutez *(listen to)* le patron *(boss)*, écoutez-le.

2. Le jeune cadre *(junior executive)* alla à son bureau *(office)* en voiture *(drive)*.

3. Il attendait, oui, il attendait sa secrétaire *(wait for)*.

4. « Elle entra précipitamment », dit-il. Puis il ajouta *(added)* : « Elle entra précipitamment dans son bureau » *(rush)*.

5. Je suis responsable, je suis entièrement *(entirely)* responsable de ce service *(department)*.

6. Regardez-le, regardez, il est sorti en courant *(run)*.

7. Allumez la lumière *(light)*, éteignez le poste *(radio set)* *(on-off-switch)*.

8. Il posa son attaché-case sur la chaise et brancha le chauffage électrique *(electric fire)*.

38. Les mots de liaison

On les appelle aussi « *mots charnières* ». Ils ont pour fonction de *lier* entre eux des mots ou groupes de mots, des membres de phrases (propositions) ou des phrases. Ce sont des *prépositions* (sur, dans..., cf. chapitre 37), des *conjonctions de coordination* (et, ou, mais...) ou de *subordination* (parce que, bien que...), parfois des *adverbes* ou *locutions adverbiales* (premièrement, de plus, cependant...). Ils servent à résumer ou expliquer sa pensée, à apporter des arguments, des réserves, à introduire des nuances... Il importe de les connaître pour suivre la démarche de celui qui s'exprime. Voici par ordre alphabétique, les mots de liaison les plus courants, illustrés par des exemples.

AFTER (*après*, préposition ; *après que*, conjonction)
I'll come **after** dinner
I watched television **after** I had dinner

ALSO (*aussi, également*)
I will come **also** (too, as well)

ALTHOUGH, THOUGH (*bien que, quoique*)
I will come **although** am tired (*fatigué*)

AND (*et*)
I have a brother **and** a sister

AND SO (*... aussi*)
I speak English **and so** does my brother (*mon frère aussi*)
(notez la construction, cf. p. 48)

AS (*comme, au moment où ; comme, puisque, étant donné que ; comme,* introduisant une comparaison)
As I came in, the telephone rang (*sonna*)
As it was raining I went to the cinema (*comme il pleuvait...*)
These rich people do not live **as** we do (like us)

AS FOR... (*quant à...*)
I like classical music, **as for** John, he likes jazz

AS LONG AS (*tant que*)
I'll work **as long as** I am able to
Je travaillerai tant que j'en serai capable

AS SOON AS *(dès que)* (cf. p. 38)
I'll come **as soon as** I have the time
Je viendrai dès que j'en aurai le temps

AS THOUGH, AS IF *(comme si)*
He did **as though** he knew nothing
Il a fait comme s'il ne savait rien

AT ANY RATE, IN ANY CASE *(en tout cas, quoi qu'il en soit)*
I'll come **at any rate**, even if it rains *(même s'il pleut)*

BECAUSE *(parce que)*, **BECAUSE OF** *(à cause de)*
He was angry *(en colère)* **because** you did not come
He was angry **because of** your carelessness *(négligence)*

BEFORE *(avant*, préposition ; *avant que*, conjonction)
I'll do it **before** Tuesday
I'll do it **before** you come back *(revenir)*

BOTH *(deux, à la fois)* (cf. p. 90)
Both Alan and John smoke a lot, they are **both** heavy smokers
(gros fumeurs), they smoke **both** cigarettes and cigars

BUT (*mais ; sauf, excepté*, **EXCEPT**)
I will come **but** I won't stay late *(rester tard)*
Give any book **but** (except) that one

BY THE WAY, INCIDENTALLY *(à propos, pendant que j'y pense)*
By the way, did he tell you that he would come?
À propos, est-ce qu'il t'a dit qu'il viendrait ?

CONSEQUENTLY, IN CONSEQUENCE, THEREFORE *(en conséquence, par conséquent, donc)*
You have lied, **consequently** you will be punished
Tu as menti, en conséquence tu seras puni

EITHER... OR *(ou* [*bien*]*... ou* [*bien*]*)*
I'll go **either** to the cinema **or** to the theatre

EVEN *(même)*
Even John passed his exam
Même John a été reçu à son examen

EVEN IF, EVEN THOUGH *(même si)*
I'll go out **even if** it rains *(même s'il pleut)*

FIRST(LY), IN THE FIRST PLACE *(d'abord, pour commencer)*

   First we'll go to the cinema, then we'll go to a restaurant

FOR *(pour,* préposition ; *durant, pendant,* préposition ; *car, parce que,* conjonction de cause)

   I did it **for** her
   I'll be in London **for** six days
   I must go now **for** it's getting late *(il se fait tard)*

FOR FEAR (THAT) *(de crainte que...)*

   He held it tight **for fear (that)** it should drop
   Il le tenait ferme de crainte qu'il ne tombe

HOWEVER *(cependant, néanmoins)*; **HOWEVER + ADJECTIF ou ADVERBE** *(quelque* ou *si... que +* Subjonctif ou *avoir beau +* infinitif*)*

   They say so, I do not, **however**, believe it
 - *On le dit, je ne le crois pas cependant*
   However tall he is (may be) he can't reach it
   Si grand qu'il soit (il a beau être grand), il n'arrive pas à l'atteindre

IF *(si)*

   If you listen carefully you will hear it
   Si vous écoutez attentivement vous l'entendrez

IN A WORD, IN A NUTSHELL, IN SHORT *(en un seul mot, en bref, pour résumer)*

   It rained, the car broke down, the hotel was uncomfortable, **in a word**, it was a horrible day
   Il a plu, la voiture est tombée en panne, l'hôtel était inconfortable, en un mot, ce fut une journée affreuse

IN CASE... *(au cas où...)*

   I'll be there, **in case** you can't come
   Je serai là au cas où tu ne pourrais pas venir

INDEED *(en effet, en vérité, vraiment...)*

   Indeed he was right ou he was right **indeed**
   En effet il avait raison ou *Il avait bel et bien raison*

IN OTHER WORDS *(en d'autres termes)*
He was tipsy, **in other words** he had drunk a little too much
Il était éméché, en d'autres termes il avait un peu trop bu

IN SPITE OF *(malgré, en dépit de)*
He did it **in spite of** my advice *(conseils)*

INSTEAD OF *(au lieu de)*
He gave me the blue book **instead of** the red one
He went out **instead of** working *(au lieu de travailler)*

LASTLY, FINALLY *(enfin, finalement,* dans une énumération d'arguments...)
First(ly) we didn't have the time, secondly we did not have the money, **lastly** the weather was not favourable
Premièrement nous n'avions pas le temps, deuxièmement nous n'avions pas l'argent, enfin le temps n'était pas favorable

MOREOVER, BESIDES *(en outre, de plus)*
He is tired, he has a bad cold, **moreover** his morale is low
Il est fatigué, il a un gros rhume, en outre il a mauvais moral

NEITHER + forme interrogative *(... non plus)* (cf. p. 48)
He did not come, **neither** (or **nor**) did his brother
He did not come, his brother did **not** come **either**
Il n'est pas venu, son frère non plus

NEITHER... NOR... *(ni... ni)*
He plays **neither** the saxophone **nor** the clarinet, he plays the bass

NEVERTHELESS, NONETHELESS *(néanmoins, cependant)*
I shall go **nevertheless**, *j'irai quand même*

NO MATTER *(peu importe, tant pis)*
"Be yourself, **no matter** what they say" (Sting)
Soyez vous-même, quoi qu'on en dise

NOT ONLY... BUT... ALSO *(non seulement... mais aussi...)* (cf. p. 142)
Not only is he stupid **but** he is **also** pretentious

NOW *(or, donc:* pour reprendre la parole après une pause)
Now, it was so dark that we could not see a thing
Or, il faisait si noir qu'on ne voyait absolument rien

ON THE CONTRARY *(au contraire)*

I would not call him intelligent. **On the contrary**, I've never seen anyone so stupid

Je ne dirais pas qu'il est intelligent. Au contraire, je n'ai jamais vu quelqu'un d'aussi stupide

ON THE ONE HAND... ON THE OTHER HAND... *(d'une part..., d'autre part...)*

On the one hand I wanted to help him, **on the other hand** I wouldn't like to encourage him to be lazy

D'une part je voulais l'aider, d'autre part je ne voulais pas l'encourager à la paresse

OR ELSE, OTHERWISE *(ou bien alors..., sinon)*

Hurry up **or else** you'll be late

Dépêche-toi, sinon tu seras en retard

PROVIDED *(pourvu que..., à condition que...)*

I will go **provided** you go too *(à condition que tu y ailles aussi)*

SINCE *(depuis,* préposition ; since, *depuis que,* conjonction*)*

I have worked here **since** 1970, **since** my mother died

Je travaille ici depuis 1970, depuis que ma mère est morte

Since you're interested I'll show you the others

Étant donné que (comme) tu es intéressé je te montrerai les autres

SO *(donc, en conséquence, aussi)*

I was tired, **so** I went to bed

J'étais fatigué, aussi je suis allé me coucher

SO THAT *(tellement que...),* that est souvent omis en américain ; *afin que, afin de* + verbe, conjonction de but

He was **so** drunk **that** he could hardly stand

Il était si ivre qu'il pouvait à peine tenir debout

I'll go to the U.S.A. **so that** I can practise my English

J'irai aux U.S.A. afin de pouvoir pratiquer mon anglais

STILL *(cependant, toutefois, néanmoins)*
    He may be sincere. **Still** I don't believe him
    Il est peut-être sincère. Cependant je ne le crois pas

THAT *(que,* conjonction, omise le plus souvent à l'oral)
    I think (**that**) you're right, *je crois que vous avez raison*

THEN *(puis, ensuite, après ; par conséquent, dans ce cas, alors)*
    I had breakfast and **then** I went out
    I've lost my watch. **Then** you must buy another one
    J'ai perdu ma montre. Alors il faut que tu en achètes une autre

THEREFORE *(en conséquence, par conséquent, aussi, donc)*
    I wasn't present, **therefore** I couldn't tell you
    Je n'y étais pas, aussi je ne saurais vous dire

THOUGH (cf. **ALTHOUGH** ; *cependant, pourtant,* adverbe)
    It was hard work. We enjoyed it **though**
    Ce fut une rude besogne. Ça nous a plu cependant

THUS *(ainsi, donc, par conséquent)*
    There has been no rain. **Thus**, the crops will suffer
    Il n'y a pas eu de pluie. Donc les récoltes vont en souffrir

TILL, UNTIL *(jusqu'à, jusqu'à ce que,* préposition et conjonction de temps)
    I'll be there **till** January 31st
    I'll wait **till** she comes
    J'attendrai jusqu'à ce qu'elle arrive

UNLESS *(à moins que... ne)*
    I'll be there **unless** I am taken ill
    Je serai là à moins que je ne tombe malade

WHATEVER *(quoi que ce soit que ou qui, quoi que)*
    Whatever he asks for, he is sure to get
    Quoi qu'il demande, il est certain de l'obtenir

WHEN *(quand,* cf. p. 38)
    When I have finished I'll have a cup of tea

WHENEVER *(toutes les fois que ; à quelque moment que)*
    Whenever we see him we speak to him
    Toutes les fois que nous le voyons nous lui parlons

Come **whenever** you like
Venez quand vous voudrez (n'importe quand)

WHEREAS (*tandis que, alors que...*, marquant l'opposition)
I want a house, **whereas** she would rather live in a flat
Je veux une maison alors qu'elle préférerait vivre dans un appartement

WHETHER (*si... ou non*), souvent remplacé par if dans la conversation
She asked **whether** he was coming
Elle m'a demandé s'il venait (ou non)

WHILE (*pendant que ; tandis que, alors que*, marquant l'opposition, comme **WHEREAS**)
I'll be watching TV **while** he will be reading
Je regarderai la télé pendant qu'il lira
You like sport **while** I prefer reading
Vous aimez le sport alors que je préfère la lecture

YET (*cependant, pourtant*)
He is ill, **yet** he goes out
Il est malade, pourtant il sort

Annexes

Auxiliaires modaux

■ Conjugaison

à partir de l'exemple **can**
(substitut ou équivalent : **be able to**)

N.B. : Comparez formes pleines et formes réduites (p. 174).

Présent	Prétérit	Present perfect		
Affirmatif			(Substitut ou équivalent)	
I can (see) etc.	I could (see) etc.	I You We They	have 've	been able (to see)
		He She It	has 's	been able (to see)
Négatif				
I cannot (see) etc. I can't (see) etc.	I could not (see) etc. I couldn't (see) etc.	I You We They	have not haven't	been able (to see)
		He She It	has not hasn't	been able (to see)
Interrogatif				
Can I (see)? etc.	Could I (see)? etc.	Have	I you we they	been able (to see)?
		Has	he she it	been able (to see)?

Pluperfect	*Futur*	*Conditionnel*
(Substitut) I { had / 'd } { been able / (to see) } etc.	(Substitut) I { will / 'll } { be able / (to see) } etc. On trouve parfois, avec I et we : I { shall We { 'll } { be able / (to see) }	(Substitut) I { would / 'd } { be able / (to see) } etc.
I { had not / hadn't } { been able / (to see) } etc.	I { will not / won't } { be able / (to see) } etc. On trouve parfois shall avec I et we : I { shall not We { shan't } { be able / (to see) }	I { would not / wouldn't } { be able / (to see) } etc.
Had I been able (to see)? etc.	Shall { I / we } { be able / (to see) }? Will { you / he / she / it / they } { be able / (to see) }?	Would I be able (to see)? etc.

Forme simple

■ Conjugaison

à partir des exemples **talk** (parler), verbe régulier
et **speak, spoke, spoken** (parler), verbe irrégulier

N.B. : Comparez formes pleines et formes réduites (p. 174).

	Présent	*Prétérit*	*Present perfect*
Affirmatif	I You We They } talk/speak	Verbe régulier I talk**ed** etc.	I You We They } have 've } talk**ed** (v. régulier)
	He She It } talk/speak	V. irrégulier I sp**o**ke etc.	He She It } ha**s** **'s** } **spoken** (v. irrégulier)
Négatif	I You We They } do not don't } talk/ speak	I { **did** not **did**n't } talk/ speak etc.	I You We They } have not haven't } talk**ed** (v. régulier)
	He She It } does not doesn't } talk/ speak		He She It } ha**s** not ha**s**n't } **spoken** (v. irrégulier)
Interrogatif	Do { I you we they } talk?/ speak?	**Did** I { talk?/speak? etc.	Have { I you we they } talk**ed**? (v. régulier)
	Doe**s** { he she it } talk?/ speak?		Ha**s** { he she it } **spoken?** (v. irrégulier)

Pluperfect	*Futur*	*Conditionnel*
I { had talk**ed** (v. régulier) 'd **spoken** (v. irrégulier) } etc.	I { will / 'll } talk/ speak etc. On trouve parfois, avec I et we : I { shall We { 'll } talk/ speak	I { would / 'd } talk/ speak etc.
I { had not talk**ed** (v. régulier) dn't **spoken** (v. irrégulier) }	I { will not / won't } talk/ speak etc. On trouve parfois shall avec I et we : I { shall not We { shan't } talk/ speak	I { would not / wouldn't } talk/ speak etc.
Had I { talk**ed**? (v. régulier) **spoken**? (v. irrégulier) }	Shall { I / we } talk?/ speak? Will { you / he / she / it / they } talk?/ speak?	Would I talk?/speak? etc.

Forme progressive

■ Conjugaison

à partir de **talk** (parler)

N.B. : Comparez formes pleines et formes réduites (p. 174).

Présent	*Prétérit*	*Present perfect*
Affirmatif I am ('m) You We } are They } 're } talking He She } is it } 's	I He She } was } talking It You We } were } talking They	I You } have } been We } 've } talking They He She } has } been It } 's } talking
Négatif I am not ('m not) You We } are not They } aren't } talking He She } is not it } isn't	I He } was not } talking She } wasn't It You We } were not } talking They } weren't	I You } have not } been We } haven't } talking They He She } has not } been It } hasn't } talking
Interrogatif Am I Are { you { we { they } talking? Is { he { she { it	Was { I { he { she } talking? { it Were { you { we } talking? { they	Have { I { you { we } been { they } talking? Has { he { she } been { it } talking?

Pluperfect	*Futur*	*Conditionnel*
I { had / 'd } been talking etc.	I { will / 'll } be talking etc.	I { would / 'd } be talking etc.
	On trouve parfois, avec I et we : I { shall / 'll } be We { } talking	
I { had not / hadn't } been talking etc.	I { will not / won't } be talking etc.	I { would not / wouldn't } be talking etc.
	On trouve parfois shall avec I et we : I { shall not / shan't } be We { } talking	
Had I been talking? etc.	Shall { I / we } be talking? Will { you / he / she / it / they } be talking?	Would I be talking? etc.

Les formes réduites ou contractées

A l'exception de **let**'s où **'s** remplace **us** (let's speak English cf. p. 146), *la contraction porte sur l'auxiliaire et la négation*, comme on le constate dans la conjugaison (pp. 168 à 173) et dans la liste des formes réduites ci-dessous. A l'écrit, une forme réduite se reconnaît à la présence d'une *apostrophe* qui remplace un ou plusieurs éléments manquants. Remarquez les cas particuliers de **will not** contracté en **won't** et de **may not** dont la contraction est très rare.

Liste des formes réduites ou contractées

I'm (I am)	didn't (did not)
I've (I have)	hadn't (had not)
He's (he is, he has)	won't (will not)
I'll (I will, I shall)	shan't (shall not)
I'd (I would, I should, I had)	wouldn't (would not)
Isn't (is not)	shouldn't (should not)
Aren't (are not)	can't (cannot)
Wasn't (was not)	couldn't (could not)
Weren't (were not)	mustn't (must not)
Haven't (have not)	mayn't (may not), très rare
Hasn't (has not)	might (might not)
Doesn't (does not)	
Don't (do not)	

Les formes réduites ou contractées s'emploient presque toujours dans la *conversation*. S'il arrive qu'on leur préfère les *formes pleines*, c'est presque toujours parce qu'on veut *insister*, affirmer son point de vue, contredire... etc. Si négation il y a, la voix porte alors sur celle-ci (en italique dans un texte imprimé, soulignée dans un texte manuscrit ou dactylographié) :

I won't come. *Je ne viendrai pas.*
I will **not** come! *Pas question que je vienne !*

Les formes réduites ou contractées s'emploient aussi *de plus en plus dans la langue écrite* d'aujourd'hui.

Les préfixes et les suffixes
(formation des mots, mots dérivés)

Il est très utile pour acquérir du vocabulaire nouveau de connaître le rôle des *préfixes* (placés *devant* les mots de base) et des *suffixes* (placés *derrière*). Voici les principales combinaisons possibles :

1. *Adjectifs de sens contraire* obtenus à l'aide des préfixes **un-, in-** et **dis-**
   Comfortable → **un**comfortable
   visible → **in**visible
   honest → **dis**honest

N.B. : Soyez très prudent si vous vous risquez à former vous-même de tels adjectifs. Il arrive que les Anglais se trompent, notamment dans le choix entre **un** et **in**...

2. *Adjectifs en* **-ful** *et* **-less** accolés à des noms :
   Joyful *(joyeux)* ≠ joyless *(triste)*

   Le suffixe **-less** *peut se trouver aussi après des noms :*
   a child**less** couple, *un couple sans enfants*

3. *Adjectifs en* **-y**, à partir de noms :
   rain *(pluie)* → rainy *(pluvieux)*

4. *Adjectifs en* **-ish** (idée d'approximation, appliquée notamment aux couleurs) ; **-ish** est accolé à des noms, des adjectifs ou même des nombres...
   green *(vert)* → greenish *(verdâtre)*
   small *(petit)* → smallish, *plutôt petit*
   sixty → sixtyish *(qui a) dans les soixante ans*

5. *Adjectifs en* **-able**, à partir de verbes (qui peut être...)
   drink *(boire)* → drinkable *(potable)*
   bear *(supporter)* → bearable *(supportable)*

6. *Adjectifs en* **-ly** dérivés de noms :
   friend *(ami)* → friendly *(amical)*

7. *Adverbes en* **-ly** à partir d'adjectifs
   sincere → sincerely, *sincèrement*
   La plupart des adverbes de manière (p. 140) sont ainsi formés.

8. *Noms abstraits en* **-ness** dérivés d'adjectifs :
   gentle *(doux)* → gentle**ness** *(douceur, gentillesse)*

9. *Noms d'agent en* **-er** dérivés de verbes, désignant ceux qui font l'action :
   drive *(conduire)* → driv**er** *(conducteur)*

10. *Noms verbaux en* **-ing** (p. 148-150), très courants en anglais :
    read *(lire)* → read**ing** *(la lecture)*
    swim *(nager)* → swimm**ing** *(la natation)*

11. *Noms en* **-ship, -hood, -dom,** accolés à des noms :
    friend *(ami)* → friend**ship** *(amitié)*
    adult → adult**hood** *(l'âge, l'état d'adulte)*
    king *(roi)* → king**dom** *(royaume)*

Remarque : Préfixes et suffixes peuvent se trouver ensemble dans un même mot dérivé :
care *(soin)* → care**less** *(négligent)* → care**lessness** *(négligence)*
fortunate *(heureux)* → fortunate**ly** *(heureusement)* → **un**fortunately *(malheureusement)*. Notez enfin qu'en français aussi on retrouve généralement les mêmes procédés.

Les principales modifications orthographiques

1. *Doublement de la consonne finale*

   Il se produit dans les mots *d'une seule syllabe* (ou de plusieurs syllabes) *dont la dernière* est *accentuée:* begin [bɪˈɡɪn] → begi**nn**ing mais develop [dɪˈveləp] → develo**p**ing) terminée par une *seule consonne* précédée d'une *seule voyelle:*

   -rub *(frotter)*, ru**bb**ing, mais speak, spea**k**ing (deux voyelles avant la consonne).

   On peut trouver le doublement de la consonne finale :

   a) dans le *participe présent*, le *gérondif*, le *prétérit* et le *participe passé* des verbes réguliers.

      It sto**pp**ed ra**ini**ng (n précédé de *deux* voyelles). *Il a cessé de pleuvoir.*

   b) dans les *comparatifs* et les *superlatifs:*

      fat *(gras),* fa**tt**er, the fa**tt**est

   c) dans les *mots dérivés* de verbes, de noms... etc. :

      a begi**nn**er, *un débutant*

      sun *(soleil),* su**nn**y *(ensoleillé)*

2. **y** *final*

   a) Il devient **ie** *devant s s'il n'est pas précédé d'une voyelle* (a, e, i, o, u, y).

      Le problème se pose notamment :

      — à la *3ᵉ personne du singulier du présent des verbes:*

        spy on *(espionner)* → he spi**e**s on us

      — pour le *pluriel des noms:*

        a famil**y** – famil**ies**

        mais a boy → two bo**y**s

      — pour des *nombres ordinaux correspondant aux dizaines:*

        twenty → twent**i**eth *(vingtième)*

        thirty → thirth**i**eth *(trentième)*

   b) Il devient **i**

      — dans le *prétérit et le participe passé des verbes réguliers:*

        study *(étudier)* → I stud**i**ed French

      — dans le *comparatif et le superlatif des adjectifs courts:*

heavy *(lourd)* → heav**ier**
— devant les suffixes -**ness**, -**less**, -**ly** :
happy *(heureux)* → happ**iness** *(bonheur)*, happ**ily**
(heureusement)
penny → penn**iless** *(sans le sou)*

c) *Il se maintient devant* -**ing** (notamment au participe
présent, à la forme progressive et au gérondif) :
study → He was study**ing** in his room

3. ie *final*
Il devient **y** devant -**ing** :
lie *(mentir)* → stop l**ying**!

4. *Addition de* e
a) à la troisième personne du singulier (he, she, it) du
présent des *verbes terminés par* **s, x, z, ch, sh** :
brush *(brosse)* : she brush**es** her teeth *(dents)* every
evening
b) au pluriel des *noms terminés par* **s, x, z, ch, sh** :
a brush *(une brosse)*, two brush**es**
c) *dans certains noms et verbes terminés en* **o** :
a potato → a few potat**oes**
a tomato → some tomat**oes**

5. *Suppression de* e
a) dans les *verbes terminés en* **e**, notamment au prétérit et
au participe passé des verbes réguliers, au participe
présent et au gérondif :
like *(aimer)*, lik**ed** (like + d seul), li**king**
b) dans les *adjectifs terminés en* **e**, notamment au comparatif et au superlatif des adjectifs courts : fine *(beau)*, fin**er**
(fine + r seul), the fin**est**.
c) dans les *adjectifs en* -**able** *dérivés de verbes en* **e**, *sauf si
ces verbes se terminent par* **ce** *ou* **ge** :
compare *(comparer)*, compar**able**
manage *(manœuvrer, manier)*, manag**eable** *(facile à
manœuvrer, maniable)*
d) dans les *adverbes dérivés d'adjectifs en* -**able**
admirable → admirab**ly**

6. *Suppression d'un* l *final*
On a fu**ll** *(plein)* avec deux l mais on a beautifu**l**, joyfu**l**
(joyeux), wonderfu**l** *(merveilleux)*... etc., avec **un seul l**.

Verbes irréguliers

Infinitif	Prétérit	P. passé	
awake	awoke / awaked	awoken / awaked	*éveiller*
be	was, were	been	*être*
bear	bore	borne	*porter*
		be born	*naître*
beat	beat	beaten	*battre*
become	became	become	*devenir*
begin	began	begun	*commencer*
behold	beheld	beheld	*contempler*
bend	bent	bent	*courber*
beseech	besought	besought	*supplier*
beset	beset	beset	*assaillir*
bet	bet / betted	bet / betted	*parier*
bid	bade, bid	bade, bid bidden	*ordonner*
bind	bound	bound	*lier*
bite	bit	bitten	*mordre*
bleed	bled	bled	*saigner*
blow	blew	blown	*souffler*
break	broke	broken	*casser*
breed	bred	bred	*élever*
bring	brought	brought	*apporter*
broadcast	broadcast	broadcast	*radiodiffuser*
build	built	built	*construire*
burn	burnt (*amér.* burned)	burnt (*amér.* burned)	*brûler*
burst	burst	burst	*éclater*
buy	bought	bought	*acheter*
can	could		*pouvoir*
cast	cast	cast	*jeter*
catch	caught	caught	*attraper*
choose	chose	chosen	*choisir*

Infinitif	Prétérit	P. passé	
cling	clung	clung	*s'attacher*
come	came	come	*venir*
cost	cost	cost	*coûter*
creep	crept	crept	*ramper*
cut	cut	cut	*couper*
deal	dealt	dealt	*distribuer*
dig	dug	dug	*creuser*
do, does	did	done	*faire*
draw	drew	drawn	*tirer, dessiner*
dream	dreamt (*amér.* dreamed)	dreamt (*amér.* dreamed)	*rêver*
drink	drank	drunk	*boire*
drive	drove	driven	*conduire*
dwell	dwelt (*amér.* dwelled)	dwelt (*amér.* dwelled)	*demeurer*
eat	ate [et, eit]	eaten	*manger*
fall	fell	fallen	*tomber*
feed	fed	fed	*nourrir*
feel	felt	felt	*sentir*
find	found	found	*trouver*
fling	flung	flung	*lancer*
fly	flew	flown	*voler*
forbid	forbade forbad	forbidden	*interdire*
forecast	forecast	forecast	*prévoir*
foresee	foresaw	foreseen	*prévoir*
foretell	foretold	foretold	*prédire*
forget	forgot	forgotten	*oublier*
forgive	forgave	forgiven	*pardonner*
forsake	forsook	forsaken	*abandonner*
freeze	froze	frozen	*geler*
get	got	got (*amér.* gotten)	*obtenir, devenir*
give	gave	given	*donner*

Infinitif	Prétérit	P. passé	
go	went	gone	*aller*
grind	ground	ground	*moudre*
grow	grew	grown	*croître, devenir*
hang	hung	hung	*pendre (à)*
hang	hanged	hanged	*pendre (pendaison)*
have	had	had	*avoir, posséder*
hear	heard	heard	*entendre*
hide	hid	hidden, hid	*cacher*
hit	hit	hit	*frapper*
hold	held	held	*tenir*
hurt	hurt	hurt	*blesser, faire mal*
keep	kept	kept	*garder, conserver*
kneel	knelt (*amér.* kneeled)	knelt (*amér.* kneeled)	*s'agenouiller*
knit	knitted, knit	knitted, knit	*tricoter*
know	knew	known	*savoir, connaître*
lay	laid	laid	*poser*
lead	led	led	*mener, conduire*
lean	leant (*amér.* leaned)	leant (*amér.* leaned)	*pencher*
learn	learnt (*amér.* learned)	learnt (*amér.* learned)	*apprendre*
leave	left	left	*laisser, quitter, partir*
lend	lent	lent	*prêter*
let	let	let	*laisser (faire), louer*

Infinitif	*Prétérit*	*P. passé*	
lie	lay	lain	*être couché*
light	{ lit { lighted	{ lit { lighted	*allumer,* *éclairer*
lose	lost	lost	*perdre*
make	made	made	*faire,* *fabriquer*
may	might		*pouvoir* *(permission,* *probabilité)*
mean	meant	meant	*signifier,* *vouloir dire*
meet	met	met	*rencontrer*
mislay	mislaid	mislaid	*égarer*
mislead	misled	misled	*induire en* *erreur*
mistake	mistook	mistaken	*prendre* *(pour) par* *erreur*
misunder- stand	-stood	-stood	*mal* *comprendre*
mow	mowed	mown mowed	*faucher*
overcome	overcame	overcome	*surmonter*
overdo, overdoes	overdid	overdone	*exagérer*
overhang	overhung	overhung	*surplomber*
oversleep	overslept	overslept	*dormir trop* *longtemps*
overtake	overtook	overtaken	*dépasser*
overthrow	overthrew	overthrown	*renverser,* *vaincre*
pay	paid	paid	*payer*
put	put	put	*mettre*
quit	{ quitted { (*amér.* { quit)	{ quitted { (*amér.* { quit)	*abandonner,* *arrêter*
read[ri:d]	read	read	*lire*

Infinitif	Prétérit	P. passé	
rend	rent	rent	*déchirer*
repay	repaid	repaid	*rembourser*
rid	{ rid { ridded	{ rid { ridded	*débarrasser*
ride	rode	ridden	*monter (à cheval, à bicyclette...)*
ring	rang	rung	*sonner*
rise	rose	risen	*se lever*
run	ran	run	*courir*
saw	sawed	{ sawn { sawed	*scier*
say	said	said	*dire*
see	saw	seen	*voir*
seek	sought	sought	*chercher*
sell	sold	sold	*vendre*
send	sent	sent	*envoyer*
set	set	set	*placer*
sew	sewed	{ sewn { sewed	*coudre*
shake	shook	shaken	*secouer, trembler*
shear	sheared	{ shorn { sheared	*tondre*
shed	shed	shed	*verser*
shine	shone	shone	*briller*
shine	shined	shined	*cirer*
shoe	shod	shod	*chausser, ferrer*
shoot	shot	shot	*tirer, abattre*
show	showed	{ shown { showed	*montrer*
shrink	shrank	shrunk	*rétrécir*
shut	shut	shut	*fermer*
sing	sang	sung	*chanter*
sink	sank	sunk	*sombrer, couler*

Infinitif	*Prétérit*	*P. passé*	
sit	sat	sat	*être assis, siéger*
sleep	slept	slept	*dormir*
slide	slid	slid	*glisser*
slit	slit	slit	*fendre*
smell	smelt	smelt	*sentir*
sow	sowed	sown sowed	*semer*
speak	spoke	spoken	*parler*
speed	{ sped { speeded	{ sped { speeded	*faire hâte*
spell	spelt (*amér.* spelled)	spelt (*amér.* spelled)	*épeler, orthographier*
spend	spent	spent	*passer*
spill	{ spilt { (*amér.* { spilled)	{ spilt { (*amér.* { spilled)	*verser, renverser*
spin	spun, span	spun	*filer*
spit	spat	spat	*cracher*
split	split	split	*fendre*
spoil	{ spoilt { (*amér.* { spoiled)	{ spoilt { (*amér.* { spoiled)	*gâter*
spread	spread	spread	*répandre*
spring	sprang	sprung	*s'élancer*
stand	stood	stood	*être debout*
steal	stole	stolen	*voler*
stick	stuck	stuck	*coller*
sting	stung	stung	*piquer*
stink	stank, stunk	stunk	*puer*
strew	strewed	{ strewn { strewed	*répandre*
stride	strode	{ stridden { strid	*marcher à grands pas*
strike	struck	struck	*frapper*
strive	{ strove { strived	{ striven { strived	*s'efforcer*

Infinitif	*Prétérit*	*P. passé*	
swear	swore	sworn	*jurer*
sweep	swept	swept	*balayer*
swell	swelled	{ swollen { swelled	*enfler*
swim	swam	swum	*nager*
swing	swung	swung	*se balancer*
take	took	taken	*prendre*
teach	taught	taught	*enseigner*
tear	tore	torn	*déchirer*
tell	told	told	*dire, raconter*
think	thought	thought	*penser*
thrive	{ throve { thrived	{ thriven { thrived	*prospérer*
throw	threw	thrown	*jeter*
thrust	thrust	thrust	*lancer*
tread	trod	trodden, trod	*fouler, piétiner*
undergo	underwent	undergone	*subir*
understand	understood	understood	*comprendre*
undertake	undertook	undertaken	*entreprendre*
undo, undoes	undid	undone	*défaire*
unwind	unwound	unwound	*dérouler*
uphold	upheld	upheld	*soutenir*
upset	upset	upset	*renverser*
wake	{ woke { waked	{ woken { waked	*éveiller*
wear	wore	worn	*porter*
weave	wove	woven	*tisser*
weep	wept	wept	*pleurer*
wet	{ wet { wetted	{ wet { wetted	*mouiller*
win	won	won	*gagner*
wind	wound	wound	*enrouler*
withdraw	withdrew	withdrawn	*retirer*
wring	wrung	wrung	*tordre*
write	wrote	written	*écrire*

Corrigés des exercices

1. Be, *auxiliaire et verbe (pp. 13,15)*

A'. Entre parenthèses les formes réduites ou contractées presque toujours employées en conversation.
   1. I **am** (**'m**) **very** hot, I **have** (**'ve**) a temperature. **2.** He **is**
   (**'s**) never ill. **3.** How old **is** the patient? He **is** (**'s**) sixty years
   old. **4.** This man **was** as fit as a fiddle. **5.** They **were** taken ill
   last year. **6.** The poor woman **was** very weak, she **was** about
   to faint. **7. Are** you hungry? No I **am** (**'m**) thirsty and I **am**
   (**'m**) out of sorts. **8.** We **are** (**'re**) **going to** send for the
   doctor. **9.** Aids **is** (**'s**) an infectious disease. **10.** The nurse
   was tending the patients while the surgeon **was operating**.
   11. You **will** (**'ll**) **be operated** on next week. **12.** She **was**
   taking her medicines when the sister came in. **13. Will the**
   injured man be taken to hospital? **14. Are** you afraid? It **is**
   (**'s**) only an injection. **15. How far is** the hospital? **16.** Is it
   cancer or tuberculosis? **17. Will** your mother always **be** in
   good health?... **18. Would you be** an ambulance man by any
   chance? **19. Was** Peter ashamed of having this contagious
   disease?

B'. **1. There is** (**'s**) an epidemic. **2. There was** an intensive care
   unit in this hospital. **3. There are** (**'re**) very serious diseases
   like cancer. **4. Are there** many young people who suffer
   from heart diseases? **5. There will** (**'ll**) **be** a lot of nervous
   breakdowns if it goes on like that. **6. There are not (aren't)**
   enough junior hospital doctors (interns). **7. There may be**
   better hospital facilities in this town. **8. There would be** less
   lung cancer if people did not smoke as much. **9.** It is a very
   small town but **there must be** a dentist. **10.** After a few
   days'treatment **there should be** a change for the better.
   11. There **is** (**'s**) no danger ou **there is not (there isn't)** any
   danger in taking an aspirin or two. **12.** I had the flu **a month**
   ago. 13. There is (**'s**) a problem of blood pressure, **isn't**
   there? 14. There used to be a lunatic asylum in our district.
   15. Is **there** an emergency ward? Yes, **there is. 16.** It **is ten**
   years since he had a stroke.

2. Have, *auxiliaire et verbe (p. 17)*

A'. 1. He **has** bought a second-hand car. 2. I **have** just put the suitcase into the boot. 3. Mr. Leadbeater **had** lost his ignition key. 4. Do you **have** good tyres? No I don't. (ou Have you got good tyres? No, I haven't.) 5. He **had** just had the sparking plugs changed. 6. **Have** you ever driven an estate car? 7. He **has** not changed gear. 8. The price of petrol **has** just gone up. 9. **Has** the pump attendant checked the pressure? 10. We **have** driven bumper to bumper for hours. 11. They **had** stopped at a filling station. 12. We **have** had the engine repaired in a local garage. 13. He does not **have** alcoholic drinks when he has to take the wheel. 14. Her car **has** just broken down, she has taken a taxi. 15. **Have** you noticed that your car consumes a lot of petrol? 16. A careful motorist **has** his car serviced regularly.

3. Do (does, did), *auxiliaire et verbe (p. 19)*

A'. 1. **Do** you understand it? You **don't** understand it. You **do** not understand it. 2. **Did** she realize it? She **didn't** realize it. She **did** not realize it. 3. **Does** Peter notice everything? Peter **doesn't** notice everything. Peter **does** not notice everything. 4. **Did** Mr. Campbell mistake one word for another? Mr. Campbell **didn't** mistake one word for another. Mr. Campbell **did** not mistake one word for another. 5. **Did** old Mr. Jones tend to mix things up? Old Mr. Jones **didn't** tend to mix things up. Old Mr. Jones **did** not tend to mix things up. 6. **Does** Mrs. O' Neil ignore her neighbours in the street? Mrs. O' Neil **doesn't** ignore her neighbours in the street. Mrs. O' Neil **does** not ignore her neighbours in the street. 7. **Did** Jackie misunderstand what I said? Jackie **didn't** misunderstand what I said. Jackie **did** not misunderstand what I said. 8. **Does** David remember it very well? David **doesn't** remember it very well. David **does** not remember it very well. 9. **Did** the student grasp everything the teacher explained? The student **didn't** grasp everything the teacher explained. The student **did** not grasp everything the teacher explained. 10. **Did** the boss take it into account? The boss **didn't** take it into account. The boss **did** not take it into account. 11. **Does** your old aunt get mixed up? Your old aunt **doesn't** get mixed up. Your old aunt **does not** get mixed up. 12. **Did** Mrs. MacDonald gather that her friend would not come? Mrs. MacDonald **didn't** gather that her friend would not come. Mrs. MacDonald **did not** gather that her friend would not come. 13. **Did** Mr. Leigh suppose you were right? Mr. Leigh **didn't** suppose you were right. Mr. Leigh **did not** suppose you were right. 14. **Do** you suspect something will go wrong? You **don't** suspect something will go wrong. You **do not** suspect something will go wrong. 15. **Did** Robert make up his mind yesterday? Robert **didn't** make up his mind yesterday. Robert **did not** make up his mind yesterday. 16. **Did** John forget to learn his lesson? John **didn't** forget to learn his lesson. John **did not** forget to learn his lesson. 17. **Did** his grandfather miss the point? His grandfather **didn't** miss the point. His grandfather **did not** miss the point.

---

4. *Les auxiliaires modaux :* can, may, must... *(pp. 19-27)*

A'. 1. **He must be** at the football match. 2. **Mr. Smith may go** to the concert. 3. **She must be** at the theatre. 4. **Jane may go** to the restaurant tomorrow. 5. **We may visit** our friends over the weekend. 6. **His children must be** at the disco every evening. 7. **The Smiths may go** hiking next weekend. 8. **John must be** rock climbing again. 9. **Mr. and Mrs. Davies may go** for a walk in the forest during the weekend. 10. **They must be** spending the long weekend in their second home. 11. **Jackie may go** to the museum on Sunday. 12. **They must be** at skating-rink with the children. 13. **Mr. and Mrs. Lancaster may go** sailing with their friends this coming weekend.

B'. 1. You **must** practise sports, it is good for your health. 2. I **can** ride a bicycle but I **cannot (can't)** ride a horse. 3. You **must** not mow the lawn, it is bad for your back. 4. The doctor says you **may** play tennis again in a month's time but not before. 5. "**Can** I go to the swimming pool?" he asked his father. "No you **cannot (can't)**. You have not finished your homework." 6. **I won't be able to** do any jogging next weekend, I have sprained my ankle. 7. We **may** go to the country but I am not sure we will. 8. John **won't be allowed to** go skiing during the weekend if he does not work hard during the week. 9. My brother **can** play chess but my sister **can't (cannot)**. 10. He has stopped doing odd jobs about the house, he **must** be very tired. 11. **I'll have to** do some decorating next weekend or my wife won't leave me in peace *(laisser en paix)*. 12. We **may (might)** go cycling if the weather is fine. 13. You **must** not gamble, it is strictly forbidden. 14. We **might** go to the seaside. God knows!

C'. 1. **Shall** we have a game of cards? 2. He is good with his hands. He **will** spend hours every weekend pottering about the house. 3. We **would** go to the funfair quite often. We loved it. 4. We **should (ought to)** adopt a child rather than buy a weekend cottage. 5. **Shall** I help you to do some repairs in your holiday home? 6. **Will** you come and have dinner with us next Saturday? 7. Mr. Parhill **would** go fishing every Sunday. He loved it. 8. We **should (ought to)** ask him to dinner, he feels a little depressed these days. 9. You **should (ought to)** get some fresh air after working so hard at the office. 10. **Shall** we go to the jazz club on Saturday night? 11. Car accidents **will** happen every weekend. 12. We **would** entertain friends every evening when we were on holiday. 13. You **should (ought to)** go boating, it will do you good. 14. **Shall** we listen to some music? 15. We **should (ought to)** help the homeless instead of building second homes.

D'. 1. **You needn't go** shopping this weekend. 2. "**Need I go** to the museum?" he asked his father. 3. **She daren't refuse** the invitation. 4. **You needn't take** a long weekend. 5. The Browns **daren't ask** the Smiths to dinner. 6. **Mrs. Page needs to take** some fresh air. 7. **She needed to** listen to some music to calm down. 8. **You don't need to** mow the lawn. 9. How **dare you say** such a thing?

E'. 1. John **must have gone** dancing. 2. **We may go** to the party. 3. **I must do** some gardening next weekend. 4. Mr. Salmon **must have taken** three days off. He **must have spent** them in his second home. 5. He **may (might) have taken** advantage of the weekend to wash his car. 6. **She may have gone** to the restaurant for a change. 7. The children **might have gone** to the youth club. **8. You must tidy up** your room this weekend.

---

5. *La forme progressive et la forme simple (pp. 29,31)*

A'. 1. I **was shopping** yesterday when I **saw** him. 2. He only **sells** retail, not wholesale. 3. He never **pays** cash. 4. She **was window-shopping** the other day when her friend **called** her. 5. I **was lingering** in a bookshop. Intellectuals **love** lingering in bookshops. 6. We generally **buy** our Christmas presents long in advance, to avoid queueing. 7. We **were waiting** in the car while they **were making** some purchases. It was not great fun. 8. She **uses** neither credit cards nor cheques. 9. Many people **prefer** small shops to supermarkets. 10. Who **forgot** to take his cheque-book last week? 11. He was fed up. He **was standing** in the queue. It **was raining**. 12. How much **did you pay** for that? I **paid** £ 10 a year ago. 13. A mail-order business **sends** goods by post. 14. My grandmother **orders** what she **needs** from the local grocer. She **was ordering** vegetables on the phone the other day when I **arrived**.

B'. 1. Look! Mrs. Smith **is doing** her shopping. She **does** her shopping every morning. 2. He **did not buy** that car because he could not afford it. It was far too expensive. 3. **Did you buy** it on credit? No I **did not buy** it on credit, I **gave** 5,000 francs on the nail and I **sent** a cheque for 10,000 francs. 4. She always **makes** good bargains. Why **does she make** good bargains? Because she **looks** round the shops and **takes** her time. 5. People who **do not have** much money **prefer** to pay in monthly instalments. 6. I **was queueing** at the butcher's while **she was queueing** at the baker's. 7. I **am going** to the hairdresser's tomorrow, I **go** to the hairdresser's every month. 8. She **thinks** (that) it is a mistake to go shopping locally, she always **goes** to department stores. 9. He was swindled, he **did not get** his money's worth. 10. The shop-assistants were busy, the customers **were hunting** for sales. 11. He **hates** queueing. **Who likes** it?... 12. It was ten o'clock. Mr. Marrow **was driving** his wife to the shopping-centre. He **drives** her there every Tuesday. He **does not** like it at all!

---

6. *Le prétérit et le present perfect.* For, since, ago *(pp. 33-37)*

A'. 1. I **went** to the travel agency **three days ago**. I **spent** three hours there! 2. I **visited** that old town three years **ago**. I **took** lots of photographs. 3. Which hotel **did you stay** in last year? We **stayed** at the Red Lion. It **was** a wonderful stay. 4. Yesterday the guide **showed** us round the city. We **were** delighted. It **was** such a sight! 5. I **did not enjoy** that guided tour very much yesterday. There **were** too many ruins to visit. 6. The poor tourists **have been sitting** on that coach **for** hours and hours. They are tired out. 7. How long **have you been working** in the tourist office? I **have been working** there **for** three years, **since** the day I **left** school. 8. This **has been** a tourist trap **for** years and years. Nobody complains. 9. Mr. Law **has been** responsible for the tourist trade in the town council **for** many years, **since** the end of the war. 10. We **bought** a good map of the town yesterday, before we **went** sightseeing. 11. Unfortunately the package tour **did not include** the Lake District last year. We **were** disappointed.

B'. 1. They **went** on a tour to Italy six months **ago**. They **enjoyed** it very much. It **was** a wonderful journey. 2. I **have worked** as a tour operator in this town **for** many years now, **since** 1970, **since** I **got** married. 3. It **is** a long time **since** I **travelled** abroad. The last time I **travelled** abroad, it **was** in Germany. 4. When **did they leave** home for England? They **left** a fortnight **ago**. They **have been** there a fortnight now. 5. When **did you buy** your ticket? I **bought** it a couple of days **ago**. 6. I **have had** my old camera **for** ten years now. I **got** another one the other day. It **cost** me a lot of money. 7. We **went** on a cycling tour in Wales a year **ago**. 8. I **have travelled** to distant places **for** the last twenty years. I **flew** to Alaska six months **ago**. 9. We **had been touring** Scotland **for** three weeks, **since** July 1st when our father **telephoned** and **asked** us to come back urgently. Our mother **had been** dangerously ill **for** two days. In fact she **died** a week after our return.

C'. 1. I **have been trying** to learn that **for** days but I **have not succeeded** yet. **2.** I am fed up. I **have been queuing for** hours. **3.** I **was writing** a letter when he **came** in. **4.** You don't know that and you **have been learning** English **for** four years! Congratulations! **5.** I am tired. I **have been cooking for** hours. **6.** Look! What a waste! That lamp **has been burning** all night! **7.** We **were watching** television when the phone **rang. 8.** You **have broken** the vase. It is useless now. **9.** He **has been trying** to convince me **for** a quarter of an hour. He is wasting his time! **10.** I can't go skiing because I **have broken** my leg. **11.** She **has been reading for** hours and hours. She does nothing else!

---

7. *Le futur, l'avenir, les projets (pp. 39,41)*

A'. 1. He **will get** married **as soon as** he **has** finished his studies. **2.** God knows how long they **will remain** man and wife. **3.** He says he **will have** a large family if he earns enough money to support them. **4. As soon as** my baby is born I **will give up** my job. **5. Will they have** a church wedding? **6.** She **will divorce** her husband **as soon as** she **learns** that. **7. When** she is married and **has** children she **will bring** them up herself. **8.** It **will be** a terrible blow to him when he **hears** about their separation. **9.** He **will go** mad the day **when** his wife **dies. 10.** She **will** not (ou **won't**) marry him. **11.** I am sure their marriage **will be** a failure. **12.** You **will not** (ou **won't**) **understand** that **as long as** you **have** not fallen in love with someone. **13. When** some time **has** elapsed he **will forget** about that tragic death. He **will look** after his grandchildren.

B'. 1. I think it **is going to** end up in a marriage. **2.** They are always quarrelling. They are **about to** split up. **3.** They **are to go** to Scotland on their honeymoon next Sunday. **4.** They **are getting** married next week. **5.** He says he **is going to** remain single. **6.** We **leave** the house at nine o'clock tomorrow morning. The funeral **is to begin** at ten o'clock. **7.** She hopes she **is going to** get a divorce. **8.** She has been pregnant for nearly nine months. She **is about to** give birth to a baby girl. 9. I hope he **is not going to** start divorce proceedings. 10. My parents **are celebrating** their silver-wedding anniversary next week.

---

8. *Le conditionnel : hypothèses, souhaits (p. 43)*

A'. 1. We **would accept** your kind invitation if we were free. 2. I **would not make** friends with that man! 3. As soon as he **had** more time he **would entertain** all his close friends. 4. He said he **would call** on us when he **was** in better health. 5. She **would** never **get** along with such neighbours. 6. They **would introduce** me to him as soon as we **saw** one another again. 7. **Would you feel** so lonely if your friends visited you a little more often? 8. They are on such bad terms that if they met they **would not** (ou **wouldn't**) even **shake hands**. They **would ignore** each other.

B'. 1. I **wish** he **came** to our party. 2. **If only** they were on friendly terms I **would** invite them together. 3. I **wish** he **mixed** with other people a little more. 4. **It's time** we **asked** them to dinner. 5. I **wish** he **became** more sociable, I **wish** he **did not keep** himself to himself. 6. **It's high time** they stopped hating each other.

---

9. *Le passé récent et le futur proche (p. 45)*

A'. 1. I have just shaved, I am going to comb my hair. 2. I have just combed my hair, I am going to dress. 3. I have just dressed, I am going to have breakfast. 4. I have just had breakfast, I am going to get my things ready. 5. I have just got my things ready, I am going to put on my overcoat. 6. I have just put on my overcoat, I am going (about) to go to work. 7. I have just gone out, I am going (about) to lock the door. 8. I have just locked the door, I am going (about) to rush for the bus. 9. I have just rushed for the bus, I am about to board it. 10. I have just got off the bus, I am about to enter the office. 11. I have just walked out of the office, I am going to get back home. 12. I have just got back home, I am going to have a bath. **13.** I have just had a bath, I am going to have tea. **14.** I have just had tea, I am going to listen to a record. **15.** I have just listened to a record, I am going to read the newspaper. **16.** I have just read the newspaper, I am going to phone a friend. **17.** I have just phoned a friend, I am going to watch the telly. **18.** I have just watched the telly, I am going to take a cup of tea. **19.** I have just taken a cup of tea, I am going to undress. **20.** I have just undressed, I am going (about) to put on my pyjamas. **21.** I have just put on my pyjamas, I am going to clean my teeth. **22.** I have just cleaned my teeth, I am about to go to bed. **23.** I have just gone to bed, I am going to have a little read. **24.** I have just had a little read, I am about to go to sleep. **25.** I am going to switch off the light.

---

10. *Question-tags* (hein?, non?, si?, n'est-ce pas?) *et autres tournures elliptiques (pp. 47,49)*

A'. 1. It's going to rain, **isn't it? 2.** The sky grows dark before a storm, **doesn't it? 3.** It never snows in this part of the country, **does it? 4.** It was getting cold, **wasn't it? 5.** There was a storm brewing, **wasn't there? 6.** It will soon clear up, **won't it? 7.** It started pouring, **didn't it? 8.** They would not go out on a rainy day, **would they? 9.** The sun won't shine bright until July, **will it? 10.** There were not many bright intervals, **were there? 11.** We'll go out when the wind dies away, **won't we? 12.** You can feel the atmosphere is damp, **can't you? 13.** You must be soaked to the skin, **mustn't you? 14.** I am very sensitive to cold, **aren't I? 15.** It will be stifling hot again, **won't it? 16.** Let's go for a picnic, **shall we?** Weather permitting. **17.** You should not go out when it is freezing cold, **should you? 18.** Everybody prefers sunny days to wet days, **don't they? 19.** You don't listen to the weather forecast every day, **do you?**

B'. 1. Isn't it a wonderful climate? **2. Didn't they go out** although it was raining cats and dogs? **3. Wasn't the barometer** rising? **4. Won't you stay** at home if the roads are slippery? **5. Couldn't you go out** on a dry day like this? **6. Didn't we have** lovely weather? **7. Wouldn't it be** too hot for us? **8. Shouldn't the fog lift** before midday? **9. Wasn't it** a chilly day? **10. Don't you think** you'll be chilled to the bone? **11. Won't there be** a nice spell before the end of the summer?

C'. 1. My mother hates thunder, **so does my sister. 2.** Fog is unpleasant, **so is black ice. 3.** My uncle did not like sultry weather, **neither did my aunt. 4.** You won't go out in such foul weather, **neither will your** friends. **5.** Poor people dread severe winter, **so do old people. 6.** They went out because the weather was fine, **so did their parents.**

---

11. *Le passif* (pp. 51,53)

A'. 1. That church **was decorated** by Michael Angelo. **2.** Lots of cathedrals **were built** in those days. **3.** This painter is **praised** by everybody without exception. **4.** This type of painting **will be appreciated** by real connoisseurs. **5.** Old paintings **must be looked after** very carefully. **6.** This young sculptor **was highly thought of. 7.** Our local museum **was designed** by a foreign architect. **8.** This art gallery is **visited** by thousands of tourists every year. **9.** The children **were told off** by the guide because they were talking during the visit. **10.** This work of art **is looked upon** as a masterpiece. **11.** More time **should be devoted** to drawing in schools. **12.** A brush and a palette **are used** by a painter. **13.** His sculptures **will be exhibited** next year. **14.** The fine arts **should be** much more **encouraged** by governments. **15.** He **is referred to** as a forerunner.

B'. 1. A museum **is being built** here. **2.** The column **was being cleaned up. 3.** New materials like plastics **are being used** by modern sculptors these days. **4.** A new statue **was being set up** in this square last week.

1. She was given a scholarship by the government to go to the art school. **2. The art student was awarded the first prize** by the examiners unanimously. **3. They were told** by the policeman that the famous artist's studio was not very far from there. **4. We were shown** round the exhibition by an old guide. **5. He will be taught** architecture by a famous professor. 6. **I was asked** by my friend if I had been to the British Museum in London. 7. **I was sent** a few sketches by my brother. 8. **She was offered** a job as a model; **she was told** she could start in a week's time. 9. **We have been offered £** 700 for this picture.

---

12. *La proposition infinitive avec* expect... *(s'attendre à...)* *(p. 55)*

A'. 1. The teacher **wanted them to** keep quiet. **2.** She **would like us to** make progress. **3.** Does the teacher **expect me to** read all those books? **4.** I **expect you to** learn this poem by heart. **5.** I **hate** pupils **to** answer my questions all together. I **want** them **to** put up their hands. **6.** It is **vital for him not to** overwork himself. **7.** He has started working but it is too **late for him to** pass his exam. **8.** Do you **want me to** help you to do your homework? Yes I **would like** you to help me to translate this passage into English. **9.** I **expected them to** make that mistake in the dictation. **10.** He **wanted us not to** wander from the subject. **11.** It is **important for her to** learn two foreign languages. **12.** He **prefers us not to** translate word for word.

---

13. *L'expression des penchants naturels, des habitudes :* will, would *(p. 57)*

A'. 1. Parents **will** (always) **repeat** the same things to their children. **2.** As my father **would** (often) **say:** "Boys **will** be boys." **3.** The same subjects **would** (always) **crop up** between my father and my brother. **4.** My mother **will insist** on our coming back home in time for meals. **5.** This father **will** (always) **criticize** whatever his son does. **6.** He **would** (always) **get up** late. **7.** He **would** never **switch off** the lights, which made his mother angry. **8.** "He **will spend** hours reading instead of doing his homework" his mother **would** (always) **repeat. 9.** Parents **will** (always) **give** advice to their children who, in any case, **will have** their own way. **10.** "She **will behave** foolishly. She can't help it" her parents

would (always) **repeat**. 11. Their daughter **will** (always) **come back** home late whatever the parents **will say**.

---

14. *Le passé révolu :* used to *(p. 59)*

A'. 1. When he was a young man **he used to have** quite a few girlfriends. **2. You used to go** out quite a lot in those days. **3. They used to go** dancing every Saturday night. **4.** I have changed now but **I used to be** an idealist. **5. He used to collect** stamps at the time. **6. You used to cycle** a lot when you were in your teens. **7. He used to go** to the cinema quite often. **8. I used to sing** in the choir every Sunday. **9. He used to do** a lot of sports; **he used to practise** tennis, badminton... **10. They used to work** hard at their studies. **11. John used to have** a terrific energy. **12. We used to spend** hours with our friends at the pub. **13.** Peter **used to read** like mad. **14.** Jack and **I used to go** to the youth club regularly. **15. We used to play** golf in Scotland every Summer. **16. He used to discuss** politics with passion, **he used to be** a militant at one time. **17. We used to go** to discos, **we used to love** dancing.

---

15. *Les verbes de perception :* see *(voir)*, hear *(entendre)*, feel *(sentir) etc. (p. 61)*

A'. 1. Did you see the baby **going** on all fours? **2.** We could hear the old man **shuffling** along. **3.** Did you see the hare **jump** off? **4.** Look at him **striding** along the street. **5.** You often see little old women **take** short steps across the streets. How dangerous! **6.** We could hear the rain **falling**. **7.** Did you hear him **fall** off the ladder? **8.** I could feel the insect **running** on my hand. **9.** We saw the thief **steal** into the room and disappear in no time. **10.** Watch him **reeling** like a drunken man. **11.** You should have seen her **leap** from her chair when she heard the news. **12.** It makes me **laugh** to see people **slip** on banana skins. **13.** I saw her **lean** out of the window, **fling** an object and **rush** across the room. It did not take long! **14.** Look at John **bending** over his bicycle, **trying** to repair it.

---

16. Make, let..., *suivis de la base verbale (p. 63)*

A'. 1. He is no handy man. You won't **get** him to drive in a nail!
He had rather Ø read a book than Ø mend a cupboard.
2. Don't **let** the baby Ø play with the hammer. **3.** She had
the living-room **decorated** by the painters. **4.** You had better
buy a new screwdriver. **5.** You must take your time unless
you want to burgle it. **6.** I don't want to watch TV this
afternoon, I would prefer to tinker about the house. **7.** I had
the lawn mower **repaired** in case you wanted to mow the
lawn. **8.** She made me Ø fix some shelves, she wanted to do
some tidying up. **9.** We had all the plugs **changed**, we
preferred to be on the safe side. **10.** I'll have him Ø do some
odd jobs about the house. I won't **let** him stay there doing
nothing. **11.** We need some screws, **let's** go to the do-it-
yourself department, **let's** see if they have what we need.
12. **Let** me give you a hand with the gardening, I want to be
useful.

---

17. *Passage du style direct au style indirect: concordance des
temps (p. 65)*

A'. 1. He told me he would note down my car number. **2.** The
policeman asked him if his car came from the right. **3.** She
told me I would have a car accident, driving so fast. **4.** The
policeman asked if there was any witness. **5.** He told me I
had knocked in his wing. **6.** She asked him if he had used
his brakes. **7.** He told the lorry-driver to pull over to the side
of the road. **8.** He told us we were in the wrong. **9.** He told
me I had jumped the lights. **10.** He told the other driver
(that) they would find the cheapest way to settle this.
11. The traffic warden told the cyclist not to get excited like
that. **12.** The policewoman said to the cyclist (that) he had
come from the left. **13.** He said there had been a terrible
clash. **14.** The insurance agent told us the responsibility was
ours. **15.** He told her it would cost her a fortune to put it
right. **16.** The policeman asked the motorist if he had the
right of way. **17.** He said proudly (that) he had a clean
record. **18.** He told me I had made a mess of his bumper.

18. *L'article indéfini* : a, an *(pp. 67,69)*

A'. 1. A vegetarian never eats Ø meat. 2. Drink a cup of tea, Ø tea will do you good. 3. He is an admirable man. He is full of energy. 4. Buy Ø greens not Ø frozen foods. 5. I'll just have a piece of toast, Ø toast is all right. 6. French people drink Ø coffee. The English prefer Ø tea to Ø coffee. 7. You should eat Ø vegetables not Ø sweets. 8. I had a mutton chop for lunch. I like Ø mutton, I prefer it to Ø pork. 9. Take an umbrella, it's going to rain. 10. I wouldn't say he's a humble man. I wouldn't call that Ø humility!

B'. 1. I couldn't do without Ø mustard. 2. What a delicious meal! 3. That was such Ø good marmalade. 4. Monsieur Dupont, a French chef, is very popular in our town. 5. What a shame you can't eat such Ø wonderful kippers! 6. Mrs. Jones is a grocer, not a butcher. 7. What a big piece of cake! 8. It's such a pity you can't touch such Ø delicious jam! 9. You'll have to do without Ø crackers. 10. He always has his coffee without Ø sugar and without Ø milk. 11. What Ø bad luck! The steak is overdone again! 12. He is a teetotaller (He never drinks Ø alcohol).

C'. 1. He drinks two pints of milk a day. 2. There is one delicatessen in our small town. 3. The baker comes twice a week. 4. Do you know him as a man or only as a shopkeeper? 5. I'll come back another day. 6. How much is it? Thirty francs a liter. 7. It took him a quarter of an hour to do it. Not half an hour. 8. Be reasonable, take one glass of brandy, not two! 9. It's too strong a beer for me! 10. This wine-merchant sells over a hundred bottles of whisky a month.

---

19. *L'article défini* : the *(pp. 71,73)*

A'. 1. The council flats were not very comfortable. 2. He lives near the industrial estate. 3. The townplanner was speaking about the green areas. 4. They live in the blind alley. 5. He is no longer the honorable man he used to be. 6. The ringroad is always crowded. 7. The garden city is very pleasant to live in. 8. We listened to the hourly news bulletin during the war.

B'. 1. Ø Shopwindows are full of toys at Christmas time. 2. The districts we visited were full of semi-detached houses. 3. We could hardly see the sun for the highrises in that American city. 4. Ø People sit and relax in the public gardens of the town. 5. Ø Pedestrians should use Ø pedestrian crossings. 6. Always be very careful at Ø crossroads. Ø Car-drivers tend to ignore Ø traffic-lights. 7. The housing estates I was telling you about are located in the suburbs of our town. 8. Oh please, John, tell the kids to be quiet.

C'. 1. A man sitting on the pavement was playing the accordion. 2. Edinburgh is the capital of Ø Scotland. 3. The young must go to Ø school up to the age of sixteen. 4. Ø Prince Charles came to Ø France Ø last month. 5. The French think Ø Russian is a difficult language. 6. What do you think of Ø English breakfast? 7. Where will you go Ø next year? I'll visit Ø Poland. 8. The elderly often refuse to go to Ø hospital. 9. I pity the poor and I don't envy the rich. 10. Ø President Roosevelt was rather popular with the French, I think. 11. Which language do you prefer, Ø German or Ø English? 12. The blind are often musical.

---

20. *Les démonstratifs* this *et* that *(p. 75)*

A'. 1. Take **these** knives, not **those**. 2. Put **this** serviette in the serviette-ring. 3. **This** is a soup-plate, **that** is a dinner-plate. 4. Will you put **this** tablecloth in **that** sideboard over there? 5. **This** is Mr. Law. Very pleased to meet you. 6. Can you pass me **those** dishes over there? 7. Come and get **these** teaspoons, put them in **that** drawer over there. 8. I'll never forget **those** days in the U.S.A. in 1950. 9. What's **this** here? And what's **that**? 10. Come and wash **these** cups and saucers. 11. Do you remember **those** glasses they gave us as a wedding present? 12. Which glass is yours? **This** one or **that** one? It's **that** one over there. 13. **This** is a teapot, **that** is a coffee-pot. 14. I can't forget **that** terrible day we spent in **that** storm years ago.

---

21. *Les quantificateurs* some, any, no *(pp. 77,79)*

A'. 1. Is there **any** water in the jug? No there isn't **any**. 2. He bought **some** sausages at the butcher's. 3. Let's have **some** porridge for breakfast. 4. He didn't have **any** cereals this morning. Did you have **any**? 5. Drink **some** orange juice, it'll do you good. 6. There were **no** eggs in the fridge, **none** at all. 7. Have **some** cream with your coffee. 8. She didn't have **any** soup, she never has **any**. 9. He always eats **some** fruit at the end of the meal. 10. **No** sweets for you! You are too greedy! Leave **some** for your brother. 11. There wasn't **any** tea in the teapot. 12. You may drink **some** whisky but not too much. So the doctor said.

B'. 1. Can you buy **some** pepper? 2. **Any** doctor will tell you you must drink a lot of water. 3. If there are **any** tomatoes, they will be welcome. 4. Would you like **some** lemonade? No thanks, I won't have **any** for lunch today. 5. Will you bring me **some** beans and **some** peas? We'll have **some** for lunch today. 6. Take **some** ham if you can find **any**. 7. **Any** grocer will sell you that. 8. You will find that in **any** little village. 9. Can I have **some** lettuce please? 10. If you have **any** objections, please tell us.

C'. 1. There is **no coffee left** in the coffee pot. There is **not any** left. 2. Will you have **some more** doughnuts? 3. I'll have **some more** cocoa. 4. He did **not** see **anybody** (or anyone) in the street, absolutely **nobody**. 5. We have **some** ale and **some** stout **left**. 6. I won't go **anywhere** this summer. **Nowhere**. 7. **Anybody** will tell you that. 8. He **never** says **anything**. Others say **anything**. 9. She does **not** want **any more** orange juice. 10. She would like **some more** milk and **some more** sugar too.

22. *Les quantificateurs* much, many, (a) little, (a) few *(pp. 81, 83,85)*

A. 1. There are not **many** pedestrian crossings in this street. 2. Motorists often show **little** patience, yes, very little indeed. 3. Are there **many** traffic lights in this town? Not many. 4. There is **little** traffic at twelve o'clock. 5. You see very **few** vehicles at four in the morning. 6. The careless driver did not pay **much** attention at the crossroads. 7. There are not **many** street lamps in these alleys. 8. There is very **little** noise in this sidestreet and not **much** traffic. 9. **Lots of** cars were running round the roundabout. 10. You won't see **many** bicycles in this thoroughfare at six o'clock in the evening. 11. If you don't drive at rush hours, there is not **much** danger. 12. Foreign visitors do not take **much** interest in this metropolis.

B'. 1. There are not **as many** streetsweepers **as** before. 2. Dustmen have **so much** work in a big city! 3. The town is **too Ø quiet** in summer. So **many** people are away on holiday. 4. You drive either **too Ø fast** or too Ø carelessly. 5. **How many** foreign cars did you count? Not **as many as** yesterday. 6. You should not drive for **so Ø long**. Driving **too Ø long** is dangerous. **Too many** motorists forget this. It isn't **as Ø easy** as all that to remember. 7. Town-dwellers are **so Ø irritable!** They show **so little** patience! 8. I didn't arrive in time. There was **too much** traffic. 9. You sleep **too much**. You don't work **as much as** you should. I wish you spent **as much** time at your desk **as** you do in your bed!

C'. 1. There is **less traffic**, there are **fewer lorries**. 2. There are **more taxis** around the station, there is **more bustle** too. 3. A van makes **less noise** than a big lorry. 4. There are **fewer tramcars** and there is **less din** too. 5. **Fewer double deckers** are to be seen these days. 6. There are **many more** policemen in this district. 7. There is **much less** noise in this cul-de-sac. 8. You see **many more** drug pushers in these side streets. 9. There are **many more** traffic jams at these crossroads.

---

23. *Les nombres cardinaux et ordinaux (pp. 87-91)*

A'. 1. Two minus two is **nought**. 2. Four multiplied by three is **twelve**. 3. Twelve plus one is **thirteen**. 4. **Forty** divided by ten is four. 5. Seventy minus one hundred is **thirty**, not **thirteen**. 6. How many inhabitants are there in France? There are **fifty-five million** inhabitants. 7. There are **sixty** minutes in an hour, not **sixteen**! 8. It is **twenty-five** minutes past **eight** by my watch. **9.** He is an old man, he is **eighty**, not **eighteen**. **10.** He gave **seventy-five** pence.

B'. — twenty-ninth (29th) — thirty-third (33rd) — eighty-first (81st) — forty-second (42nd) — eightieth (80th) — eighth (8th) — ninetieth (90th) — ninth (9th) — three thousandth (3000th) — two hundredth (200th) — three thousand eight hundred and ninety first (3891st) — seven hundred and third (703rd) — twelfth (12th) — thirtieth (30th).

C'. 1. Millions of flowers are sold every year, **several million**. **2.** I bought **two dozen** roses yesterday morning. **3.** There were thousands of daffodils in the fields. **4.** That horticulturist sold hundreds of hyacinths last month, **five hundred, six hundred** perhaps. **5.** They have picked **a few dozen** buttercups. **6.** All these tulips have cost more than **three hundred** francs.

D'. — eight hundred **and** three — two hundred **and** thirty-three — two thousand **and** nine — five hundred **and** forty two — four thousand **and** seventy six — six thousand seven hundred **and** fifty seven — eighty two thousand **and** eighty eight. — three hundred **and** six — seven thousand four hundred **and** thirty-five — twelve thousand **and** twenty-seven.

E'. 1. I don't like his (her) **last two** novels. **2. February 14th (the fourteenth)** is Saint Valentine's Day. **3.** The Allied Forces landed in Normandy on **June 6th (the sixth)** 1944 **(nineteen forty four)**. **4.** How did you like the **first two** acts? **5. February 23rd (the twenty-third)** is Shrove Tuesday. **6.** Henry VIII **(the eighth)**, Louis XIV **(the fourteenth)** are very famous kings. **7.** Lily of the valley is associated with **May 1st (the first)**.

F'. 1. I saw **them both (both of them)** yesterday morning. **2.** He'll come **once**, not **twice**. **3.** He is **both** a poet and a novelist. **4.** We went to the U.S.A. **four times**. **5.** She is learning **both** English and German. **6. Both** are American. They are **both** American. **Both of them** are American. **7.** He spoke to **both of us**. **8. Both languages** are very difficult. **9.** She writes **both** short stories and novels.

24. *Le pluriel des noms (pp. 93,95,97)*

A'. 1. There are a lot of potatoes this year. 2. The thieves were arrested yesterday. 3. Have you seen the cliffs of Dover? 4. Housewives have a lot of work every day. 5. Have you visited the churches in our town? 6. Don't forget to lock your safes. 7. I like white pianos. 8. I bought a dozen knives and forks. 9. There were lots of cars and lorries. 10. I took these photos last summer. 11. Put these pictures in these boxes. 12. Lay the dishes on the table. 13. His favourite hobbies are music and painting. 14. Where are the keys? 15. It is autumn. The leaves are yellow.

B'. 1. There are a lot of taxi-drivers in this town. 2. The street was full of passers-by. 3. I prefer the Smiths to the Jacksons. 4. I like cherry-tarts. 5. Peter and Bob met their girl-friends outside the cinema. 6. The MPs (or Mp's) walked into the House of Commons. 7. What do you think of our fellow-travellers? 8. They came in with their pipes in their mouths. 9. Those ladies are all mother-hens. 10. They all lost their lives in that terrible accident. 11. They all came on their bicycles. 12. Did you go to the zoo yesterday? Did you see the baby-elephants? 13. All our friends, who were many, came in their cars.

C'. 1. She never eats fish. 2. I have two very bad teeth. 3. These men and these women were demonstrating in the street. 4. This farmer has a hundred sheep and four or five oxen. 5. Is the news good? 6. How many children does she have? 7. Look at your feet! They are all dirty! 8. Your hair is too long. 9. Information is free. 10. This is a good piece of information. 11. The advice she gives you is quite useless. 12. There were people in the street. 13. This little boy has two white mice. 14. Your luggage is light. 15. He gave me a piece of advice. I always take his advice. 16. He eats fruit every day. 17. I prefer these people to the Wilsons. 18. Furniture is expensive.

25. *Le génitif (ou cas possessif) (p. 99,101,103)*

A'. 1. I don't like my sister's new bathing suit. 2. I don't like Jane's blue raincoat. 3. I don't like the children's white socks. 4. I don't like Old Brown's red dressing gown. 5. I don't like these workers' caps. 6. I don't like Mummy's new blouse. 7. I don't like these young ladies' short skirts. 8. I don't like the senior executives' umbrellas. 9. I don't like my brother's new shoes. 10. I don't like businessmen's bowler hats. 11. I don't like these people's red ties. 12. I don't like soldiers' uniforms.

1. The little girls' pyjamas were too long. 2. Look at the dog's tail. 3. The worker repaired the roof of the old house. 4. Did you notice President George Bush's dinner jacket? 5. The buttons of her blouse were white. 6. My mother has mended the sleeve of my raincoat. 7. I don't like the colour of Uncle John's tracksuit. 8. Think of the difficulties of the poor. 9. What do you think of the colour of her (his) gloves? 10. The two women's furcoats were identical. 11. The zip of my trousers is broken.

B'. 1. We took a three hours' walk. 2. We had a week's holiday in England. 3. I'll buy tomorrow's newspaper. 4. What do you think of the party's decision? 5. Poland's crisis is given front page coverage. 6. It was a fortnight's visit. 7. Let us have a moment's rest. 8. It's a man's job, not a woman's (job). 9. What do you think of Turkey's entry into the Common Market? 10. The schoolboys are having a ten minutes' break. 11. Did you listen to last night's weather forecast? 12. How long does it take to get a doctor's degree?

C'. 1. Aunt Mary's handbag is big, Aunt Helen's is small. 2. She went to the butcher's. 3. Jane's tights are black, Betty's are brown. 4. Shall we go to our old friends'? 5. We go to St Peter's every Sunday. 6. This man's slippers are old, that man's are brand new ones. 7. Robert and Jack's bedroom is very large. 8. What do you think of Margaret's and Joan's new aprons? 9. These young ladies'suits are red, those old ladies' are green. 10. Let us stay for a week at our uncle's.

26. *Les possessifs (p. 105,107)*

A'. **1.** This anorak belongs to me, it is **my** anorak, it is **mine**. **2.** Mary takes great care of **her** equipment. Do you take care of **yours**? **3.** I like this instructor, I like **his** way of teaching. **4.** Look at this motorbike! Look at **its** size. **5.** This tent belongs to Peter and Paul, it is **their** tent, it is **theirs**. **6.** Can you pass her **her** skisticks? **7.** Is this Jane's racket? Yes it is **her** racket, it's **hers**. **8.** We enjoyed **our** skiing holidays. Did you enjoy **yours**? **9.** The young boy has lost **his** skates. **10.** The poor fellow has broken **his** fishing-rod again! **11.** Where is **your** riding-school? It is near here. Is **yours** far from here? **12.** That gentleman is quite rich, **his** sailing boat is quite big. **Mine** isn't as big! I am not as rich! **13.** They always go there. It is **their** favourite winter sports resort. It is not **ours**, we do not like it so much. **14.** Whose gloves are these? They are the young lady's, they are **hers**.

B'. **1.** The two scouts went away with **their** rucksacks on **their** backs. **2.** Look at the Wilsons in **their** motorboat. They bought it yesterday. It is **theirs**. **3.** The young man was standing on the golf links; he had **his** golf club in **his** hand. **4.** The young ladies came in **their** bicycles. **5.** Everybody came in **their** cars. **6.** All the hunters had to show **their** hunting permits. **7.** I saw it with my **own** eyes. **8.** He goes swimming with **a friend of his** every afternoon. **9.** All these rich people spend hours on **their** yachts doing nothing. **10.** Mind your **own** business, I'll see to **mine**. **11.** One should always wear **one's** life jacket on **one's** boat. **12.** She went skiing with **a sister of hers**. **13.** She goes to the riding school but it is her **own** horse. **14.** It is his ball. It's **his**. **15.** He broke his **own** record. Breaking **one's own** record is quite an event. **16.** We play tennis with **two friends of ours**. **17.** Skiing with **one's** friends is great fun.

27. *Les adjectifs qualificatifs (pp. 109-113)*

A'. 1. Sitting-rooms are very **large** in modern houses. **2.** We have **a very small bathroom. 3.** A house is never **big enough. 4.** Our children have **a very pleasant rumpus-room. 5. The others** were sitting in front of the beautiful fireplace. **6.** Is there **anything interesting** on the telly? **7.** There were **glasses full of whisky** on the round table. **8.** What do you think of **these modern kitchens? 9.** They have **an attic full of dusty furniture. 10.** They are very rich. They have **a splendid second home. 11.** His study is full of **very old books. 12.** It is a **small spare room** but it is very useful. **13.** Have you visited the other second homes?—The others? No, I haven't.

B'. 1. Not **all the blind** play musical instruments, but I know **many blind people** who do. **2.** You shouldn't envy **the rich. 3.** There are **a lot of unemployed people** in Britain. **The unemployed** receive unemployment benefits. **4. The French** have a world-wide reputation for their cuisine. **5.** I visited **an elderly woman** yesterday. She said she often felt lonely. **6.** This **blind girl** plays the piano very well. She is only nine years old. **7. Some handicapped men** are very optimistic. **8.** I pity **the poor**, but I don't do much for them. **9.** Take the big box not the small **one. 10. The British** drink tea all day. **11.** I saw **a poor woman** in the street; she was begging. **12.** Which dress do you prefer, the long **one** or the short **one? 13.** Mrs. Shaw is very devoted to **the elderly. 14.** The tall girls are English, the small **ones** are French. **15.** I like **the English**. I like **English** too, it is a beautiful language. **16.** How many **Englishmen** are there in the room? (en un seul mot!). **17. The Welsh** are fond of music. **18. The blind boy** crossed the street. He was accompanied by his father. **19.** Wasn't it terrible to see those **poor children** playing in the slums? We should think of **the poor** a little more. **20.** Who is Mr. Brown? The tall man or the small **one**?

C'. 1. He is an **extraordinary old** man. **2.** There was an **immense green** field. **3.** It is a **young grey** cat. **4.** He was wearing a **new blue** suit. **5.** She is a **charming old** woman. **6.** We have an **old red** car. **7.** It was a **large round** table.

8. She was a **tall young** woman. 9. Take the **big oval** box. 10. It was a large old town.

D'. 1. A **red-roofed** bungalow. 2. A **dirty-looking** kitchen. 3. A **home-made** cake. 4. A **green-shaded** lamp. 5. A **snow-covered** cottage. 6. A **horse-drawn** cart. 7. A **three-storeyed** house. 8. A sailor who is **sea-sick**. 9. A **black-hatted** gentleman. 10. A **many-coloured** rumpus-room. 11. A **comfortable-looking** drawing-room. 12. A **three-legged** table. 13. A **long-nosed** lady. 14. A **home-sick** exile. 15. Bob is **left-handed**. 16. A rabbit is a **long-eared** animal. 17. A **white-walled** second home.

---

28. *Le comparatif et le superlatif (pp. 115,117,119)*

A'. 1. This bedside lamp is **more modern than** mine. 2. Your standard-lamp is **nicer than** the red one. 3. Is this grandfather clock **older than** the one we bought? 4. This video tape recorder is **the most expensive** and **the most sophisticated** of all. 5. This record player is **worse than** the others. 6. Is this television set **better than** yours? No it's **worse**. 7. A dishwasher is **as** useful **as** a washing-machine. 8. This chest of drawers is **the biggest** of the three. 9. This writing-table is **the least convenient** of all. It is not **as** convenient **as** yours. 10. Do you find this bed-settee **more comfortable** or **less comfortable than** the other one? 11. It is **the biggest** wardrobe that I have ever bought. 12. You won't find **bigger** cushions **than** this one; it's really **the biggest** one that I have found. 13. These paintings are not **as** rare **as** yours. 14. I think that the Browns' furniture is **plainer** than the Smiths'; but it is **more expensive** too.

B'. 1. It is **more and more difficult** to find old furniture. 2. He was **all the happier** to have an answering machine **as** he was often absent. 3. Telephone books are **less and less** available. 4. **The older** we get **the more attached** to our house we become. 5. Today wall-to-wall carpet is **thicker and thicker** and **more and more expensive**. 6. A room looks **all the more crowded as** we collect trinkets in it. 7. His typewriter is **more and more** useful; he is **busier and busier**. 8. This sitting-room is **all the cosier as** there are lots of curtains in it.

9. He needs **bigger and bigger** filing-cabinets; he is a **more and more** important business man. 10. Wallpapers are **all the more popular as** they are washable. 11. **The more numerous** T.V. channels are **the more hesitant** you become when choosing your programme. 12. A writing-desk is **all the more convenient as** it has many drawers.

C'. 1. There were two big fridges. We bought **the more expensive** one. 2. They have **no other** deep-freeze **than** this one. 3. We have the **same** gas cooker **as** the Smiths. 4. See those two geyser; **the less efficient** of the two is this one. 5. There are **no other** saucepans **than** the red one and the blue one; take **the bigger** of the two. 6. We don't have the **same** household appliances here **as** in our second home.

---

29. *Les pronoms personnels (p. 121, 123)*

A'. 1. He was playing with **them**. 2. **She** was with **him**. 3. **They** went out together. 4. Look at **her**, she's playing with **it**. 5. **She** has been living in **it** since 1960. 6. **She** spoils **him**. 7. Have you seen **them**? 8. I saw **him** and I told **him** about **it**. 9. **She** is jealous. 10. How old is **he**? 11. **They** went to the cinema with **them**. 12. Don't speak to **her** like that! 13. **He** is a widower. 14. **She** has never accepted **it**. 15. **They** don't always get on well. 16. **He** is an orphan. 17. **They** are interested in **it**. 18. I visited **them** last week. 19. **It** is near **it**. 20. **They** are twins. 21. **They** enjoy **it**. 22. **She** is English. 23. Have you met **him**?

B'. 1. **My brother and I** are fond of sports. 2. I'll come on Tuesday and **he**'ll come on Wednesday. 3. She is younger **than me (than I am)**. 4. **You** never know. **One** never knows. 5. **You and I** don't always agree. 6. Put on your raincoat, yes, put **it** on, it is raining. 7. "**We** drink a lot of wine in France" Monsieur Dupont said. 8. Who did it? **He** did. 9. His sister and **he** came yesterday morning. 10. Who will come tomorrow? **I** will. 11. If **you** do that, **you** look for trouble. 12. She let **him** in. 13. **They** say he is a very good teacher. 14. You did not see her but **she** saw you. 15. Don't let **her** down. 16. She drives faster than **he** does. 17. **We** can always try. 18. Who would accept that? **She would**. 19. **You** could not tell if she is happy or not. **20. One** has to pay income taxes.

---

30. *Les pronoms réfléchis et réciproques (pp. 125,127)*

A'. **1.** Don't be selfish. Don't think of **yourself** all the time. **2.** They are enemies, they hate **each other**. **3.** She blushed. She was ashamed of **herself**. **4.** He is self-centred, he is always talking about **himself**. **5.** These two people admire **each other**. **6.** John and Peter often laugh at **one another**. **7.** I did it, I only have **myself** to blame. **8.** Defend your interests, young men, defend **yourselves**! **9.** We kissed **each other** and went away. **10.** Did you enjoy **yourselves** at the party, you two? (s'amuser). **11.** We could not stand **one another**. **12.** John and Mary fell in love with **each other**. **13.** They did it **themselves**, nobody helped them. **14.** Richard and Mary felt attracted to **one another**. **15.** I don't like the city **itself**, I prefer the suburbs. **16.** The mother and the daughter dote on **each other**. **17.** We should always control **ourselves**. **18.** Mr. Brown and I were not very fond of **each other**. **19.** I cursed **myself** for being so stupid. **20.** This old man talks to **himself**. **21.** They hardly know **one another**. **22.** Those two girls can't bear **each other**, they loathe **each other**. **23.** Let me do it. I will do it **myself**.

N.B. : On peut remplacer **each other** par **one another** et vice versa.

B'. **1.** He was in despair, he killed **himself**. **2.** They were in love with **each other**. **3.** If only you could see **yourself**! You look ridiculous! **4.** Respect **one another**. **5.** She could not imagine **herself** in that situation. **6.** At what time did you **wake up** yesterday? **7.** They took to **each other**. **8.** I **shave** and **dress** in ten minutes. **9.** They are very angry **with one another**. **10.** They often **quarrel**, they bear a grudge against **each other**. **11.** The demonstrators will **gather** at ten o'clock. **12.** My cousins are very **close to one another**. They often **meet** and talk for hours. **13.** Stop **fighting**. **14.** You are a selfish lot, you think only of **yourselves**. **15.** She **got (was) killed** in a car accident. **16.** They do not even listen to **one another**. They do not feel respect for **one another**. **17.** I am not sure of **myself**. 18. We cannot rely on them, we must rely on **ourselves**. 19. One must do it **oneself**. 20. She was **by herself**. She was very unhappy. 21. One should not think of **oneself** only. 22. Did you spend the evening **by yourself**?

---

31. *Les relatifs* who *et* which, that, *etc. (pp. 129,131,133)*

A'. 1. This man, **who** is an industrialist, works twelve hours a day. 2. He is the G.P. **who** lives next door. 3. Have you been to the garage **which** he recommended? 4. Is he the mechanic **who** repaired your car? 5. He is a bookseller who **knows** his onions. 6. It is a job **which** demands a lot of patience. 7. Do you remember the vet **who** came for the dog? 8. The plumber **who** came was not very efficient. 9. It is a salary **which** is hardly sufficient to survive. 10. Publishing is a trade **which** attracts him. 11. He is a journalist **who** works for the *Financial Times*. 12. It is an area **which** does not offer many job opportunities.

B'. 1. Is he the butcher you were speaking **about**? 2. It is the tool the technician worked **with**? 3. The newspaperman I had an argument **with** was not sincere. 4. These are the scissors the hairdresser cut her hair **with**. 5. The barrister I was speaking **to** was quite famous. 6. This is the oven the baker makes such good bread **in**. 7. That was the dentist he was so angry **with**. 8. Mary is a typist he is madly in love **with**.

C'. 1. He is a dentist **whose wife** is English. 2. Do you remember the pharmacist I was talking **about** (about whom I was talking). 3. He was operated on by a surgeon **whose reputation** is worldwide. 4. In this country **whose output** is so high, unskilled workers, **whose** wages are so low, can hardly survive. 5. Do you know the florist **he is talking about**? (about whom he is talking). 6. He is a lawyer **whose integrity** is unquestionable. 7. My friend Peter **I told you about** (about whom I told you) is a professor. 8. It is a house **with large windows, whose proprietor** (the proprietor of which) is a famous scientist. 9. He is the jeweller **whose shop** was burglarized last week.

32. *Les relatifs* what *et* which, those who... *(p. 135)*

A'. **1.** Tell me **what** you know, all (**that**) you know about this great musician. **2.** **What** I like best of all is going to the concert. **3.** He practises the violin every day, **which** pleases his parents. **4.** I envy **those who** can play a musical instrument. **5.** **The one who** is sitting on the right is a famous opera singer. **6.** He played out of time, **which** made the conductor mad. **7.** **What** I can't bear is people singing at the top of their voices. **8.** He gave up the cello, **which** was a big mistake. **9.** **All** (**that**) I can say is that acoustics in that concert hall are not very good, **which** is a pity. **10.** **What** you must have is a good ear, especially if you play a wind instrument.

---

33. *Les interrogatifs* who? *et* whose?, what? *et* which? *(pp. 137,139)*

A'. **1.** **Who** was that actress? Vivien Leigh. **2.** **Whose** wife was Vivien Leigh? Laurence Olivier's. **3.** **What** is he? He is a film director. **4.** **What** sort of film was it? A thriller. **5.** **Which** film star is your favourite, Fay Dunaway or Jane Birkins? **6.** **What** do you think of the dubbing? **7.** **What** was on at the Gaumont? **8.** **Which** detective film did you prefer, the English one or the American one? **9.** **Whose** film made a hit that season? Woody Allen's. **10.** **What** do you like most? Documentary films. **11.** **Whose** job is that? It's the scriptwriter's. **12.** **Who** won the oscar? An Italian actress. **13.** **Whose** film won the oscar? Hitchcock's. **14.** **Who** is the famous actor who is also well-known as a stuntman? Jean-Paul Belmondo. **15.** **Whose** film was entirely shot in the open? I think it was that American producer's. **16.** **Which** cinema did you go to, the Gaumont or the Realto?

B'. **1.** **What** were you talking about? **2.** **Who(m)** was he referring **to**? **3.** **Which** performance will you go **to**? **4.** **What** was the cinema made **of**? **5.** **What** is she fond **of**? **6.** **Who** does he look **like**? **7.** **What** did this film remind her **of**? **8.** **Who(m)** did he play **with** in "Hamlet"?

C'. **1.** **When** did she have an ice-cream? **2.** **Where** were the

shots on location taken? **3. Why** was the film a flop?
4. Where are they showing that film? **5. When** did she
watch that film? **6. Why** didn't you enjoy the film? **7. How
long** does the film last? **8. When** do you go to the movies?

---

34. *La place des adverbes de manière, de lieu, de temps, etc.*
(pp. 141,143)

A'. 1. I'll go to the circus **tomorrow**. 2. He likes conjuring
tricks **very much**. 3. We are going to a show **next week**.
4. **Perhaps** we'll go to the fun fair with them. 5. The
children liked the pantomime **very much**. 6. She does not
fancy musical comedies **too much**. 7. The interval was **long
enough**, wasn't it? 8. **Perhaps** we'll go to a disco. 9. I could
not see the jugglers **very well** from my seat. 10. I don't like
this company **very much**. 11. Actors should speak **loud
enough** for everybody to hear them. 12. I know this ballet
dancer **very well**. 13. This play is **complicated enough** for
us. 14. They hissed the clowns **very loudly** the other day.
15. The audience was **enthusiastic enough**, wasn't it?
16. He read the programme **very conscientiously in his
office** the day before.

B'. 1. Has the little girl **ever** been on that merry-go-round? No
she has **never been**. 2. We **often** go to a show during the
weekend. 3. They **usually** have outstanding performances at
this theatre. 4. We **rarely** book stalls, we are not **rich
enough**. 5. He **sometimes** books his seats long in advance.
6. He **nearly** went out of the house in the middle of the
performance. The actors were **bad enough**. 7. I have **never**
heard such a bad performance of Bach / Never **have I
heard**... 8. Hardly **had the curtain risen** when the audience
started clapping their hands. 9. I **rather** liked her performance of Gisèle. 10. I have **never** been to that nightclub.

35. How *adverbe interrogatif et exclamatif (pp. 145,147)*

A'. 1. **How long** did the journey last? **How many hours** did the journey last? 2. **How often** do you take the plane? 3. **How far is it** from London to Liverpool? 4. **How much is** the railway ticket? 5. **How old** is that jet? 6. **How often** do you travel from New York to Boston? 7. **How much** luggage do you have? **How many** suitcases do you have? 8. **How many** carriages does this train have? How long is it? 9. **How high is** a double-decker bus? 10. **How many** passengers were there on the coach? 11. **How wide** is the track? 12. **How long** did it take you to pack your luggage? **How many** hours did it take you to pack your luggage? 13. **How much** petrol does your car consume...? **How many** gallons does your car consume? 14. **How often** do you check the tyre pressure?

B'. 1. **How good** it is! 2. **How old** it is! 3. **How** sturdy it was! 4. **How reckless** he was! 5. **How high** it had been! 6. **How** slippery they will be! 7. **How** crowded it is! 8. **How** dangerous it was! 9. **How** wonderful it is! 10. **How** eventful it was!

---

36. *Le gérondif ou nom verbal (pp. 149,151)*

A'. 1. I am not interested in **doing** the housework all day. 2. **Polishing** the floor is hard work. 3. I'm fed up with **making** the beds in this house. 4. It's **her knitting** all the time that annoys me! 5. I'll dust the furniture before **sweeping** the floor. 6. **Sewing** damages your eyesight. 7. **Hoovering** a carpet is not more interesting than sweeping! 8. John hates **tidying** up his room. 9. I much prefer **making** cakes to **washing** up the dishes. 10. I don't like **the children's playing** about when I am doing a room. 11. You can't very well darn socks without **using** a needle, can you?

B'. 1. I **feel like reading**, not like **doing** the housework. 2. She **can't help knitting** when she watches television. 3. It is **no use dusting** the furniture every five minutes. 4. She **looks forward to watching** television after doing the chores. 5. I **prefer sewing** to knitting. 6. She **prevented** me **from doing** the washing up. 7. I **consider hiring** a charwoman. 8. She

intends ironing before making the beds. 9. **Using** a sewing machine is not always so simple. 10. The operation which **consists in doing** all the rooms thoroughly is called spring-cleaning.

---

37. *Les prépositions de lieu et de temps (pp. 153-159)*

A'. 1. The businessman walked **into** his office. 2. The firm was prosperous **till** 1982. 3. The junior executive travelled **from** London **to** New York every month. 4. Who was the accountant talking **to**? He was talking to the boss. What was he talking **about**? He was talking about the company. 5. The manager held a meeting in his office **till** four o'clock. 6. There was a big slogan written **across** the front of the company building. 7. Business was brisk **till** 1929. 8. The head-office is **in** Brussels. 9. The clerk commuted **from** home **to** work. 10. He'll be doing clerical work **till** November. 11. The General Manager travels **as far as** Japan for business. 12. She is a typist **in** a joint-stock company. 13. Wait **till** six o'clock, when I come back **from** the office. 14. The paper knife went **through** the sheet of paper.

B'. 1. The Board of Directors met **for** three hours **on** February 3rd. 2. Business was slack **during** the summer. 3. The staff met **in** the morning, not **in** the afternoon. 4. I'll learn shorthand **one** day. 5. Inflation was rampant Ø last year. 6. The secretary did not come to work **on** Thursday. 7. That senior executive usually spends three weeks in Spain **during** his holidays. 8. I must buy a typewriter **one** day. 9. The executive worked in the City for a month Ø last winter. 10. I worked in that firm **for** years **during** the war.

C'. 1. I am not interested **in** book-keeping. 2. The secretary asked the boss **for** a pay rise. 3. The manager's desk was covered **with** dossiers. 4. It was not easy to deal **with** the industrial dispute. The staff were very angry **with** the boss. 5. It depends **on** the order-books. 6. Executives often go Ø home late in the evening. 7. You must not make the boss wait **for** you. 8. The manager was not satisfied **with** his employee. 9. Will you remind me **of** that letter I have to type? If you don't, I'll never think **about** it. 10. The boss is responsible for the running of the business. He must work hard **in order to** run it properly. **11.** A multinational is not very different **from** another. **12.** He entered Ø his office at 8 o'clock sharp. **13.** He did not have enough money, he had to borrow some **from** a friend.

D'. 1. Listen. Listen **to** the boss, **listen to him**. **2.** The junior executive **drove to** his office. **3.** He was **waiting**, yes, he was waiting **for** his secretary. **4.** "She **rushed in**" he said. Then he added "She rushed **into** her office." **5.** I am **responsible**, I am entirely responsible **for** this department. **6. Look at** him. Look. He has run out. **7. Switch on** the light, **switch off** the radio set. **8.** He put his attaché case **on** the chair and **switched on** the electric fire.

Index

BUS

BUILDING
LAYOUT

By W. P. Jackson

Craftsman Book Company
6058 Corte del Cedro / P.O. Box 6500 / Carlsbad, CA 92018

Contents

Chapter 1

The Transit

A transit is used to measure horizontal and vertical angles. An engineer normally measures angles from the north-south meridian in surveying, so the engineer's transit is equipped with a compass. The builder's or contractor's transit, or transit-level, does not normally include a compass because buildings are laid out from an existing fixed point at or near the building site, such as the lot corner stake or monument.

A theodolite is essentially a more precise transit. Instead of a vernier scale, a theodolite is equipped with an optical micrometer scale. This permits readings that are not possible on a vernier, such as readings directly to 10'' (0°00'10''). On some models the readings are directly to one second (0°00'01''). Figure 7-15 shows the accuracy of these readings. The theodolite has an optical plummet, and the sensitivity of the level tube is usually 45'' or better. Theodolites are used where precision work is essential.

The operation of a builder's transit (or transit-level) is not complicated. You don't need an engineering degree or any technical knowledge to use one. More and more trades are using them to save time, cut costs, and insure accuracy in their work.

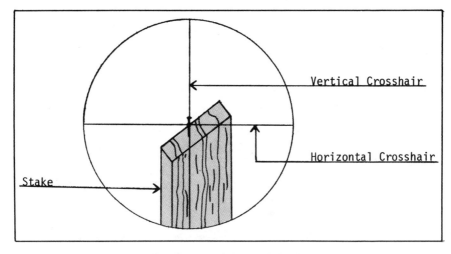

View of Objective Through Telescope
Figure 1-1

1. Builders need them to lay out foundations, plot lot lines, establish grades and excavations, and for many other uses.

2. Plumbers need them to lay out sewer lines.

3. Masons need them to level walls and foundations.

4. Concrete contractors need them for grades on floors, driveways and walks.

5. The list can include farmers, landscapers and many others.

There are three main parts to any transit — the *telescope,* the *leveling vial,* and the *circle.*

1. *The telescope* This is a precision optical sighting device that produces a clear magnified image. The degree of magnification of a telescope is called its *power* (x). For example, a 20x telescope makes a distant object appear 20 times closer than if

viewed with the naked eye. Crosshairs in the telescope permit the object sighted to be centered in the field of view. See Figure 1-1. The power of the telescope can vary. The less expensive instruments have a lower power and are used for shorter range. An 18x instrument is usually used in work up to about 120 feet. A 26x instrument may be used for work up to 500 feet. Telescopes come in one of two types: fixed lens or zoom lens, sometimes called variable power type. The fixed lens type has a fixed power, such as 18x or 26x. The variable powers of the zoom lens type depend on the model of the instrument; some adjust from 18x to 34x, others from 24x to 37x. The advantage of the zoom lens is that it compensates for dim light and changes in distance.

2. *The leveling vial* This is a bubble that works like the bubble on a carpenter's level, but it is much more sensitive and accurate. Leveling vials are available in various degrees of sensitivity. For precision work use a more sensitive vial. A level vial with a sensitivity of 90 seconds ('') per 2 mm is more sensitive than one whose sensitivity is 14 minutes (') per 2 mm. A vial with a sensitivity of 45 seconds ('') per 2 mm is more sensitive than one with a 90 seconds ('') per 2 mm sensitivity. Level tube sensitivity is explained later in the chapter.

3. *The circle* This is the plate on which the telescope rotates. It is marked in degrees and has a vernier scale that subdivides each degree in minutes on the better models. Instruments designed for still greater precision have a vernier that further subdivides each minute into seconds. Figure 7-15 shows what different vernier readings mean in linear distance. Thus, a transit whose vernier reads to 15 minutes can have a linear error of 5 ¼'' in 100 feet. One whose vernier reads to 5 minutes can have a linear error of 1 ¾'' in 100 feet. But the instrument with a vernier reading of 20 seconds may have a linear error of only 1/8'' in 100 feet. The theodolite is recommended for work that requires

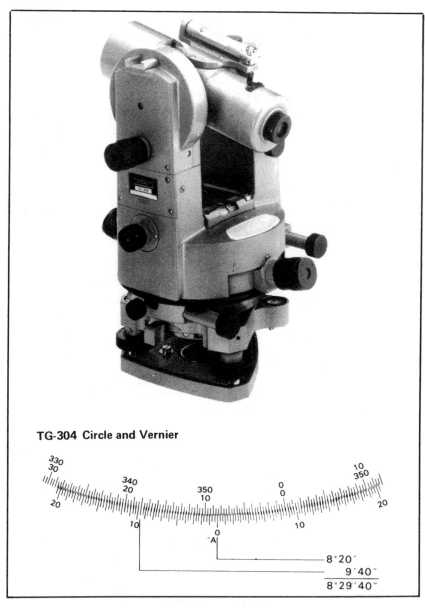

David White Path Transit
Figure 1-2

greater precision than an instrument with a 20 second vernier reading. See Figures 1-2 and 1-3. These are extremely precise instruments.

The *optical plummet* is a device for centering a transit over a point. It replaces the plumb bob used in most transits. By sighting horizontally through a right angle prism, you see the point over which the transit is centered. When the instrument is properly set up it is directly over the mark. The optical plummet serves the same purpose as a plumb bob, but is more accurate because it is not affected by the wind.

Purchase the most precise transit you can afford. You may not need that degree of precision now, but you probably will need it later when your skills increase and you take on other types of jobs. Since you use a transit for its accuracy, there is no substitute for an accurate instrument regardless of the size of the job.

Figure 1-2 shows a transit with a 20 second vernier reading. The divisions on the circle and vernier are very fine. It takes practice to read a vernier with this precision. The circle and vernier in this illustration read 8° 29' 40''.

Figure 1-3 shows two theodolites, each with a micrometer scale. The T-308AT theodolite reads directly to 20 seconds on the optical micrometer. Its horizontal (H) reading in the illustration is 285° 56' 20''. The vertical (V) reading is 169° 36' 20''. The T-208AT theodolite reads directly to 10 seconds on the optical micrometer. The horizontal reading shown is 268° 45' 50''. The vertical reading on the T-208AT is 152° 25' 50''. As shown in the illustration, both horizontal (H) and vertical (V) circles are viewed simultaneously. This helps you make error-free readings.

The right transit for you depends on your job requirements.

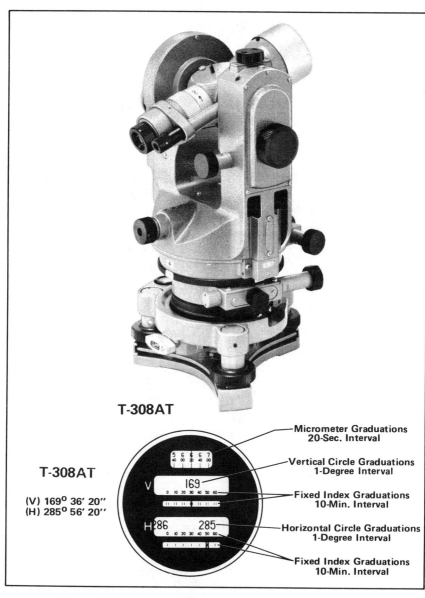

Theodolite - Fully Numbered Optical Micrometer
and Scale (Reads Direct to 20'')
Figure 1-3A

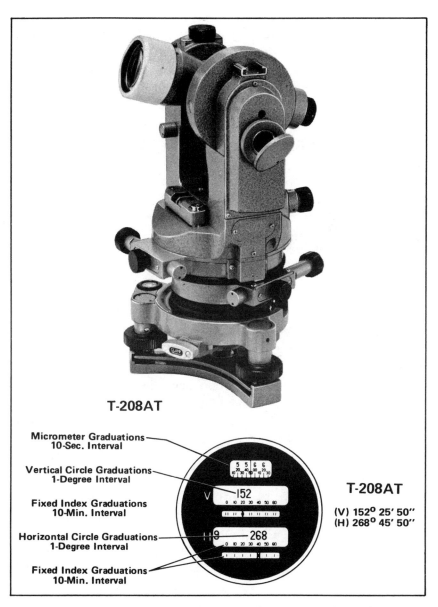

T-208AT

Micrometer Graduations
10-Sec. Interval

Vertical Circle Graduations
1-Degree Interval

Fixed Index Graduations
10-Min. Interval

Horizontal Circle Graduations
1-Degree Interval

Fixed Index Graduations
10-Min. Interval

T-208AT

(V) 152° 25′ 50″
(H) 268° 45′ 50″

Theodolite - Fully Numbered Optical Micrometer
and Scale (Reads Direct to 10'')
Figure 1-3B

The range of the work and the accuracy required are two factors you must consider before selecting any instrument. Be sure the transit you select has the power, the precision, and the versatility you need to meet all your requirements for the present and the future.

Level Tube Sensitivity

The more sensitive the level tube, the greater the precision that may be obtained. A 75 second ('') per 2 mm level tube is approximately 60% more accurate than one with a sensitivity of 120 seconds per 2 mm.

Level tubes are ground to specific radii. If the radius is large, a small vertical movement on one end of the tube causes a large displacement of the bubble. If the radius is small, the same vertical movement causes only a small displacement of the bubble. Thus the radius of the tube is a measure of its sensitivity. The more sensitive the level tube, the longer it takes to center the bubble. A bubble that travels more with small movement takes longer to settle with each movement of the leveling screw. When the bubble moves even slightly on any transit, you will see a movement in the line of sight as indicated by the crosshairs in the field of vision.

Table 1-4 shows the radii of level tubes of different sensitivities. The greater the precision of the transit, the more sensitive is the level tube built into it. An instrument whose vernier only reads to 15 minutes would probably have a level tube with a sensitivity of 8 to 14 minutes (or 480''-840'') per 2 mm. An instrument with a 5 minute vernier reading would probably have a level tube whose sensitivity would be from 90 to 120 seconds per 2 mm, and an instrument with a 1 minute vernier reading would probably be in the 60 to 75 seconds per 2 mm sensitivity range.

Sensitivity in seconds (") per 2 mm division of level tube	Radius of curvature in feet
14' (840")	1'-7"
8' (480")	2'-10"
100"	13'-6"
90"	15'
75"	18'
60"	23'
45"	30'
30"	45'
20"	68'

Radii of Level Tubes of Different Sensitivities
Table 1-4

The more precise instruments whose vernier or optical micrometer scales read in the seconds would have level tubes in the 20 to 45 seconds sensitivity range.

Level tube sensitivity is normally given as the number of seconds of arc per 2 mm division on the tube. In most units, the markings on the level tubes are 2 mm apart. This means that for each 2 mm the bubble moves in the tube, it forms an angle equal to the sensitivity of the arc given. So a level tube with a sensitivity

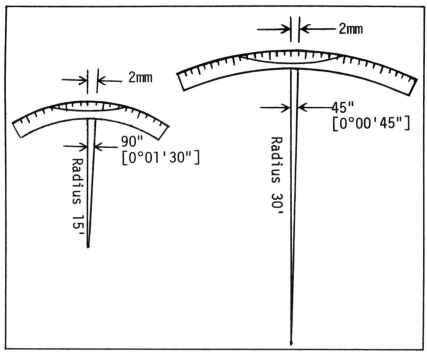

Sensitivity of Level Tubes
Figure 1-5

of 45 seconds per 2 mm would form an angle of 45 seconds at a radius of 30 feet for each 2 mm division the bubble moves in the tube. A level tube with a sensitivity of 90 seconds per 2 mm would form an angle of 90 seconds at a radius of 15 feet for each 2 mm the bubble in the tube moves. See Figure 1-5. A tube with a sensitivity reading of 8 minutes (480 seconds) would form an angle of 08' 00'' at a radius of 2 feet 10 inches (2'-10'') with each 2 mm movement of the bubble.

Setting Up The Transit

The transit is designed to produce precision work. But if it is not set up and leveled properly, accurate work is impossible regardless of how accurate the instrument is. Make sure your instrument is in perfect adjustment before you follow the instructions below.

The transit is usually set up over a fixed point such as a tack in a stake, an iron pin or a crossmark in a concrete monument. The manual that comes with each transit gives step by step instructions for setting up and leveling the instrument. They will not be covered here, but you should know the reason for some of the operations and how they can affect the accuracy of your work.

Set the tripod on firm ground and make sure the tripod points are stuck well into the ground. If you are setting up on a paved surface, be sure the points are secure. Position the tripod legs so the center of the tripod head is approximately over the centering point and the tripod head appears level. If the center of the tripod head is not approximately over the point, centering the transit with the plumb bob or optical plummet isn't possible. You must then reposition the tripod. If the tripod head is too far out of level, the transit can not be leveled with the leveling screws.

Leveling is the most important operation you perform before you use your instrument. The accuracy in all readings and surveying tasks requires a level instrument at all times. Figure 1-6 shows a serious error due to an instrument out of level. Points *A, B,* and *C* have been located. The instrument is set up over *A* to locate *D.* The line of collimation (the line of sight when the telescope is at 0° elevation) is perpendicular to the vertical axis. See Detail 1, Figure 1-6. The instrument is set up over *A,* centered over the tack and properly leveled. A 90° angle is turned from *B,* and *D* is located at the proper distance from *A.* But after setting up at *A,* say the instrument is *not* level. See Detail 2, Figure 1-6. The vertical axis is *not* centered over *A,* even though

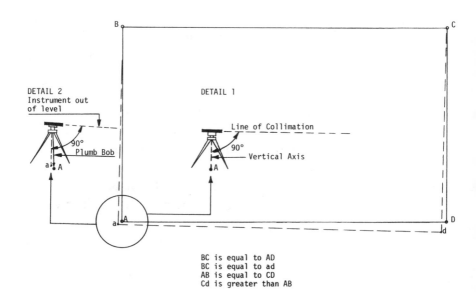

The Importance of a Level Instrument
Figure 1-6

the plumb bob might be. Instead it will be centered over another point, *a*, resulting in an erroneous reading. This gives *d* instead of D. As a result, the angles *AdC* and *BCd* are not 90° and the distance from C to *d* differs from that of B to A when they should be the same.

Using a transit with an optical plummet provides a faster and more accurate method of centering than the plumb bob. The wind has no effect on the optical plummet; it can be a factor with the plumb bob. Figure 1-7 shows the principle of the optical plummet. Line *a-b* is parallel to the line of collimation of the telescope and is perpendicular to *b-c*, which is the ray of light from the right angle prism at *b* to the target at *c*. Therefore, if the instrument is level when it is set up and centered at point A as shown in Figure 1-6, sighting through the optical plummet *a-b* will center the tack at A.

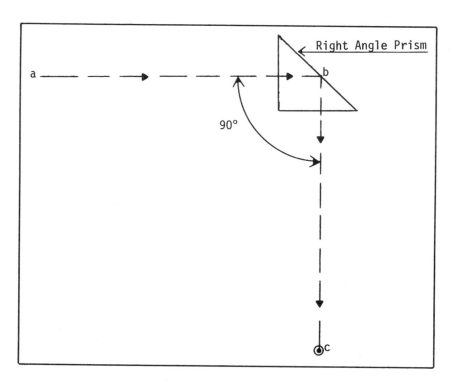

The Principle of The Optical Plummet
Figure 1-7

If the instrument is not level, as shown in Detail 2, Figure 1-6, the optical plummet will not be centered over *A* throughout a complete 360° revolution. It will be centered on different points such as *a* when the telescope is revolved. If this condition exists, recheck the instrument for level and do not proceed with any readings until the optical plummet is centered over the reference point throughout the entire 360°.

Chapter 2

Reading Survey Maps

Contour lines on a map are imaginary lines connecting points of constant ground elevation, usually above sea level. A contour map should always be prepared by a qualified surveyor because of the precise and specialized work involved.

Plot plans may or may not show the contour lines as the elevations of the lot. Contour lines have the advantage of far greater accuracy than ordinary symbols. The surveyor uses a permanent marker, such as a concrete monument, as a bench mark for a starting point in his contour survey. From this bench mark an accurate picture of the lot elevations can be made.

On any contour map, note the following:

1. The lines are at uniform intervals. These intervals may be either 1, 2, 5, 10, 20, 50 or 100 feet, depending on the scale of the map and the terrain. Whatever interval is used, *all* contour lines on one map have the same interval.

2. The steeper the slope, the closer the contour lines are to

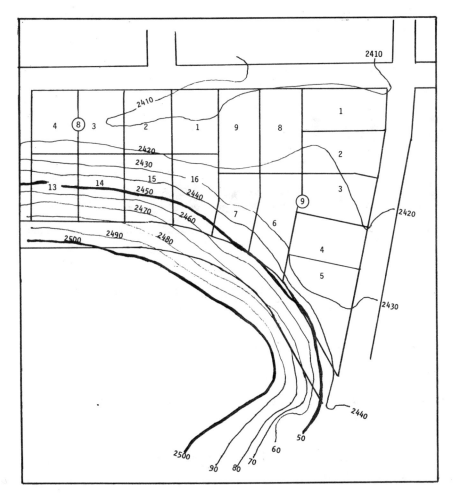

Contour Map
Figure 2-1

each other. Lines are bunched together on steep terrain and are farther apart on flatter ground.

3. A closed contour line — one that forms a circle — indicates a summit or a depression.

4. Different contour lines do not cross each other or merge except at a cliff, cave or overhanging ground.

Contour intervals vary depending on the scale of the map and the terrain. Often each fifth contour line is heavier than the rest and the elevations are written on them.

Figure 2-1 shows a contour map. From it we get the following information.

1. The contour lines have a 10' interval.

2. Lots 1, 2, 3, 4, 8 and 9 in section 9 are nearly level. The elevation at the front of lot 8, section 9 is 2410 feet above sea level, and the back property line is only 2420 feet above sea level. This is a grade of 6.7%.

3. Beginning with lots 13, 14, 15 and 16 in section 8, and the back part of lots 6 and 7 in section 9, there is a steep slope upward. The elevation rises from 2430 feet above sea level to 2500 feet in approximately 160 feet. This is a grade of 43.8%.

When contour lines are shown on plot plans, the existing elevations may be indicated in solid lines and the finish grade in dotted lines. Occasionally dotted lines may be used for the existing grade and solid lines for the finish grade. The contour map should have a legend with an explanation of its symbols as in Figure 2-2.

Metes And Bounds

At one time, land was recorded with descriptions of natural or artifical features of the terrain such as streams and ridge lines. As years passed and land was developed, many of these features

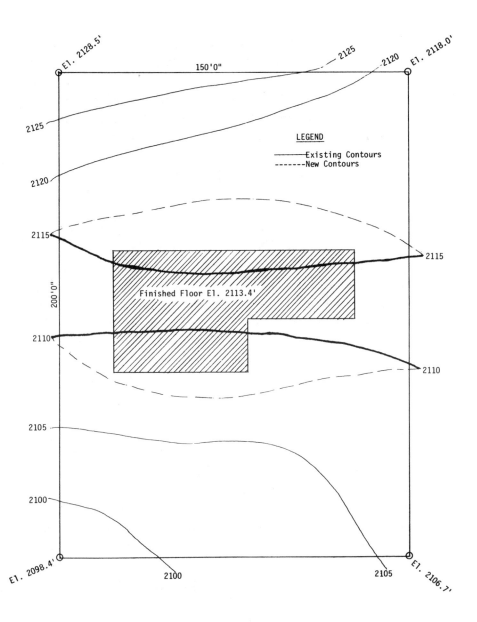

El. 2128.5'
150'0"
2125
2120
El. 2118.0'

2125

2120

LEGEND
——— Existing Contours
- - - - New Contours

2115

2115

200'0"

Finished Floor El. 2113.4'

2110

2110

2105

2100

El. 2098.4'
2100
2105
El. 2106.7'

Contour Map With Legend
Figure 2-2

ceased to exist. Needless to say, numerous disputes resulted. It became more common to describe lengths and directions of boundaries by compass and measurements. When bearings and lengths are given to describe a tract of land, the description is by "metes and bounds." This system dates back to colonial days and is used in most of the eastern part of the United States. The surveyor locates a corner of the property and follows the direction and the distances of the property lines until the perimeter is described back to the starting point.

The compass reading or direction of the property line is given in one of the four quadrants (N.E., S.E., N.W., or S.W.). The angles are never more than 90° and they are taken from either the north meridian or the south meridian, whichever gives the lesser angle. For example, in Figure 2-3 the bearing N 10°-17' W means that it is 10°-17' from the north meridian and is in the N.W. quadrant. N 79°-43' E is the N.E. quadrant and is 79°-43' from the north meridian, and S 10°-17' E is in the S.E. quadrant and is 10°-17' from the south meridian.

From the compass readings on each bearing in Figure 2-3, note that the property line falls in two quadrants. The property line with a bearing of N 10°-17' W and a distance of 188.0' is in the N.W. quadrant and the S.E. quadrant (180° apart), and the property line whose bearing is N 79°-43' E is in the N.E. and S.W. quadrants. The location of the property line in the quadrant given on the map by the surveyor depends on which direction (clockwise or counterclockwise) he makes his survey around the perimeter of the property. He should indicate his starting point by noting the P.O.B. (Point of Beginning) with an arrow in the direction he takes his survey.

It is important for the builder to know the direction the surveyor takes in surveying the property. If the corner stakes are

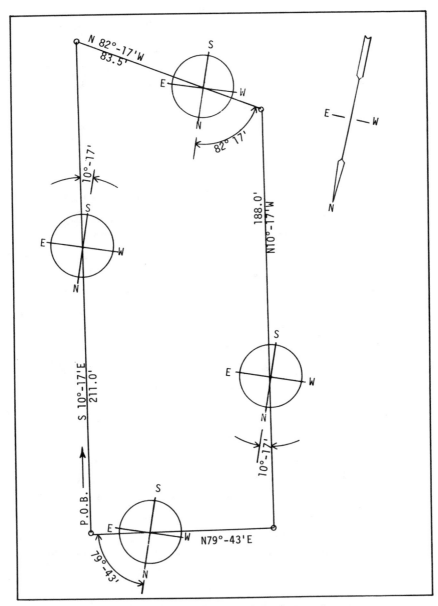

Compass Readings on Each Bearing
Figure 2-3

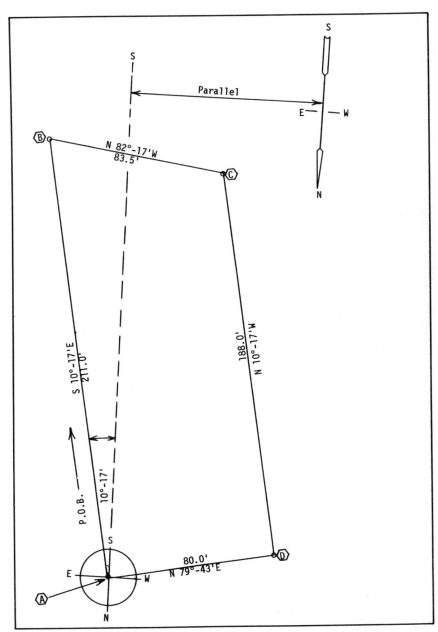

Determining The Direction of Survey
Figure 2-4

lost, knowing the survey direction can save a lot of time and money in relocating lost stakes from the stakes that are intact. Assume that in Figure 2-4 the corner stake at *B* was lost but the stake at *A* remained. By knowing the direction of the survey, the builder would know immediately when he set up his transit at *A* whether the compass reading should be S 10°-17' E or N 10°-17' W in locating *B*.

When the direction of the survey is *not* known, it can be determined by the following method. See Figure 2-4:

1. Draw a parallel North and South meridian from the compass direction on the map through one of the lot corners. At right angles to the N-S meridian draw the east and west line bisecting the point of the lot corner.

2. In this example the compass reading on the map was transferred to lot corner *A* where property line *A-B* falls in the S.E. quadrant, and the property line *A-D* falls in the S.W. quadrant.

3. The bearings of line *A-B* as shown on the map are S 10°-17' E, telling us this property line is in the S.E. quadrant. The property line from *A* toward *B* on the compass drawing at *A* locates *A-B* in the S.E. quadrant. Thus, the surveyor made his survey from *A* to *B*, *B* to *C*, *C* to *D* and back to *A*, or in a clockwise direction. Note that property line *A-D* from *A* falls in the S.W. quadrant and the bearings of line *A-D* on the map are N 79°-43' E (N.E. quadrant). Therefore, the surveyor was not making his survey from *A* toward *D* or counterclockwise, but from *D* toward *A* or clockwise.

Bearings Of Property Lines

Angles and directions on maps are defined as bearings or

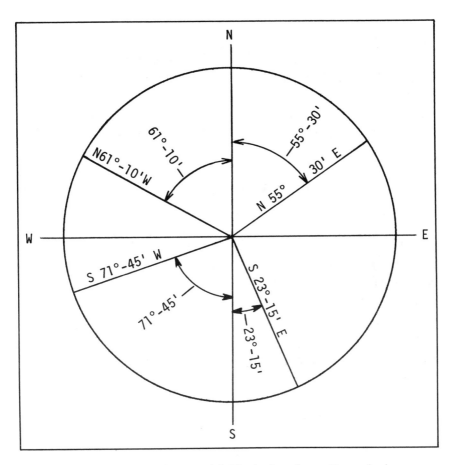

Four Lines as Bearings With Their Quadrant Descriptions
Figure 2-5

azimuths. Builders are likely to see bearings more than azimuths on survey maps. But you should know both methods, since you must occasionally convert bearings to azimuths to establish a property line.

The bearings of a line always fall in either the northeast, southeast, northwest, or southwest quadrant. A bearing is an acute angle from 0-90 degrees measured from either the North or

South meridian. If the line is parallel to the North or South meridian it is written as N-0° (called *due north*), or S-0° (called *due south*). If it is perpendicular to the N-S meridian it would be N-90° E (called *due east*) or N-90° W (called *due west*). In Figure 2-5 the line in the N.E. quadrant whose bearing is N 55°-30' E forms an angle of 55°-30' from the North meridian. The property line whose bearing is S 71°-45' W in the S.W. quadrant is 71°-45' from the South meridian; S 23°-15' E is 23°-15' from the South meridian and N 61°-10' W is 61°-10' from the North meridian.

Converting Bearings To Azimuths

An azimuth is a measurement of arc from 0-360 degrees running clockwise, usually from the North meridian (although it can be measured from the south). Figure 2-5 shows four lines as bearings with their quadrant descriptions, each line an acute angle from the N.S. meridian. Figure 2-6 shows the same lines and azimuths for those lines in compass readings measured from the North meridian in a clockwise direction.

Converting bearings to azimuths is essential in calculating the interior angles of lot corners, as shown later in this chapter. These conversions are not difficult, but the bearing in each quadrant has a different solution. See Figure 2-6.

1. *If the bearing is in the N.E. quadrant, the bearing and the azimuth are the same.* The property line whose bearing is N 55°-30' E has an azimuth of 55°-30'.

2. *If the bearing is in the S.E. quadrant, subtract the bearing reading from 180° to get the azimuth reading.* The property line whose bearing is S 23°-15' E has an azimuth of 156°-45'. It is computed as follows:

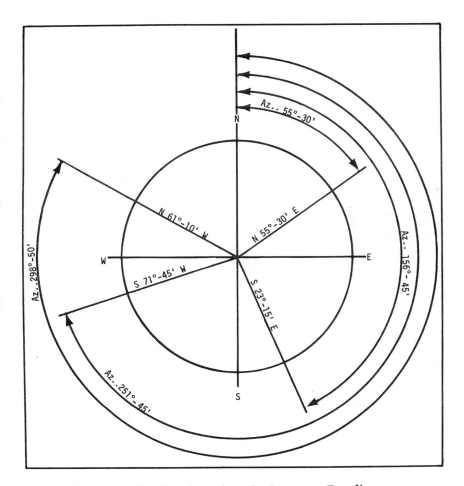

Azimuths For Bearing Lines in Compass Readings
Figure 2-6

$$180°\text{-}00' = 179°\text{-}60'$$
$$\underline{ -23°\text{-}15'}$$
$$\text{Azimuth} = 156°\text{-}45'$$

3. *If the bearing is in the S.W. quadrant, add the bearing reading to 180° to get the azimuth reading.* The property line

whose bearing is S 71°-45' W has an azimuth of 251°-45'. It is
computed as follows:

$$180°\text{-}00'$$
$$+71°\text{-}45'$$
$$\text{Azimuth} = \overline{251°\text{-}45'}$$

4. *If the bearing is in the N.W. quadrant, subtract the bearing
from 360° to get the azimuth reading.* The property line whose
bearing is N 61°-10' W has an azimuth of 298°-50'. It is computed
as follows:

$$360°\text{-}00' = 359°\text{-}60'$$
$$-61°\text{-}10'$$
$$\text{Azimuth} = \overline{298°\text{-}50'}$$

When the conversion is done by calculation as shown here, the
azimuth is said to be "calculated." When the conversion is done
in the field by measurement, it is said to be "observed."

Curves And How To Understand Them

As explained earlier, property lines can be described by
direction and by distance until the perimeter has been completely
traced back around to the starting point. Curved lot lines are
described by giving their radius and the length of their arc. The
sharper curve has a shorter radius and a flatter curve has a longer
radius.

The radius of the curve is selected to fit the terrain and the
proposed use of the line. The construction of these curves is the
work of a qualified surveyor, but it is helpful for builders to know
about them, what the symbols mean and how their values are
calculated.

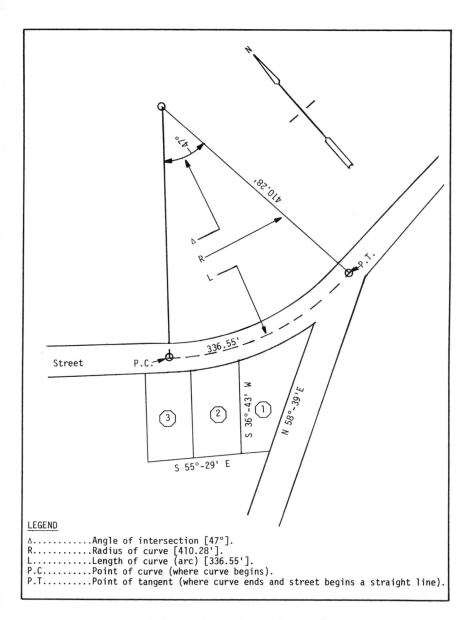

LEGEND

Δ............Angle of intersection [47°].
R............Radius of curve [410.28'].
L............Length of curve (arc) [336.55'].
P.C..........Point of curve (where curve begins).
P.T..........Point of tangent (where curve ends and street begins a straight line).

Calculating a Curved Lot Line and Street
Figure 2-7

Figure 2-7 shows a typical curved street and its adjacent lots. The symbols shown here are not always included on a typical map, but they are part of the surveyor's calculations and will help you understand curves.

$\triangle$ . . . . Angle of intersection

R . . . . Radius of curve

L . . . . Length of arc (curve)

P.C. . . . . Point of curve (where curve begins)

P.T. . . . . Point of tangent (where curve ends and street begins a straight line)

In Figure 2-7 we see that the length of the arc (L) at the center of the street from point *P.C.* to point *P.T.* is 336.55', the radius (R) is 410.28' and the angle of intersection ($\triangle$) is 47°. Knowing any two of these values, find the third as follows:

1. To find the length of arc (L) given the angle of intersection ($\triangle$) and radius (R):

$$L = \frac{\triangle}{360°} \times 2R\pi \ (\pi = 3.1416)$$

$$L = \frac{47°}{360°} \times 2 \times 410.28' \times 3.1416 = 336.55'$$

2. To find the radius (R) given the angle of intersection ($\triangle$) and length of arc (L):

$$R = \frac{L \times 360° \div \triangle° \div \pi}{2}$$

$$R = \frac{336.55' \times 360° \div 47° \div 3.1416}{2} = 410.28'$$

3. To find the angle of intersection (△) given the radius (R) and length of arc (L):

$$\triangle = \frac{L \times 360°}{2 \times R \times \pi}$$

$$\triangle = \frac{336.55' \times 360°}{2 \times 410.28' \times 3.1416} = 47°$$

Converting Bearings To Interior Angles

A builder must know the exact boundaries of the lot he is building on. The setback restrictions are given from the property lines. Any encroachment on the setback can result in legal action. Sometimes one or more of the lot corners cannot be seen, or they may be lost. Knowing the interior angles of the lot can help the builder establish a property line under these conditions. Interior angles of lot corners are seldom given on a map. *Know how to calculate them.* For example, in Figure 2-8 if lot corner *B* is not visible from lot corner *A*, and lot corner *D* is visible from *A*, set up your transit on *A* and sight on *D*. By turning an angle of 90° from *D* toward *B*, property line *A-B* can be established. If lot corner *B* is not visible from *C*, and *D* can be seen from *C*, set your instrument up at *C* and sight on *D*. By turning an angle of 108°-00' from *D* toward *B*, property line *B-C* can be established.

When a surveyor surveys any property, whether it is a single lot with four interior angles or a large tract of land with many lines and interior angles, the perimeter of the property must *close* or return to the point of origin if the survey is accurate. A survey is said to close when the sum of the interior angles (or exterior angles, as shown in Figure 2-9) totals the sum of all interior angles of a closed figure with the same number of sides. Any land bounded by four lines has four interior angles and the sum of the four angles is always 360°.

To convert bearings to interior angles, do the following:

1. Convert the bearings of property lines to azimuth, as explained earlier in the chapter.

2. Subtract the azimuth of the two adjacent property lines to obtain the deflection angle. See the detail in Figure 2-8.

3. If the deflection angle is less than 180°, subtract this angle from 180° to obtain the included angle. See the detail in Figure 2-8.

4. If the deflection angle is more than 180°, subtract 180° from the deflection angle to obtain the included angle.

5. If there is an exterior angle within the perimeter of the property lines as shown at lot corner *C* in Figure 2-9, add 180° to the deflection angle to obtain the included angle.

Example 1: Corner A, Figure 2-8
1. The two adjacent property lines have bearings of N 79°-43' E and S 10°-17' E, respectively.

2. Convert the bearings to azimuth and subtract as follows:

Bearing	Azimuth
S 10°-17'E	169°-43'
N 79°-43'E	79°-43'
Deflection Angle =	90°-00'

3. The deflection angle is less than 180°, so it is subtracted from 180° to obtain the included angle *A*.

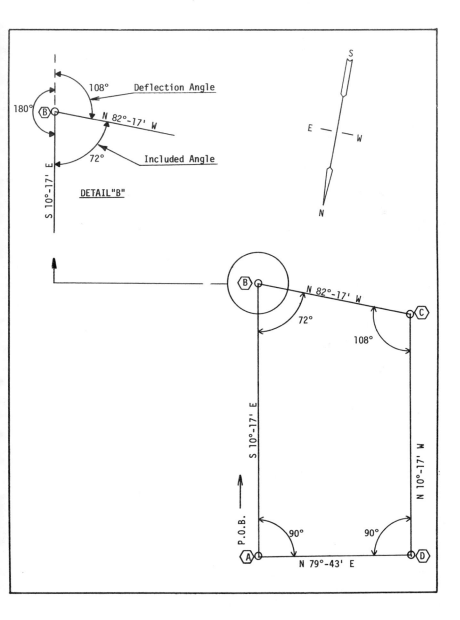

Interior Angles of Lot Corners
Figure 2-8

$$
\begin{aligned}
&\phantom{\text{Deflection Angle}} 180°\text{-}00' \\
\text{Deflection Angle} &= \underline{90°\text{-}00'} \\
\text{Included Angle } A &= 90°\text{-}00'
\end{aligned}
$$

Example 2: Corner B, Figure 2-8

1. The two adjacent property lines have bearings of S 10°-17' E and N 82°-17' W, respectively. Convert the bearings to azimuth and subtract.

	Bearing	Azimuth
	N 82°-17' W =	277°-43'
	S 10°-17' E =	169°-43'

Deflection Angle (see detail of corner *B* in Figure 2-8) = $\overline{108°\text{-}00'}$

2. The deflection angle, since it is less than 180°, is subtracted from 180° to find the included angle *B*.

$$
\begin{aligned}
&\phantom{\text{Deflection Angle}} 180°\text{-}00' \\
\text{Deflection Angle} &= \underline{108°\text{-}00'} \\
\text{Included Angle } B &= 72°\text{-}00'
\end{aligned}
$$

Interior angles *C* and *D* are calculated the same as angles *A* and *B*. The deflection angle at *D* is more than 180°, therefore 180° must be subtracted from the deflection angle to obtain the included angle *D*.

Example 3: Corner D, Figure 2-8

1. The two adjacent property lines have bearings of N 10°-17' W and N 79°-43' E, respectively.

2. Convert the bearings to azimuth and subtract.

$$
\begin{array}{rl}
\text{Bearing} & \text{Azimuth} \\
\text{N } 10°\text{-}17' \text{ W} = & 349°\text{-}43' \\
\text{N } 79°\text{-}43' \text{ E} = & 79°\text{-}43' \\
\hline
\text{Deflection Angle} = & 270°\text{-}00'
\end{array}
$$

3. The deflection angle is more than 180°, so 180° is subtracted from this angle to obtain the included angle D.

$$
\begin{array}{rl}
\text{Deflection Angle} = & 270°\text{-}00' \\
& 180°\text{-}00' \\
\hline
\text{Included Angle } D = & 90°\text{-}00'
\end{array}
$$

Since there are four interior angles within the boundary of this property, the sum of the four angles must equal 360°.

$$
\begin{array}{rl}
\text{Corner } A = & 90°\text{-}00' \\
\text{Corner } B = & 72°\text{-}00' \\
\text{Corner } C = & 108°\text{-}00' \\
\text{Corner } D = & 90°\text{-}00' \\
\hline
& 360°\text{-}00'
\end{array}
$$

The interior angles total 360° so you can assume that the survey is correct.

When the perimeter of the property has more than four interior angles, use the following rule to calculate the total number of degrees of the interior angles. See Figure 2-9.

$$
\begin{array}{l}
(\text{N-2}) \times 180° = \text{Total number of degrees} \\
(\text{N} = \text{Number of sides})
\end{array}
$$

Example 1: Figure 2-9 has five sides $[5\text{-}2 = 3]$

$$(5\text{-}2) \times 180° = 540°$$

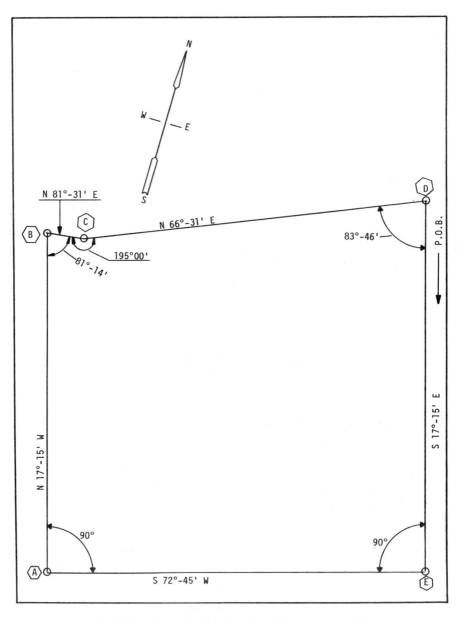

Calculating the Total Number of Degrees of the
Interior Angles of a Lot
Figure 2-9

or

$$3 \times 180° = 540°$$

1. The two adjacent property lines at corner *B* have bearings of N 17°-15' W and N 81°-31' E.

2. Convert the bearings to azimuth and subtract.

$$
\begin{array}{rl}
\text{Bearing} & \text{Azimuth} \\
\text{N 17°-15' W} = & 342°\text{-}45' \\
\text{N 81°-31' E} = & \underline{81°\text{-}31'} \\
\text{Deflection Angle} = & 261°\text{-}14'
\end{array}
$$

3. The deflection angle is more than 180°, so subtract 180° from this angle for the included angle *B*.

$$
\begin{array}{rl}
\text{Deflection Angle} = & 261°\text{-}14' \\
 & \underline{180°\text{-}00'} \\
\text{Included Angle } B = & 81°\text{-}14'
\end{array}
$$

Example 2: Corner C, Figure 2-9. [This corner is an exterior angle but is included in the five interior angles that make up the boundary of this property.]

1. The two adjacent property lines have bearings of N 81°-31' E and N 66°-31' E, respectively.

2. Convert the bearings to azimuth and subtract.

$$
\begin{array}{rl}
\text{Bearing} & \text{Azimuth} \\
\text{N 81°-31' E} = & 81°\text{-}31' \\
\text{N 66°-31' E} = & \underline{66°\text{-}31'} \\
\text{Deflection Angle} = & 15°\text{-}00'
\end{array}
$$

3. Remember the rule for exterior angles (Rule 5 above): *add 180° to the deflection angle to obtain the included angle C.*

$$180°\text{-}00'$$
$$+ \ \ 15°\text{-}00'$$
$$\text{Included Angle } C = \overline{195°\text{-}00'}$$

The total of the five interior angles in Figure 2-9 must be 540° if the survey is correct.

$$\text{Angle } A = \ \ \ 90°\text{-}00'$$
$$\text{Angle } B = \ \ \ 81°\text{-}14'$$
$$\text{Angle } C = 195°\text{-}00'$$
$$\text{Angle } D = \ \ \ 83°\text{-}46'$$
$$\text{Angle } E = \ \ \underline{\ 90°\text{-}00'}$$
$$\overline{539°\text{-}60'} = 540°\text{-}00'$$

The survey *closes* and is assumed to be correct.

Most plats for residential construction give the bearings of the property lines in degrees (°) and minutes (') because a minute reading is accurate enough for most of these surveys. But there are times when a more precise reading is required, and in these cases the surveyor gives the bearings in degrees (°), minutes (') and seconds (''). For example, a bearings might read S 85°-30'-15'' E, N 71°-45'-18'' W.

The following shows the relation of degrees, minutes and seconds:

$$60 \text{ seconds ('')} = 1 \text{ minute (')}$$
$$60 \text{ minutes (')} = 1 \text{ degree (°)}$$
$$360 \text{ degrees (°)} = 1 \text{ circumference (circle)}$$

$$\begin{array}{cccc} Circumference & Degrees & Minutes & Seconds \\ 1 & = \ 360 \ = & 21,600 \ = & 1,296,000 \end{array}$$

One degree is one three hundred and sixtieth part of a circumference, regardless of the size of the circle. One minute is 1/21,600 part of a circle and one second is 1/1,296,000 part of a circle. For each one second angular bearing the linear distance is only 1/200 of an inch in 100 feet. For each one minute the linear distance is 3/8 inch in 100 feet. And for each degree the linear distance is 1 ft. 8 15/16 inches in 100 feet. See Figure 7-15 for other linear distances.

You can subtract degrees, minutes and seconds to obtain an azimuth reading. Proceed as follows:

Subtract S 85°-30'-15'' E from 180°

$$180°-00'-00'' = 179°-60'-00'' = 179°-59'-60''$$
$$\underline{\quad -85°-30'-15''}$$
$$\text{Azimuth} = 94°-29'-45''$$

Chapter 3

Locating The Building On The Lot

Deed restrictions and zoning codes specify the minimum structure setback distances from the front, side and rear property lines. There is usually some flexibility in selecting the exact location of the house on the lot. With some advance planning, you can increase the attractiveness and utility and save many dollars in developing costs.

You probably will not have an up-to-date contour map or other elevation points for the lot. Start by taking the lot elevations at 10 to 15 foot intervals within the buildable limits of the lot. These elevations should be recorded in scale on a plat map. See Figure 3-1.

After the elevations on the plat plan have been recorded, the best location for the building on the lot can be found by testing different locations within the setback requirements. Obviously, staking out the foundation at more than one location is too time-consuming and costly. A fast and inexpensive way to test each

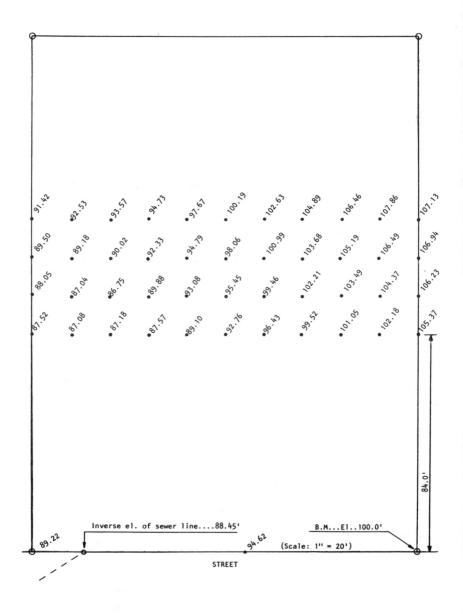

Lot Elevations Recorded On a Plat Map
Figure 3-1

Ink drawing of
Foundation Plan
Plexiglas   (same scale as plat plan)

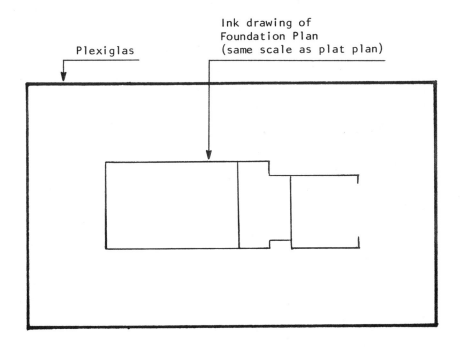

Foundation Plan Drawn To Scale On Plexiglass·
Figure 3-2

possible location is to make a drawing of the foundation plan with a grease pencil or felt tip pen on an 8″ x 12″ piece of clear plexiglas. The foundation plan should be drawn to the same scale as the plat map. See Figure 3-2. Place this plexiglas with its foundation plan over the plat map to find the excavation required. Here are two examples of this procedure:

Option 1

1. The blueprints show that the house in Figure 3-3 and 3-4 has a partial basement, a crawl space area and a garage with a side entrance.

2. From the blueprints you know that the basement floor is to

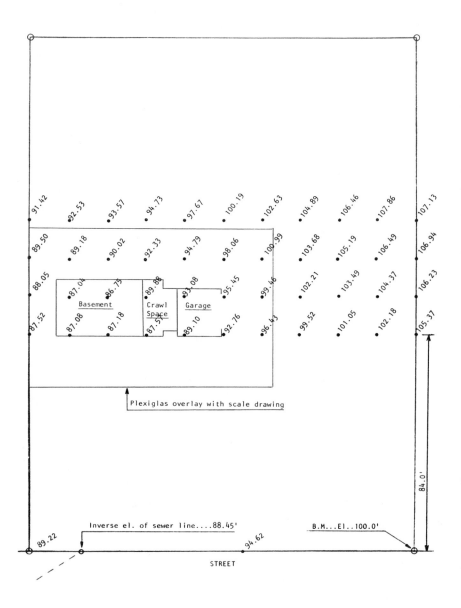

Foundation Plan Placed Over Plat Map - Option 1
Figure 3-3

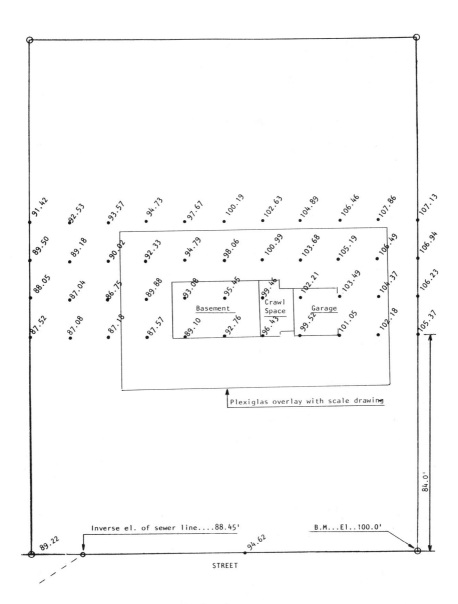

Foundation Plan Placed Over Plat Map - Option 2
Figure 3-4

be 8'-10'' (8.83') below the finish floor. The garage floor is to be 1'-0'' below the finish floor. A minimum of 2'-0'' clearance is required in the crawl space.

3. The garage door is located on the right side of the house, thus requiring a minimum of 25'-0'' from the right property line to insure easy access for cars entering and leaving the garage.

4. The minimum front setback is 75'-0'', and the minimum sideline setback is 10'-0''.

5. The owner of the property wants his house to be in line with the house on the adjacent lot. This is 84'-0'' from the front property line.

6. The only flexibility in placing this house is laterally between the side lines.

7. Assign the floor levels a temporary elevation to make the needed calculations. The first possibility was to set the house the minimum distance required from the left property line, as shown in Figure 3-3. Plumbing fixtures were to be installed in the basement. To provide natural drainage from the basement to the sewer line, the basement floor elevation was to be 3'-0'' above the inverse (lowest) elevation of the sewer line (88.45' as shown on the plat plan). This gives the basement an elevation of 91.45' (88.45' + 3.0'). The basement floor is 8'-10'' below the finish floor, thus the elevation of the finish floor is 100.28' (91.45' + 8.83'). The garage floor is 1'-0'' below the finish floor, giving it an elevation of 99.28'. The blueprint shows that the basement floor is 4 inch concrete poured over 4 inches of crushed stone. The basement grade elevation is then calculated to be 8'' (.67') below the basement floor. The elevation of the basement grade is 90.78' (91.45' less .67').

8. The grade at the crawl space requires a minimum of 2'-0''
clearance. This distance added to the height of the floor assembly
(1 foot) gives the crawl space grade an elevation of 97.28' (100.28'
less 3.0').

9. The garage floor is 4 inch concrete, thus making the garage
grade elevation 98.95' (99.28' less 4'' or .33').

10. The elevations needed to calculate the excavations and fill
dirt are as follows:

> Basement grade elevation.................90.78'
> Crawl space grade elevation..............97.28'
> Garage grade elevation...................98.95'

Placing the plexiglas overlay over the plat plan as shown in
Figure 3-3 makes the following computations possible:

1. Fill dirt will be required to bring the existing grade in the
basement up to the calculated grade elevation of 90.78'. For
example, the existing elevation near the left front corner of the
foundation is 87.08', and it will be necessary to fill 3.70' at this
location (90.78' less 87.08'). Continue to calculate the balance of
the fill that will be required for the basement area. Chapter 6 has
a detailed explanation of calculating cuts and fills.

2. The calculated crawl space grade elevation is 97.28'. The
existing grades at this location are 89.88' and 87.57', which is
below the calculated grade elevation. This will give more
clearance in the crawl space than the minimum required. No
excavation or fill will be required here.

3. Fill dirt will be required in the garage area. For example,
the calculated garage grade elevation is 98.95'. The existing

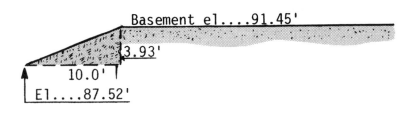

Fall From Basement Floor
Figure 3-5

grade at the right front corner of the garage is 92.76'. It will be necessary to fill this area a total of 6.19' (98.95' less 92.76'). Calculate the balance of the fill required for the garage area as shown here.

4. The driveway in front of the garage door should have a slope away from the house toward the right property line and toward the street. The existing elevation 30'-0'' away from the garage door toward the right property line varies from 99.52' to 103.68' in line with the back wall of the house. The garage floor elevation is 99.28'. Allowing a fall of 1'-0'' in 30'-0'', the finish grade of the driveway at this location will be 98.28'. Excavation will be required here, and as far toward the right and back property lines as is necessary to provide the desired aesthetics and proper drainage of the surface water away from the building. A gentle slope from the right property line to the edge of the driveway can be obtained. No retaining wall will be required.

5. The grade of the driveway from the street to the garage will be 5%.

6. The fall from the basement floor (there is an outside basement door located here) to the left property line is 3.93' in 10.0', as shown in Figure 3-5.

Option 2

Assume now that the house is to be built 30'-0'' from the right property line as shown in Figure 3-4 and that the finished floor is assigned an elevation of 103.0'. The following calculations can be made.

The garage floor elevation will be 102.0' (103.0' less 1.0') and the garage grade elevation will be 101.67' (102.0' less 4'' or .33'). The basement floor elevation will be 94.17' (103.0' less 8'-10'' or 8.83'). The basement grade elevation will be 93.50' (94.17' less 8'' or .67'). The crawl space grade elevation will be 100.0' (103.0' less 3.0'). The elevations needed to calculate the excavation and fill are:

> Basement grade elevation. . . . . .93.50'
> Crawl space elevation. . . . . 100.00'
> Garage grade elevation. . . . . 101.67'

The following information can now be obtained.

1. Both fill dirt and excavation will be required to bring the existing grade in the basement area to the calculated basement grade elevation of 93.50'. For example, a fill of 4.40' will be required to bring the existing grade of 89.10' near the left front corner of the foundation to the basement grade elevation of 93.50'. Excavation will be required in the right back corner of the basement to bring the grade down to 93.50'.

2. The existing grade in the crawl space area is below the calculated grade elevation of 100.0'. More than the minimum clearance is already present, so neither excavation nor fill will be needed here.

3. Both excavation and fill dirt will be required in the garage

area to bring the existing grade to the calculated garage grade elevation of 101.67'.

4. Excavation will be necessary all the way to the right property line for the driveway area. This area must slope away from the garage to provide drainage of surface water away from the building. This excavation should be carried to the back property line for the drainage necessary. A retaining wall will be required along the right property line because of the depth of the cut in this area.

5. The grade of the driveway from the street to the garage will be 2%.

6. There will be a fall of 6.65' from the basement door to the left property line.

Although only two options were explored in this example, you can use as many trial locations with the plexiglas overlay as necessary to provide the best possible location of the house on the lot. The time it takes to make these computations is paid back many times in lower development costs and in higher property value. Once these calculations are made, you can tell very quickly where the house should be located on the lot. After you locate the house on the lot, prepare the complete plot plan.

Information From Plot Plans

Plot plans are a vital part of the working drawings you use in building the house. They are usually drawn to a scale of 1'' = 10' or 1'' = 20'. The character of a building depends to a great extent on the land it is built on. If you use the natural characteristics of the land you greatly enhance the architectural design and make the house more enjoyable to live in. In addition to other details, this plan must show the location of the house on the lot and the elevations of each different floor level together with the grade elevations.

The plot plan should show the following minimum information:

1. Description of the lot, such as lot and section number.

2. Lot corners.

3. Metes and bounds of the property lines and their distances.

4. Compass direction showing north.

5. Location and dimensions of the house, garage, carport and other buildings.

6. Location and dimensions of walks and the driveway.

7. Location of steps, terraces and porches.

8. Location and dimensions of easements.

9. Finished floor elevations ot the dwelling, garage or carport, street where the driveway connects, and grade elevations at each corner of the dwelling.

10. Location and dimensions of water and sewer lines, and the location of electric and gas lines.

11. Location of existing trees.

The elevations can be given in feet above sea level (if they are known) or in feet above an arbitrary elevation based on a fixed point called a bench mark or B.M. If an arbitrary elevation is used, the bench mark is normally assigned an elevation of 100.0'. All other elevations on the plot plan are in reference to this point. For example, in Figure 3-6 the bench mark is a point at the edge of the pavement in front of the eastern entrance of the driveway. It has been assigned an elevation of 100.0'. The finished floor (F.F.) of the dwelling has an elevation of 104.0' or 4'-0'' above the bench mark. The back porch has an elevation of 103.5' and is 0.5' (6'') lower than the finished floor. The right or western entrance to the driveway has an elevation of 98.5' or 1.5' (1'-6'') lower than the bench mark.

The plot plan in Figure 3-6 gives the following information:

1. The legal description of the lot and its dimensions.

2. The location of the dwelling on the lot and its dimensions.

3. The location, shape and dimensions of the driveway. No front walk is required because the driveway comes up to the front entry and serves as both a walk and a driveway.

4. No easements are shown here as there are none.

5. The finished floor (F.F.) elevation of 104.0' is only 0.5' (6'') higher than the front stoop. No steps are needed or required at the front entrance. The grade elevations at each corner of the house show the direction in which surface water will run away from the dwelling.

6. The elevation at the street where the left or eastern entrance of the driveway connects is 100.0'. The elevation of the driveway at the front entrance to the house is 103.5'. This is a

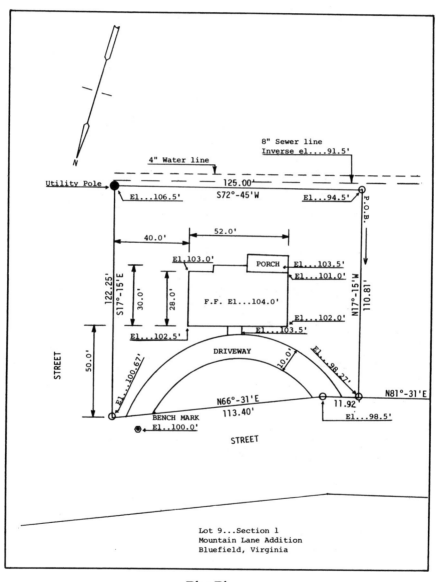

Lot 9...Section 1
Mountain Lane Addition
Bluefield, Virginia

Plot Plan
Figure 3-6

grade of 7%. The right or western entrance of the driveway has a grade of 10%.

7. The location of the utility pole is shown at the left rear corner of the lot. The electric and T.V. cable lines are located here.

8. The location and size of the water and sewer lines are shown with the inverse (lowest) elevation of the sewer line given. The finished floor (F.F.) elevation is 104.0' and, because there is no basement, the fall of the sewer line from the finished floor of the dwelling to the right rear corner of the lot where the sewer tap will be made is 12.5' (104.0' less 91.5').

No basement is planned for the building in Figure 3-6. But one could be built with laundry and bathroom facilities without raising the floor elevation of the dwelling. Raising the floor 5 or 6 feet would make the house less attractive on the lot. If a basement were planned, the basement floor would be either 8'-0'' or 9'-0'' below the finished floor which has an elevation of 104.0'. The basement floor would then have an elevation of either 95.0' or 96.0', still above the inverse elevation of the sewer line (91.5') where the sewer tap is to be made. This insures a natural flow to the sewer line. The aesthetics of the house would not be effected if a basement were included.

Chapter 4

How To Take Elevations

The most basic operation in all building layout is leveling the site and finding the level at which the foundation or floor will rest. Nearly all buildings are designed with floor levels or elevations. Finding the right level and establishing that level at all the appropriate points is an essential part of laying out every building.

Leveling is done when the building site and grades are laid out by sighting a leveling instrument at one point to a level rod placed at another point.

Subtracting the reading on the level rod from the height of the leveling instrument gives the difference in elevation between the two points or stations. For this work you need a sighting level of some type and a rod to sight to at the various points.

You can use a carpenter's rule, mason's rule, engineer's rule or a steel tape for a leveling rod. A plain piece of rigid framing lumber can also be used. At each location where the elevation is to be taken, mark the reading on this improvised level rod at the point where the horizontal crosshair viewed through the eyepiece of the sighting instrument bisects it. Measure the distance between these marks. The difference is the *elevation* difference between the points.

Level rods are made of warp-resistant materials such as maple or magnolia or a light metal such as aluminum. Graduations on level rods are large and easily identified. The foot numbers are larger and are usually painted red. The intermediate numbers are smaller and are usually painted black. Rods like that in Figure 4-1 are known as architect's or builder's level rods, or engineer's level rods. They vary in length from about 9 feet to about 15 feet. The graduations on a builder's level rod are in feet, inches and eights (such as 8'-5-3/8''). The engineer's level rod is marked in feet, tenths and hundredths of a foot (such as 8.45'). The engineer's level rod is most often used because working in feet and decimals of a foot is much easier than working in feet, inches and fractions of an inch. The following example shows why:

Using the builder's level rod
Rod reading at point *A*   = 12'- 3-1/4"
Rod reading at point *B*   =   8'- 5-3/8"

12'-3-1/4"	=	11'-14-10/8"
8'-5-3/8"	=	8'- 5- 3/8"
Difference in elevation	=	3'- 9- 7/8"

Using the engineer's level rod
Rod reading at point *A*   = 12.27'
Rod reading at point *B*   =   8.45'
Difference in elevation   =   3.82' (or 3'-9-7/8")

Note: Figure 4-10 at the end of this chapter can be used for converting decimal equivalents to inches and fractions. A detailed explanation is given in Chapter 7.

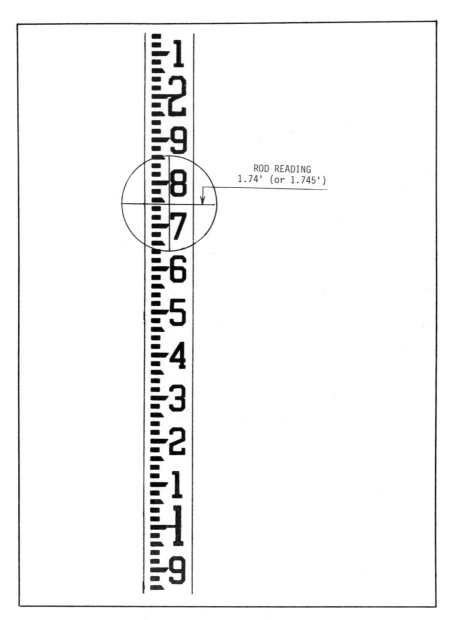

Level Rod
Figure 4-1

On the engineer's level rod the graduations are read directly in feet, tenths and hundredths. If a more precise reading is desired, a vernier target is used to give readings to thousandths of a foot. But in residential building such precise readings are seldom necessary. If they are needed, an estimation to thousandths can be made, as shown in Figure 4-1, without the use of the vernier target.

The Builder's Level

The builder's level is a combination telescope and spirit level mounted on a tripod and is the most practical instrument for determining differences in elevation. It has crosshairs in the objective lens. The telescope can be of a fixed or variable magnifying power. Some vary from around 24 to as much as 37 power. This permits a choice of magnification power for more efficient use under various light conditions and job requirements. The greater the power, the greater the distance from which readings can be taken. An instrument with 26 power has 44% more range than an instrument with 18 power, and an instrument with 30 power has 66% more range than an 18 power instrument. The more expensive instruments have a greater telescope power for longer range work.

A dumpy level cannot be raised vertically. See Figure 4-2. The transit level, Figure 4-3, can be rotated vertically for use as a transit. It can be locked at the zero vertical reading to project a horizontal line.

The leveling vial or "bubble" on the instrument works just like the bubble on the carpenter's level, but it is more sensitive. The leveling vials are in degrees of sensitivity. The sensitivity of the level vial is explained in Chapter 1.

Dumpy Level
Figure 4-2

Sensitivity may range from approximately 8 minutes (480 seconds) per 2 mm division on the level vial on the less expensive models to 45 seconds per 2 mm division on the more expensive models. The more sensitive the vial, the more precise the results.

The engineer's level is more accurate than the builder's level because it is used for more precise leveling. The telescope on the engineer's level usually has about 30 power magnification, and the level vial is usually more sensitive. An engineer's level normally does not have a graduated circle to measure horizontal angles.

For residential building and other small construction sites, the builder's dumpy level, Figure 4-2, or the transit level, Figure 4-3, will be accurate enough. The builder's level is basically the same as the engineer's level, except that its magnification power is

Transit Level
Figure 4-3

usually less (approximately 20 power), and the sensitivity of the level vial does not permit the precision required by engineers. The builder's level normally has a graduated circle that permits the reading of horizontal angles. The transit level can be used as a transit, or by locking the telescope in the "level" position it can be used as a level. This instrument is very versatile and is popular with builders.

Another popular type of level is the automatic or self-leveling level. See Figure 4-4. With this type, rough leveling is done using

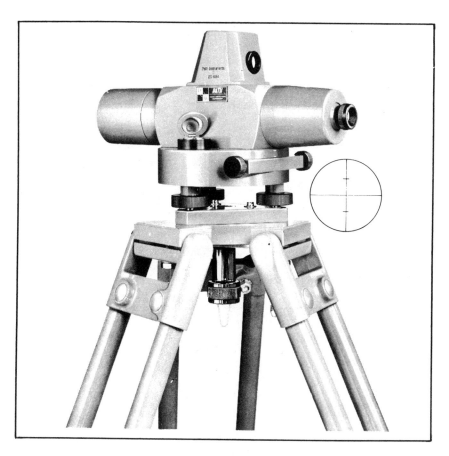

Automatic Level
Figure 4-4

a small circular bubble accurate to ± 10' (10 minutes per 2 mm division on the level). A suspended compensator then takes over and maintains a horizontal line of sight. This permits a high degree of accuracy because the level is not affected by solar radiation, wind, or traffic. See Figure 4-5.

Taking Elevations

Taking elevations is required for establishing correct floor

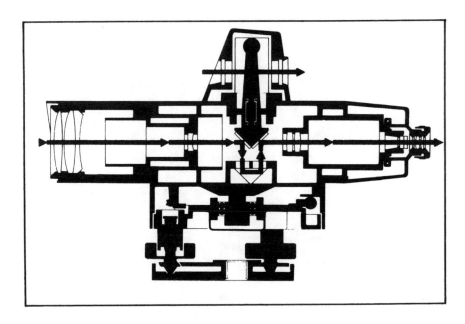

Suspended Compensator In An Automatic Level
Figure 4-5

levels, calculating cuts, fills, and excavations, and planning the grade for driveways, drainage and sewer lines. Knowing how to establish elevations yourself saves you money, time, and scheduling problems with survey crews.

Refer to Figure 4-6. Suppose you want to find the difference in elevation between the two points or stations labeled *B* and *C*:

1. Setup and level the instrument at an intermediate point between *B* and *C* called *A*.

2. Take a rod reading (R.R.) at a point of assumed or known elevation. The elevation at station *B* is not known so it is arbitrarily assigned an elevation of 100.0'. Sighting on the level rod at *B*, the R.R. is recorded as 8.45'.

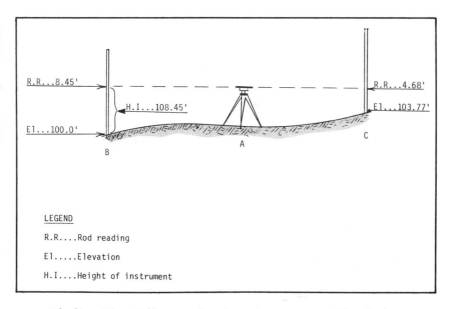

Finding The Difference in Elevation Between Two Points
Figure 4-6

3. Add this R.R. (8.45') to the assumed elevation (100.0') to get the height of instrument (H.I.) reading (100.0' + 8.45' = 108.45').

4. Without moving the instrument, have the assistant hold the level rod on each station for which elevations must be found (where they can be seen from this instrument location). Sight and record these rod readings. The level rod is then held at *C* and this R.R. is recorded as 4.68'.

5. Subtract the R.R. at each station from the H.I. to get the elevation. The R.R. at *C* (4.68') is subtracted from the H.I. (108.45') to get the elevation at station *C* -103.77'.

It is not always possible to sight on all stations from one central location of the instrument. A large difference in elevation or obstructions such as trees, shrubs, buildings and rock formations may require moving the instrument to several locations before all of the required elevations can be taken. When it becomes necessary to relocate the instrument, the new location is known as a turning point (T.P.). Each T.P. establishes a new H.I. If you need elevations on steep slopes or hillside property, or where there are obstructions in the lines of sight between points, follow the steps below (illustrated in Figure 4-7).

1. Start from a bench mark (B.M.) or from a point of known or assumed elevation.

2. Setup the level where this station and as many other stations as possible can be seen through the instrument. Take a rod reading at A (here, 6.14') and add it to the known elevation for the H.I. (100.0' + 6.14' = 106.14'). The H.I. between A and B is 106.14'. Without moving the instrument to a different location, have the assistant move the level rod to station B. Sight and record this R.R. (3.85'). The elevation at B can now be calculated; it is 102.29' (H.I. 106.14' less R.R. 3.85' = 102.29').

3. Have the assistant remain at station B with the level rod, but move the instrument to a point where B and C can be sighted and an R.R. taken and recorded. This is a turning point called T.P. (1).

4. After leveling the instrument at T.P. (1) take a R.R. on B (5.18') and add it to the elevation at B (102.29') for the H.I. at T.P. (1). The new H.I. is 107.47' (102.29' + 5.18' = 107.47').

5. Move the level rod to C and record this R.R. (1.76'). Subtract this R.R. from the H.I. at T.P. (1) for the elevation at C (107.47' — 1.76' = 105.71'). The elevation at C is 105.71'.

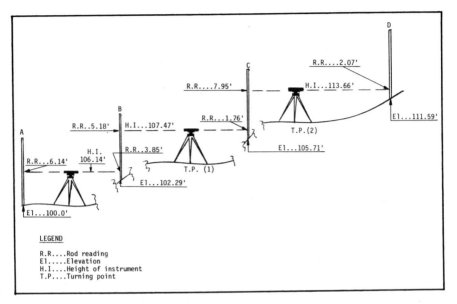

Taking Elevations On Slopes
Figure 4-7

6. Again, do not move the level rod from this station until the instrument is moved and setup at T.P. (2) and an R.R. has been taken at station *C*. The R.R. at *C* from the instrument at T.P. (2) is recorded as 7.95'. Adding this R.R. (7.95') to the elevation at *C* (105.71') gives the H.I. at T.P. (2) as 113.66' (7.95' + 105.71' = 113.66').

7. Move the level rod to station *D* and take the R.R. from T.P. (2). This R.R. is 2.07'. Subtracting this R.R. from the H.I. at T.P. (2) gives the elevation at *D* as 111.59' (113.66' — 2.07' = 111.59').

8. If there are other stations where elevations are needed, repeat the above until all stations are recorded.

9. Calculating the difference in elevation between any two of

these stations means subtracting one elevation from the other. Example:

Elevation at D = 111.59'
Elevation at A = 100.00'
D is 11.59' higher than A

Elevation at C = 105.71'
Elevation at B = 102.29'
B is 3.42' lower than C

When there are obstructions that prevent sighting all stations from one instrument setup, the procedure is the same as that outlined above for hillside property. Instead of moving the instrument up and down a steep slope, move it around the obstructions to a new T.P. Always move it to where a known point of elevation can be sighted. This establishes a new H.I. From this H.I. the other elevations can be found. In Figure 4-9, station C can not be seen from the instrument where the R.R. at A and B were taken. The instrument was moved to a new position (T.P. 1) where a new H.I. could be established from the known elevation at B. After the R.R. at C is taken, the elevation can be found. Because of other obstructions D could not be sighted from the instrument at T.P. (1). It was moved to T.P. (2), where both C and D could be sighted. From C a new H.I. was established at T.P. (2) and an R.R. was taken at D. The elevation at D can now be determined.

Figure 4-8 shows some of the elevation calculations for a typical residential lot. The bench mark has been assigned an elevation of 100.0' and the R.R. from the instrument is 5.34'. This reading added to the assigned elevation of the B.M. is the H.I. (100.0' + 5.34' = 105.34'). Take R.R. at all desired points. Subtract each R.R. from the H.I. to obtain the elevation at this

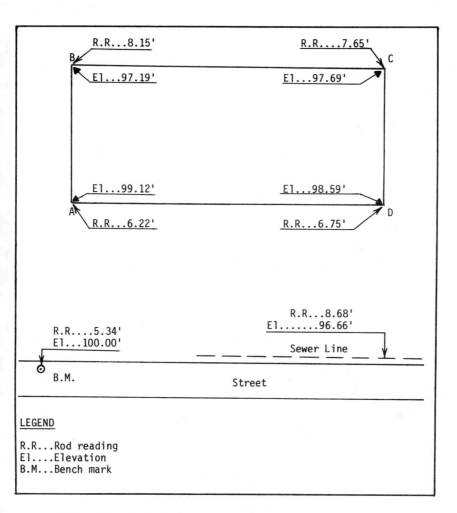

Elevation Calculations For a Typical Residential Lot
Figure 4-8

point. See the examples below.

Station *A*
H.I. = 105.34'
R.R. = −6.22'
Elevation at *A* = 99.12'

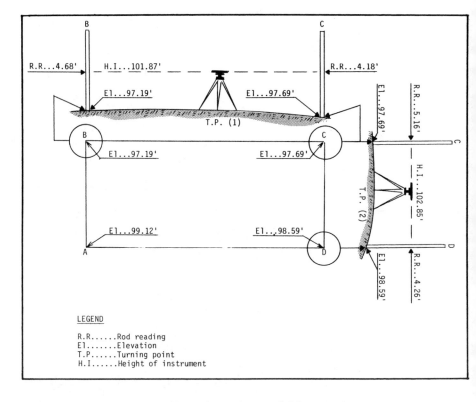

Sighting Elevations Around Obstructions
Figure 4-9

Inverse (lowest) point of sewer line
H.I. = 105.34'
R.R. = −8.68'
Elevation at sewer line = 96.66'

The calculated elevations give the following information:
A is 0.88' lower than the B.M. (100.00' less 99.12')

B is 1.93' lower than A (99.12' less 97.19')

C is 0.50' higher than B (97.69' less 97.19')

D is 0.90' higher than *C* (98.59' less 97.69')

The inverse point of the sewer line is 1.93' lower than *D* (98.59' less 96.66').

Remember these points: 1) The height of the instrument (H.I.) is the known elevation plus the rod reading (R.R.). 2) The calculated elevation is the H.I. less the R.R.

To work to a designated elevation such as the top of a foundation or the bottom of an excavation for footers, subtract the designated elevation from the H.I. for the R.R. For example, the elevation for the footers must be 92.68' and the H.I. is 105.38'. The R.R. should be 12.70' (105.38' less 92.68' = 12.70'). In checking the elevation of the footers, set the target on the level rod at 12.70'. When the horizontal crosshair of the instrument bisects this reading, the elevation is correct. This is explained more fully in Chapter 8.

Conversion Charts

Calculations are much easier using the decimal system of tenths (.1) and hundredths (.01) of a foot than inches and fractions of an inch. In residential building it is seldom necessary to work to any closer tolerance than hundredths, which can be converted to the nearest eighths of an inch. See Figure 4-10. If a more precise reading is required, use the chart in Figure 7-5, which is in thousandths of a foot and sixteenths of an inch. Chapter 7 explains how to calculate this conversion mathematically.

Table 4-10 shows inches and eighths of an inch and their equivalents in hundredths of a foot. You can convert measurements in very little time with this chart. Use the chart to make these conversions:

4TH	8TH	0″	1″	2″	3″	4″	5″	6″	7″	8″	9″	10″	11″
0	0	.00	.08	.17	.25	.33	.42	.50	.58	.67	.75	.83	.92
	1	.01	.09	.18	.26	.34	.43	.51	.59	.68	.76	.84	.93
1	2	.02	.10	.19	.27	.35	.44	.52	.60	.69	.77	.85	.94
	3	.03	.11	.20	.28	.36	.45	.53	.61	.70	.78	.86	.95
2	4	.04	.13	.21	.29	.38	.46	.54	.63	.71	.79	.88	.96
	5	.05	.14	.22	.30	.39	.47	.55	.64	.72	.80	.89	.97
3	6	.06	.15	.23	.31	.40	.48	.56	.65	.73	.81	.90	.98
	7	.07	.16	.24	.32	.41	.49	.57	.66	.74	.82	.91	.99

Eighths of an Inch to Hundredths of a Foot
Table 4-10

Convert 8¼ ″ to hundredths of a foot
   1. Go *across* the top line to the 8″ column.

   2. Go *down* this column to the line where number 1 in the 4th column (¼″) is shown at the extreme left.

   3. Read the answer. In this example it is .69'

Convert .69' to inches and fractions
   1. Find .69' in the chart.

   2. Go *up* this column to find the number of inches (8″ in this example).

   3. Go *across* this line to the 8th column at the extreme left. This is the fractional part of an inch in eighths (1/8″). The answer here is 2/8″ or 1/4″ — .69' is 8¼″.

   Another essential tool for field conversion work is the engineer's rule. This rule is similar to the carpenter's rule, except that on one side of it the graduations are in feet, tenths and hundredths. On the other side graduations are in feet, inches and

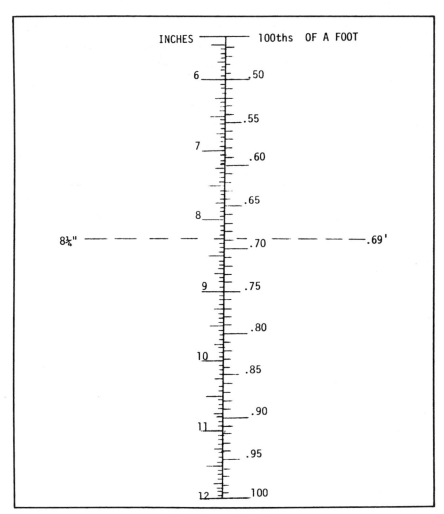

Engineer's Rule
Figure 4-11

sixteenths. Conversions are easily made by holding your thumbnail on the reading on one side and then turning the rule over and reading the conversion on the other. In Figure 4-11, if you hold your thumbnail at the 8¼ '' mark on the inch side of the rule you are at the .69' mark on the other side. Holding your thumbnail on the decimal reading on the engineer's side allows you to read the conversion in inches and fractions on the carpenter's side.

Chapter 5

Establishing Grades

Anyone who lays out building sites should be familiar with certain layout principles. The person who actually does the layout shouldn't be the first to consider how well the proposed building is suited to the site. But unfortunately, many owners and some builders don't adapt the building plan to the site. As you lay out the building on the site, you may realize that the owner is violating some of the basic planning principles in this section, is wasting money on unnecessary construction, could provide more living space with little additional investment, or is not complying with local regulations. Once your layout is complete and the foundation is poured, even little changes in the basic plan become very expensive. Be ready to suggest improvements or problems that become obvious to you as you do the layout work.

The size, shape and contours of the lot are important considerations in the design of every house. Sloping lots let you design entrances at more than one ground level. A sloping lot can be used to provide a garage in the basement area. Level lots are easy to build on, but they may present drainage problems such as water in the basement. One-story or ranch-type houses can be built on level or sloping lots. But if they are to be built on sloping lots, plan to use the high foundation wall on the lower side of the lot as one wall of a basement or garage. One and a half and two-story houses offer more living area for less money per square foot. They require less lot area than a one-story house with the same amount of living space. The bi-level or split-entry house has gained in popularity in recent years because it includes a finished basement and requires less excavation. The price per square foot of a bi-level house is usually less than that for a one-story house. The split-level or tri-level house was designed for sloping lots, but is often built on level land.

The price per square foot for a split-level house is higher than that for other types of houses mentioned above. Each of these designs has advantages and disadvantages. Only the owner (with the help of his builder) can decide on the best design for a particular lot.

There are other factors to be considered besides the contours of the lot before the final decision to buy or build on the lot is made.

- An irregular shaped lot or a lot facing a curved street may cause problems with the setback restrictions if the house is too large.

- The grade of the walks and the driveways should be acceptable.

- Is the land *virgin* soil or is it filled? Filled land can make building the foundation difficult since pilings or extra excavation may be needed to construct the house on solid earth. Rock is expensive to excavate, and the cost of removing it can eliminate the basement from your design.

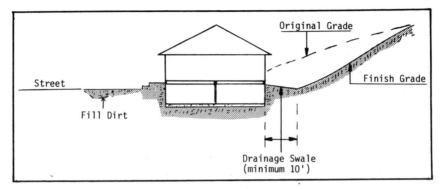

Planning For Proper Drainage
Figure 5-1

Underground springs and signs of disturbed earth also affect the choice of the lot, construction costs and schedule, final cost of the house, and marketability.

- Will the adjacent property be damaged by runoff water during and after construction? Don't invite legal problems.

- Will there be enough area around the house to insure the proper drainage of surface water away from the building? (See Figure 5-1.)

There are many other factors that should be considered before beginning work.

- Check local zoning restrictions. The area could be zoned for industrial and commercial use—or such zoning changes may be contemplated.

- The deed restrictions and the zoning codes may differ. This could affect the size and type of house that can be built on the lot. Zoning codes normally take precedence. But get legal counsel when there is a doubt.

- Check on the public utilities. Is the water supply adequate? Is it approved by the proper authority? Is there a sewage disposal system available, or will a private system be necessary? If there is a sewer line, where is it located and how deep is it? Are the electric, gas and telephone service lines available?

- Are the streets maintained by the state, county or local government, or will they have to be maintained by the property owners?

It is always wise to decide on the lot first and then plan the house that will best fit on it. The lot with the lowest purchase price may become the most expensive after development costs are included.

Match the house to the lot to:

- Enhance the appearance of the house.

- Keep the amount of excavation and fill dirt to a minimum.

- Make the walks safer because the grade is less steep.

- Keep the grade of the driveway attractive and safe.

- Cut the number of steps to a minimum.

- Eliminate many unnecessary costs.

Establishing The Correct Floor Elevation

When you plan to build a house to a predetermined floor elevation, determine the setback requirements on the plot plan before construction begins. Highways are built to predetermined elevations. So are commercial and industrial buildings. When architects design a house for a given lot they normally specify the floor elevations. Designed floor elevations save unnecessary expenses and make any house more attractive and enjoyable to live in. When the aesthetics of the house are enhanced, the value of the property is increased.

Sometimes certain conditions dictate altering the floor elevations. Trees should be saved when possible. You may want to leave rock formations on the lot intact. Underground rock, high ground water and other disturbed earth conditions may have to be considered. Changing the floor elevations, and perhaps even eliminating the basement, may be necessary. When these conditions are present only the owner of the property can make the final decision on the changes you or the architect propose.

To calculate floor elevations, first stake out the house on the lot. Pick a permanent reference point or bench mark. This mark must be some point that will not be changed during construction, such as a mark in the street or a nail in a tree that will not be removed. If the elevation of this bench mark is not known, assign it an arbitrary elevation, such as 100.0'. Then take the following elevations.

1. The existing grade at the approximate location of each corner of the house.

2. The inverse (lowest) point of the sewer line where the sewer service lateral from the house will connect to the main sewer line.

3. The point at which the driveway will connect to the street.

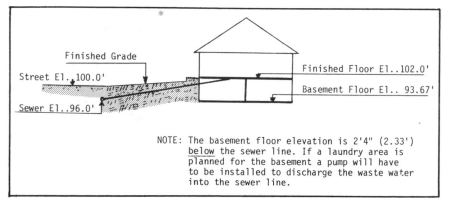

Planning The Basement Floor Elevation
Figure 5-2

4. All other elevations necessary to plan the finish grade for drainage, landscaping, walks, driveways, and the like.

Once these existing elevations are known, decide on the finished floor elevations. Here are some of the factors that influence this elevation. Often, you must compromise between two or more of them.

1. How much higher above the existing grade will the finish floor have to be to provide an ideal appearance and satisfactory surface water drainage away from the house?

2. If there is to be a basement, will the basement floor elevation be high enough above the inverse sewer line elevation to provide a natural drain? Local ordinances may require a pump or special fittings to ensure discharge of waste water in the basement to the sewer line if there is not adequate natural drainage. Raising the floor elevation may solve these problems. See Figures 5-2 and 5-3.

3. If the finished floor elevation is raised to provide a natural

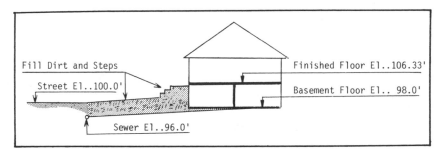

Finished Floor Elevation Raised 4.33'
to Allow Basement Drainage Without a Pump
Figure 5-3

drain from the basement into the sewer line, will this change the aesthetics of the house noticeably? See Figure 5-3.

4. Will the grade of the driveway be acceptable?

5. Will the number of steps required be acceptable?

After the primary floor elevation is determined, the other floor elevations in the house are calculated from the dimensions shown on the blueprints. The thickness of the floor assembly that comprises the plates, floor joists, sub-floor, finish floor (or floor underlayment when carpet or tile is to be the finish floor) are given in the plans or specifications. A typical framing lumber layout is shown in Figure 5-4. The height of concrete block walls by courses is shown in Figure 5-5. Table 5-6 lists actual lumber and block dimensions so you can calculate the height of the floor assembly and the foundation wall. If the finished floor in Figure 5-7 has been assigned an elevation of 102.0', the calculations to determine the basement floor elevation are as follows:

1. The basement ceiling height is given as 7'-5½'' (11 courses of blocks above the basement floor [7'-4''] plus the plate [1½'']).

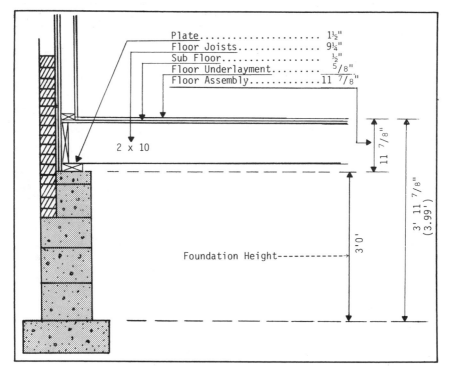

Plate...................... 1½"
Floor Joists.............. 9¼"
Sub Floor................. ½"
Floor Underlayment........ 5/8"
Floor Assembly...........11 7/8"

2 x 10

11 7/8"

3' 11 7/8"
(3.99')

Foundation Height------------→   3'0'

Typical Framing Lumber Layout
Figure 5-4

2. From the plans and specifications the actual thickness of the floor assembly, less the plate, is calculated to be 10½".

3. The basement floor to finish floor height is 7'-5½" plus 10½" or 8'-4" (8.33').

4. The basement floor elevation can now be computed by subtracting the "basement floor to finish floor" height from the finish floor elevation (102.00' less 8.33' = 93.67'). *Note:* If the predetermined elevation of the basement floor was assigned before the finished floor, then add the "basement floor to finish

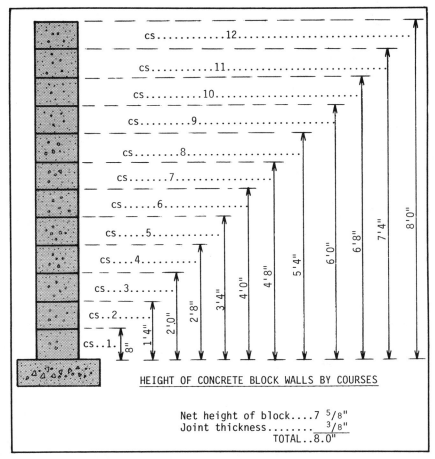

Height of Concrete Block Walls by Course
Figure 5-5

floor'' height to the basement floor elevation for the finished floor elevation.

Figure 5-8 shows existing grades on a lot and the plan of how the building will be positioned on the site. The elevation at the main entrance door is 104.20'. The elevation at the left entrance to the driveway is the bench mark (B.M.) whose assigned

NEW FRAMING LUMBER SIZES

Nominal Size	Actual Size
2" x 4"	1½" x 3½"
2" x 6"	1½" x 5½"
2" x 8"	1½" x 7¼"
2" x 10"	1½" x 9¼"
2" x 12"	1½" x 11¼"

CONCRETE BLOCK SIZES

Nominal Size	Actual Size
4" x 8" x 16"	3 5/8" x 7 5/8" x 15 5/8"
8" x 8" x 16"	7 5/8" x 7 5/8" x 15 5/8"
12" x 8" x 16"	11 5/8" x 7 5/8" x 15 5/8"

Table 5-6

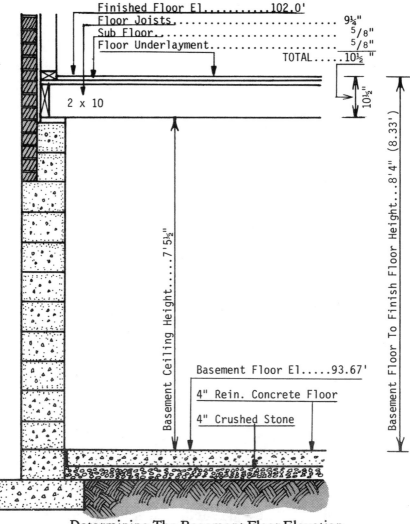

Determining The Basement Floor Elevation
Figure 5-7

elevation is 100.0'. The elevation of the right front corner of the lot is 99.87'. The inverse elevation of the main sewer line is 96.56' where the house sewage flows into the sewer.

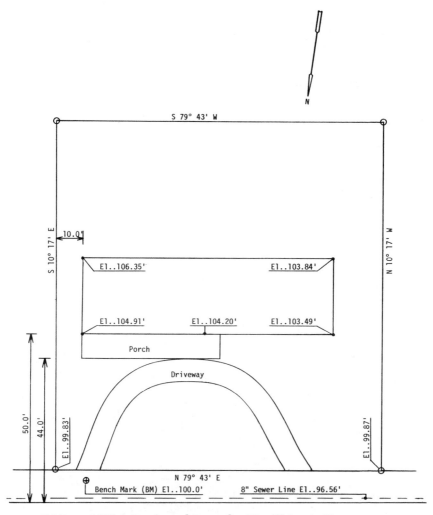

Bi-Level With Bath and Laundry Facilities in Basement
Figure 5-8

The house shown in Figure 5-8 is a bi-level with bath and laundry facilities in the basement. Figure 5-9 shows the wall section of the house as shown on the blueprints. The plan gives

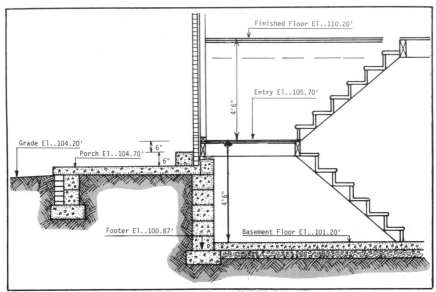

Wall Section
Figure 5-9

the height of the finished floor as 4'-6'' (4.5') above the entry
floor. The basement floor is 4'-6'' below the entry floor, or 9'-0''
below the finished floor. From the dimensions on the blueprints
and the grade elevations shown in Figure 5-8, the following
calculations can now be made:

1. The entry floor can be 1'-6'' above the existing grade at the
main entrance, as shown on the plot plan in Figure 5-8. The grade
elevation at this point is 104.20'. Add 1'-6'' (1.5') to 104.20' to get
the assigned elevation for the entry floor: 105.70'. This elevation
and other calculated floor elevations are recorded on the floor
plans as shown in Figure 5-9.

2. The main finished floor is 4'-6'' above the entry floor. Add
this figure to the entry floor elevation (105.70 + 4.5' [4'-6'']) to
get an elevation of 110.20' for the finished floor.

3. The basement floor is 4'-6'' below the entry floor (or 9'-0'' below the main finish floor). Subtract this figure from the entry floor elevation (105.70' — 4.5') to get an elevation of 101.20' for the basement floor.

4. Calculate the footer elevation by subtracting the thickness of the concrete basement floor (4'' or .33') from the basement floor elevation (101.20' — .33' = 100.87').

5. The inverse elevation of the sewer line at the street as shown in Figure 5-8 is 96.56', or 4.64' lower (101.20' less 96.56') than the basement floor. This permits drainage by gravity rather than by a pump.

The grade of the driveway is acceptable. It is only 7% at both the left and right entrances to the house. No unnecessary expense will be encountered to provide adequate drainage of the surface water away from the house. And the elevation of the entry floor eliminates any unnecessary steps, giving the house a pleasing appearance on the lot.

Driveway Grades

Driveways extend from the street or alley to the garage, carport or parking space. At one time cars were parked on the street when the house was built on a sloping lot, but today driveways are necessary because most localities require garage space, or off street parking.

When houses are built on sloping or hillside lots, the grade (or gradient) of the driveway may present a problem. Solve this problem before the actual construction of the house begins. You may have to change the floor elevations of the house, or set the house farther back on the lot than was originally planned, to

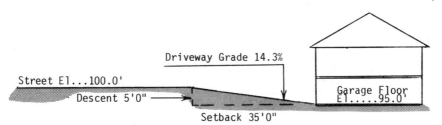

Determining the Driveway Grade
Figure 5-10

insure a satisfactory grade for the driveway.

The grade of the driveway is its rate of increase or decrease in elevation. This is usually expressed in percent. A 3% grade increases or decreases in elevation three feet in a horizontal distance of 100 feet. The formula for computing driveway grades is:

$$\text{Grade (\%)} = \frac{\text{Ascent or descent}}{\text{Horizontal distance}}$$

For example, in Figure 5-10 the house sits 35'-0'' from the street and the elevation of the garage floor is 5'-0'' below the street at the point where the driveway joins the garage floor. The grade of the driveway is 14.3%. This was computed as follows:

$$\text{Grade (\%)} = \frac{5}{35} = .143$$

Grade = 14.3%

Local codes differ in the maximum driveway grades permitted. But the grade should not exceed 14% if possible. Steep driveways are a serious access problem in wet or freezing

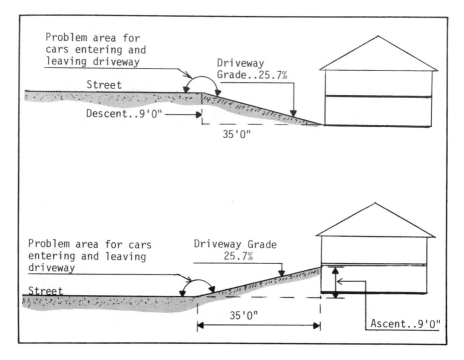

Unsuitable Grades For Driveways
Figure 5-11

weather. A steep driveway also presents a problem at the street where the car enters or leaves it, since the car's undercarriage and bumper may not accept such a change in grade. See Figure 5-11.

It is possible to decrease the grade of the driveway by either decreasing the rise or fall (see Figure 5-12), or increasing the horizontal run (see chart in Figure 5-13). You can also set the house farther back on the lot than was originally planned to reduce an excessively steep driveway grade. It may be possible to lower the floor elevations or put the garage in the basement. See Figure 5-12. Figure 5-13 shows grades in percent for horizontal runs and rises.

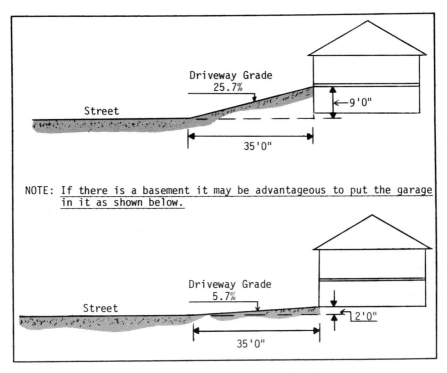

Decreasing The Driveway Grade
Figure 5-12

Aligning Floors In New Additions

Matching the floor level in a new addition to the floor level in the existing house requires careful planning. You must be very careful in your calculations and supervise construction as the work progresses.

The floor assembly in the new addition does not have to be the same size and dimension as the floor assembly in the existing house. See Figure 5-14. Your calculation should always start with the floor elevation in the existing building and work down. The

Horizontal Run in Feet	DRIVEWAY GRADES									
	Rise in Feet									
	1	2	3	4	5	6	7	8	9	10
35	2.9%	5.7%	8.6%	11.4%	14.3%	17.1%	20.0%	22.9%	25.7%	28.6%
40	2.5%	5.0%	7.5%	10.0%	12.5%	15.0%	17.5%	20.0%	22.5%	25.0%
45	2.2%	4.4%	6.7%	8.9%	11.1%	13.3%	15.6%	17.8%	20.0%	22.2%
50	2.0%	4.0%	6.0%	8.0%	10.0%	12.0%	14.0%	16.0%	18.0%	20.0%
55	1.8%	3.6%	5.5%	7.3%	9.1%	10.9%	12.7%	14.5%	16.4%	18.2%
60	1.7%	3.3%	5.0%	6.7%	8.3%	10.0%	11.7%	13.3%	15.0%	16.7%
65	1.5%	3.1%	4.6%	6.2%	7.7%	9.2%	10.8%	12.3%	13.8%	15.4%
70	1.4%	2.9%	4.3%	5.7%	7.1%	8.6%	10.0%	11.4%	12.9%	14.3%
75	1.3%	2.7%	4.0%	5.3%	6.7%	8.0%	9.3%	10.7%	12.0%	13.3%
80	1.3%	2.5%	3.8%	5.0%	6.3%	7.5%	8.8%	10.0%	11.3%	12.5%
85	1.2%	2.4%	3.5%	4.7%	5.9%	7.1%	8.2%	9.4%	10.6%	11.8%
90	1.1%	2.2%	3.3%	4.4%	5.6%	6.7%	7.8%	8.9%	10.0%	11.1%
95	1.1%	2.1%	3.2%	4.2%	5.3%	6.3%	7.4%	8.4%	9.5%	10.5%
100	1.0%	2.0%	3.0%	4.0%	5.0%	6.0%	7.0%	8.0%	9.0%	10.0%

Driveway Grades in Percent For Horizontal Runs and Rises
Table 5-13

elevation of the footers and the elevation of the top of the foundation must be computed before construction begins, and close supervision must be maintained during the construction period to insure that the footers and foundation are constructed to the correct elevations.

Figure 5-14 shows a proposed new addition for an existing

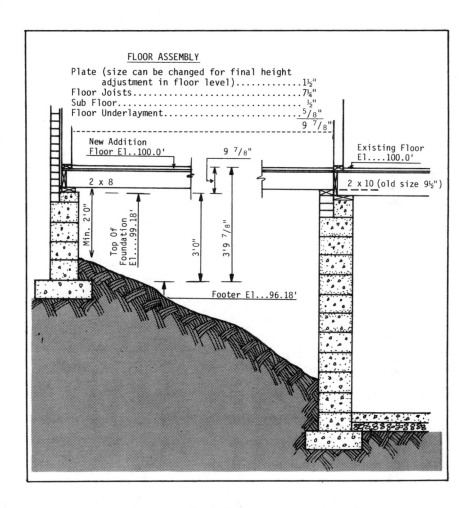

Calculating The Floor Elevation In a New Addition
Figure 5-14

house. The addition is to be built over a crawl space, and the minimum headroom in the crawl space is to be 2'-0''. According to the specifications, the floor assembly is made up as follows:

Plate (2 x 6). . . . . 1-1/2"
Floor joists (2 x 8). . . . . 7-1/4"
Subfloor (plywood) . . . .   1/2"
Floor underlayment. . . . .   5/8"
Height of floor assembly . . . . 9-7/8"

After staking out the foundation for the new addition, take the elevations at each corner of the building to determine the amount of excavation that will be required. In this example, the calculations reveal that the foundation height needs to be 3'-0" (four courses of 12" x 8" x 16" plus one course of 4" x 8" x 16" solid concrete blocks) to provide the headroom required. The calculations can now be made to determine the elevation of the footers and the elevation of the top of the foundation wall. As mentioned earlier, start with the floor level in the existing building and work down. Assign the existing floor an arbitrary elevation of 100.0'. The floor level in the addition must align with the floor level in the existing building. Thus the new floor elevation will also be 100.0'.

The height of the foundation in the addition is to be 3'-0". The height of the floor assembly is 0'-9-7/8". Adding these two heights together (3'-0" plus 0'-9-7/8") equals 3'-9-7/8". This is the distance the footers must be below the floor elevation. The footer elevation is computed as follows:

100.0' *less* 3'-9-7/8" (3.82') = 96.18'

The top of the foundation is 3'-0" above the footers, thus the top of the foundation wall elevation is:

96.18' *plus* 3.0' = 99.18'

Be sure that these two elevations are correct during construction of the addition. Minor errors can be corrected by changing the dimensions of the plate. For example, if the foundation height is ½'' too high, it can be corrected by changing the dimensions of the plate from 1 ½'' to 1''. If the foundation height is ½'' too low, a strip of ½'' plywood can be cut and nailed on top of the plate to give it the correct height. If the foundation elevation is off more than a small fraction of an inch, it may be necessary to change the floor assembly to be in perfect alignment. See Chapter 9 for precision leveling techniques for foundation construction.

Chapter 6

Calculating Cuts And Fills

After determining the location of the house on the building lot and assigning elevations to the different floor levels, calculate the cuts and fills for the foundation excavation. First, calculate the grade elevation for the basement, crawl space and garage. From the blueprints or the specifications find the distance from the basement floor to the finish floor height, the minimum clearance for headroom in the crawl space, and the thickness of the concrete floor and stone the concrete is poured over. When there is to be a basement, the blueprints may only show the headroom required (the distance from the basement floor to the bottom of the floor joists). When this information is given, add the floor assembly height (see Figure 5-7) to the basement clearance height to find the distance from the basement floor to the finish floor.

Figure 6-1 shows a house with a basement, crawl space and garage. The basement grade elevation is calculated as follows:

1. The finish floor (F.F.) has been assigned an elevation of 103.0'.

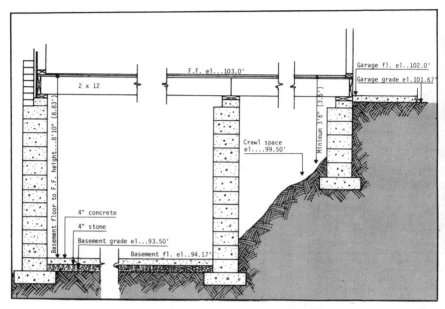

F.F. el...103.0'

Garage fl. el..102.0'
Garage grade el.101.67'

2 x 12

Basement floor to F.F. height..8'10" (8.83')

Minimum 3'6" (3.5')

Crawl space
el....99.50'

4" concrete
4" stone
Basement grade el...93.50'
Basement fl. el..94.17'

Calculating The Grade Elevation For The Basement,
Crawl Space And Garage
Figure 6-1

2. The blueprint shows the height from the basement floor to the F.F. to be 8'-10'' (8.83'). The concrete for the basement floor is to be 4'' thick and it is to be poured over 4'' of stone.

3. The basement floor elevation is calculated to be 94.17' (103.0' less 8.83' = 94.17').

4. The basement grade is 8'' (.67') below the basement floor. The basement grade elevation is then 93.50' (94.17' less .67' = 93.50').

5. From the blueprint the minimum headroom for the crawl space is 2'-6''. The floor assembly is added to this dimension for a minimum distance of 3'-6'' (3.5') from the F.F. to the crawl space

grade. The crawl space grade elevation is 99.50' (103.0' less 3.5' = 99.50').

6. The garage floor is 1'-0'' below the F.F. The blueprint shows 4'' of concrete for the garage, poured directly on the grade. The garage floor elevation then becomes 101.67' (102.0' less 4'' [.33'] = 101.67').

7. If the blueprint shows the floor system to be a slab rather than built over a basement or crawl space, the grade for the slab would be calculated the same as in 4 and 6 above. The F.F. for a slab floor system would be concrete. The slab grade would be the F.F. elevation minus the thickness of the concrete and the stone or sand it was poured over.

After the grade elevations have been calculated, the cuts and fills for the foundation excavation can now be computed. The depth of the cuts and the height of the fills is the difference between the calculated grade elevation and the existing grade elevation. For example, we can calculate the cuts and fills for Figure 6-2. The steps are shown below.

1. The calculated basement grade elevation is 93.50'. The existing grade elevation at the left front corner of the foundation is 87.22'. A fill of 6.28' will be required here (93.50' less 87.22' = 6.28').

2. A cut of 1.07' will be required at the right front corner of the basement (93.50' less 94.57' = -1.07').

3. The left back corner of the basement will require a fill of 1.51' (93.50' less 91.99' = 1.51').

4. The right back corner of the basement will require a cut of

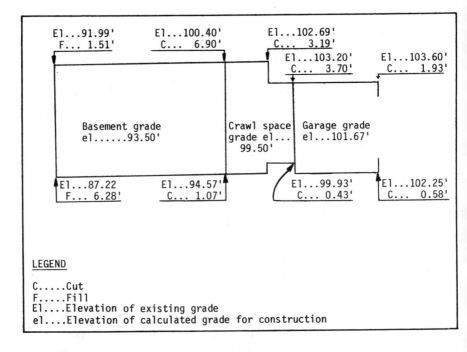

Calculating The Cuts And Fills For The Foundation Excavation
Figure 6-2

6.90' (93.50' less 100.40' = -6.90').

5. The crawl space grade elevation is 99.50'. The excavation for the basement will have to extend into the crawl space area a short distance to permit the construction of the footers and the basement foundation wall adjacent to the crawl space. Therefore, no calculations are made for the cuts and fills in this area of the crawl space.

6. A cut of 3.19' will be required at the extreme right back corner of the crawl space (99.50' less 102.69' = -3.19'). A cut of 3.70' will be required at the right back corner of the crawl space adjacent to the garage (99.50' less 103.20' = -3.70').

7. The right front corner of the crawl space adjacent to the garage will require a cut of 0.43' (99.50' less 99.93' = -0.43').

8. The garage grade elevation is 101.67'. The excavation in the crawl space will have to extend into the garage area to permit the construction of the footers and foundation wall between the two areas. No calculations are made for the cuts and fills in the garage area adjacent to the crawl space. The cuts and fills that may be required here are brought to the same elevation as the other cuts and fills that may be necessary for the garage grade elevation.

9. A cut of 1.93' will be necessary in the right back corner of the garage (101.67' less 103.60' = -1.93').

10. A cut of 0.58' will be required at the right front corner of the garage (101.67' less 102.25' = -0.58').

After all cuts and fills have been computed, the quantity of fill dirt and the amount of the excavation in cubic yards can be calculated, as explained below.

Calculating Excavation Quantities

Excavations are normally figured in cubic yards—that is, the length of the excavation in feet multiplied by the width in feet multiplied by the depth in feet and divided by 27 (L x W x D ÷ 27). Excavations are estimated in cubic yards as solid ground in place, and not as the loose dirt piled on the side or hauled away. The volume of loose dirt can be as much as 25% greater than original "in place" volume.

Calculating the average depth of the excavation on level ground is fairly easy. It is only a matter of taking the cuts and fills at each corner of the house and averaging them:

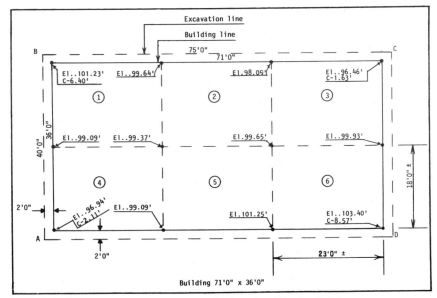

Excavating Boundaries Set Up In Grids
Figure 6-3

House Corner	Depth of Cut
A	5.00'
B	5.17'
C	4.92'
D	5.08'
	20.17'

20.17' ÷ 4 = 5.04'

The average cut is 5.04' (or 5'-0½'')

Before calculating the average depth of the excavation of sloping ground, the excavation boundaries should be set up in grids as shown in Figure 6-3. For residential work, these grids can be from 10 feet to 25 feet on a side. A stake should be driven at each corner of the grids and the elevation of each corner should be taken and recorded. To calculate the average depth, add the elevations at each grid corner and divide by the number of corners. This is the *average elevation*. Subtract this average elevation from the calculated basement grade elevation to get the average depth of the excavation.

Excavations should be a minimum of 2'-0'' beyond the building lines to allow access around the foundation. In Figure 6-3 the house dimensions are 71'-0'' x 36'-0''. The excavation line is 2'-0'' outside of each building line, making the dimensions of the excavation boundary 75'-0'' x 40'-0''.

The cuts (C) and fills (F) are marked on the stakes at each corner of the house. The cut is the excavation required to bring the existing grade of the ground down to the calculated elevation. The fill is the height fill dirt will have to be added to bring the existing grade up to the calculated elevation. Where there are both cuts and fills within one foundation, calculate each separately to determine the average depth of the cuts and the average height of the fills.

The plan for the job in Figure 6-3 assigned the finished floor an elevation of 103.50', and the bench mark was assigned an elevation of 100.00'. From the wall section of the blueprint the basement floor elevation should be 8'-0'' below the finished floor. The plans call for a 4'' concrete basement floor poured over 4'' of gravel. The basement grade elevation is then 8'-8'' (8.67') below the finish floor or at an elevation of 94.83' (103.50' less 8.67' = 94.83').

The cuts at each corner of the house are calculated by subtracting the existing elevation at each of these corners from the calculated basement grade elevation:

Basement Grade Elevation		Existing Grade Elevation	Cut or Fill
94.83'	*Less*	96.94' at *A*	= -2.11' (cut)
94.83'	*Less*	101.23' at *B*	= -6.40' (cut)
94.83'	*Less*	96.46' at *C*	= -1.63' (cut)
94.83'	*Less*	103.40' at *D*	= -8.57' (cut)

These cuts are marked on the stakes at each corner of the house:

$$A.....C-2.11' (2'-1-3/8'')$$
$$B......C-6.40' (6'-4-3/4'')$$
$$C......C-1.63' (1'-7-1/2'')$$
$$D......C-8.57' (8'-6-7/8'')$$

It is a help for the equipment operator doing the excavation to mark the cuts and fills in feet and inches rather than in feet and hundredths. Although fractions of an inch are shown above do not expect the operator of the equipment to be able to work this close. It is not necessary.

To calculate the quantity of earth to be excavated in Figure 6-3, proceed as follows:

1. Add the elevations at each corner of the grids and divide the total by the number of corners for the average elevation, as below:

96.94'
99.09'
101.25'
103.40'
99.09'
99.37'
99.65'

$$99.93'$$
$$101.23'$$
$$99.64'$$
$$98.05'$$
$$\underline{96.46'}$$
$$\overline{1194.10'} \div 12 = 99.51'$$

The average existing elevation = 99.51'

2. Subtract the existing grade elevation from the calculated basement grade elevation to determine the average depth (cut) of the excavation:

$$\begin{aligned}
\text{Basement grade elevation} &= 94.83' \\
\text{Average existing elevation} &= \underline{99.51'} \\
\text{Average cut} &= \overline{-4.68'} \ (4'\text{-}8\text{-}1/8'')
\end{aligned}$$

3. Calculate the cubic yards of excavation required.

$$\begin{aligned}
L &= 75.00' \\
W &= 40.00' \\
D &= 4.68'
\end{aligned}$$

$$\frac{75' \times 40' \times 4.68'}{27} = 520 \text{ cubic yards}$$

The amount of excavation required in Figure 6-3 is 520 cubic yards.

Make sure that the equipment operator excavates the foundation to the exact grade elevation; check the dimensions and depth of the foundation before the equipment is moved away from the job. The depth can be checked with the builder's level by the following method.

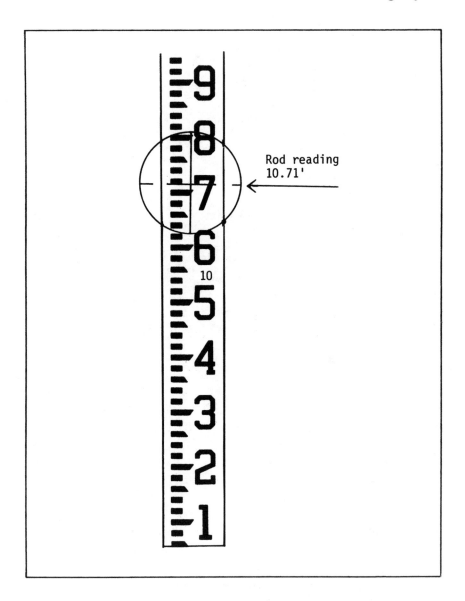

Excavation Depth Checked With a Rod Reading
Figure 6-4

1. Setup the level at a convenient point where a reading can be taken on the bench mark and on all points of the excavation.

2. Take a reading on the level rod at the B.M. and add this rod reading to the B.M. elevation for the height of instrument (H.I.).

$$\text{Elevation at B.M.} = 100.00'$$
$$\underline{\text{Rod reading at B.M.} = \quad 5.54'}$$
$$\text{Height of instrument (H.I.)} = 105.54'$$

3. Subtract the basement grade elevation from the H.I. for the rod reading to be used in checking the depth of the excavation.

$$\text{H.I.} = 105.54'$$
$$\underline{\text{Basement grade elevation} = \quad 94.83'}$$
$$\text{Rod reading} = \quad 10.71'$$

4. Set the target on the level rod at 10.71', and without moving the builder's level from the position where the H.I. reading at the B.M. was taken, sight through the instrument on the level rod at several points where the excavation is being done. When the horizontal crosshair on the instrument cuts across the target setting on the level rod (10.71') the depth of the excavation is correct. See Figure 6-4.

Chapter 7

Foundation Layouts

No building is better than the foundation it rests on. Everything the foundation supports is affected directly or indirectly by it. It must provide safe and adequate support for the building. It also must be square and level. If it isn't, the carpenters and other craftsmen will have difficulty following the plans. Trying to set cabinets and plumbing fixtures when the building is out of square can be exasperating and costly. Similar problems will occur throughout the off-square house. Unless the error is corrected early in the project, the mistakes are visible as long as the building stands.

Few foundations are laid out under perfect conditions, as any experienced builder can verify. Transferring the dimensions and other data from the blueprints and plot plans to the actual foundation sometimes seems almost impossible. One of the biggest threats to accuracy is the problem of building on uneven terrain. With knowledge, desire and proper equipment, all foundations can be constructed so errors fall well within allowable tolerances. This chapter will show you how to measure, calculate, and lay out accurate, on-square foundations on either flat or inclined sites.

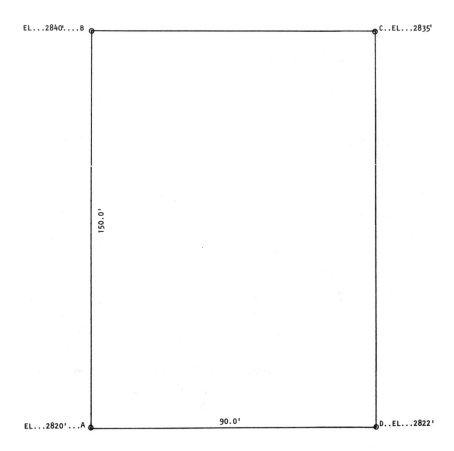

Land Measurement, Horizontal Distance
Figure 7-1

Taking Horizontal Measurements
On Steep Slopes

In land measurement, the distance between two points is understood to be in horizontal distance regardless of the difference in elevation. In Figure 7-1 the elevation of the left front

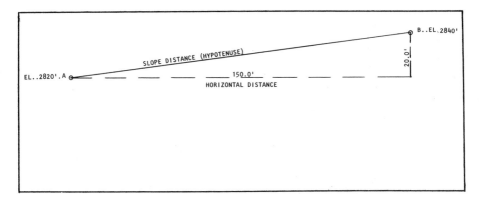

Horizontal Distance
Figure 7-2

corner (*A*) of the lot is 2,820' above sea level. The elevation of the left back corner (*B*) of the lot is 2,840' above sea level. The distance between the two points is 150.0'. This is the horizontal distance as shown in Figure 7-2, not the slope distance.

All measurements taken with a steel tape must be made with the tape held level and taut. The distance a tape can be held taut and level is limited. Therefore, when you measure distances over steep slopes you must use a plumb bob (or a straight edge held plumb). For this you need the help of another person. The procedure may involve several steps. Have the men practice holding the tape horizontal and taut so that the same precision can be obtained with horizontal measurements on steep slopes as on level ground.

Figure 7-3 shows the side view of a lot with a setback requirement of 40.0' from the front property line. The elevation of point *A* is 15.0' higher than point *D*. This horizontal distance must be measured in more than one step:

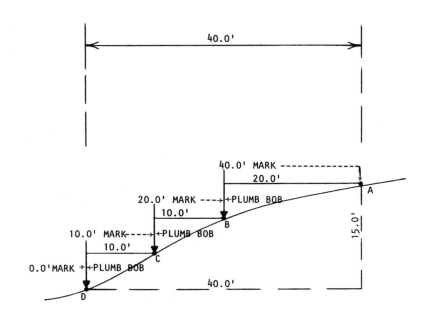

Taking The Setback Measurement of a Sloped Lot
Figure 7-3

1. One man stands at point *D* and holds a plumb bob over the mark. The zero reading of the steel tape is held against the plumb bob string. The second man stands at a convenient distance (Point *C*) where he can hold the tape horizontal and taut, and records the tape reading at this point. A stake is set in the ground at point *C* with a tack or other mark to indicate the exact point where the measurement was taken. In this example it is 10.0'.

2. The first man then proceeds to point *C* where he holds the plumb bob over this point and at the first measured distance on the tape (10.0' in this example). The second man moves to point *B*, again records the tape measurement and sets another stake with a reference mark in the ground (20.0' in this example).

3. Steps 1 and 2 are repeated until the desired horizontal distance is measured. This operation should be repeated as a check against errors when precision measurements are required.

You can also obtain horizontal distances by calculating the slope distance, as shown in Figure 7-4. (See the next section of this chapter for the mathematical solution.) Use a calculator with a square root (√) key. There are many small battery powered electronic calculators on the market with the ability to find square roots. Most of these pocket calculators sell at a reasonable price.

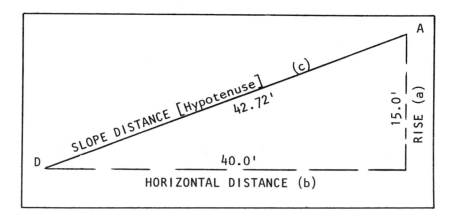

Calculating Slope Distance
Figure 7-4

Here is the formula for calculating the slope distance in Figure 7-4.

$$c = \sqrt{a^2 + b^2}$$

where : a = rise or difference in elevation

b = horizontal distance

c = slope distance (hypotenuse)

Since a = 15.0' and b = 40.0' the solution to calculating the slope distance c is:

$$c = \sqrt{15^2 + 40^2} = \sqrt{225 + 1600}$$

$$c = \sqrt{1825} = 42.72' \quad (42'\text{-}8\text{-}5/8'')$$

Calculating the slope distance can save a lot of time if you measure long distances over slopes. Precision work is impossible if the men who take the measurements are careless in the way they hold and read the steel tape. Make accurate measurements even when great precision is not required.

Mathematics For Foundation Layouts

Certain mathematical problems must be solved before the foundation is laid. This can be done either in the office or in the field. This section shows you how to convert inches and fractions of an inch into equivalent decimals of a foot, and how to find the diagonal distances between foundation corners. Once you know the diagonal distance, you can check any foundation to see if it is square.

The foundation dimensions are given on the plans in feet and inches. Sometimes dimensions are given in feet, inches, and fractions, such as 67'-11¾'' x 28'-10½''. These inches and fractions should be changed to decimal equivalents of a foot before computations are made. Calculations are always easier using the decimal system rather than inches and fractions.

Convert inches and fractions to decimal equivalents of a foot as follows:

1. Change the fraction to the decimal equivalent of an inch.

2. Add the whole number of inches to this decimal equivalent.

3. Divide this number by 12 to get the decimal equivalent of a foot. Example: Convert 8¼" to its decimal equivalent in feet.

    1) ¼" = .25" (1 ÷ 4 = .25)

    2) .25" + 8" = 8.25"

    3) 8.25" ÷ 12 = .688 feet (or .69')
       .688' (or .69') is the decimal equivalent of 8¼".

Convert decimal equivalents of a foot back to inches and fractions as follows:

1. Multiply the decimal equivalent by 12 to get inches and the decimal equivalent of an inch.

2. Subtract the whole number of inches from this figure.

3. Multiply this decimal equivalent by the fractional part of an inch desired. (Multiply by 4 to get 4ths, multiply by 8 to get 8ths, multiply by 16 to get 16ths, etc.)

4. Add the fractional part of an inch calculated in 3 to the whole number of inches calculated in 1 to get the total inches and fractions. Example: Convert .69' to inches and fractions.

    1) .69' x 12 = 8.28"

    2) 8.28" — 8" = .28"

3) .28'' x 8 = 2 (number of 8ths: 2/8'' or ¼'')

4) 8'' + ¼'' = 8¼''

8¼'' = .69'

These calculations are made more easily on an electronic calculator. But there may be times when you do not have a calculator at hand. When this happens, it helps to have a conversion chart handy. Figure 7-5 is a conversion chart that gives the decimal equivalents of fractional parts of a foot. Convert inches and fractions to the decimal equivalent in feet as follows:

Example: Convert 8¼'' to its decimal equivalent in feet.

1. *Go across* the top line to the 8'' column.

2. *Go down* this column to the line where 1 falls in the 4th column (¼'') at extreme left.

3. Where the two lines intersect read the answer.

(In this example it is .688' or .69'.)

Another valuable tool to have in the field for conversion work when there is no calculator available is the engineer's rule. This rule is similar to a 6 foot carpenter's rule except that one side of the rule has graduations in feet, tenths and hundredths, and the other side has graduations in feet, inches and sixteenths. Conversions are easily made by holding your thumbnail on the reading on one side and turning the rule over to find the conversion on the other side.

After the foundation dimensions have been converted to decimal equivalents, use the Pythagorean theorem to find all the diagonal dimensions. This theorem states that the square of the length of the hypotenuse of a right triangle equals the sum of the squares of the lengths of the other two sides. The formula is:

$$c^2 = a^2 + b^2$$

Thus, the length of the hypotenuse of a right triangle is equal to the square root of the sum of the squares of the other two sides. This formula is:

$$c = \sqrt{a^2 + b^2}$$

From the following sketch the formula could also be:

$$AC = \sqrt{BC^2 + AB^2}$$

From the tables in Figure 7-5 (or by actual computation, as explained above) the decimal equivalent of 11¾" is .979'. Then 67'-11¾" is 67.979'. The decimal equivalent of 10½" is .875', then 28'-10½" is 28.875'. The solution to solving the diagonal distance AC is:

$$AC = \sqrt{BC^2 + AB^2}$$

$$AC = \sqrt{28.875^2 + 67.979^2}$$

$$AC = \sqrt{833.766' + 4621.144'}$$

$$AC = \sqrt{5454.910'}$$

$$AC = 73.857' \text{ or } (73'\text{-}10\text{-}5/16")$$

Finding the acute angles (angles that have a value of less than 90°, such as angles *BAC* and *BCA* in the sketch on the following page) of a right triangle requires the use of trigonometry. But don't think that you have to be a master in trigonometry to compute these angles. Basically the three formulas for solving the acute angles and any side of a right triangle are:

4th	8th	16th	0"	1"	2"	3"	4"	5"	6"	7"	8"	9"	10"	11"
		0	.000	.083	.167	.25	.333	.417	.5	.583	.667	.75	.833	.917
		1	.005	.089	.172	.255	.339	.422	.505	.589	.672	.755	.839	.922
	1	2	.010	.094	.177	.260	.344	.427	.510	.594	.677	.760	.844	.927
		3	.016	.099	.182	.266	.349	.432	.516	.599	.682	.766	.849	.932
1	2	4	.021	.104	.188	.271	.354	.438	.521	.604	.688	.771	.854	.938
		5	.026	.109	.193	.276	.359	.443	.526	.609	.693	.776	.859	.943
	3	6	.031	.115	.198	.281	.365	.448	.531	.615	.698	.781	.865	.948
		7	.036	.118	.203	.286	.370	.453	.536	.620	.703	.786	.870	.953
2	4	8	.042	.125	.208	.292	.375	.458	.542	.625	.708	.792	.875	.958
		9	.047	.130	.213	.297	.380	.464	.547	.630	.714	.797	.880	.964
	5	10	.052	.135	.219	.302	.386	.469	.552	.635	.719	.802	.885	.969
		11	.057	.141	.224	.307	.391	.474	.557	.641	.724	.807	.891	.974
3	6	12	.063	.146	.229	.313	.396	.479	.563	.646	.729	.813	.896	.979
		13	.068	.151	.234	.318	.401	.484	.568	.651	.734	.818	.901	.984
	7	14	.073	.156	.240	.323	.406	.490	.573	.656	.740	.823	.906	.989
		15	.078	.161	.245	.328	.411	.495	.578	.661	.745	.828	.911	.995

Sixteenths of an Inch to Thousandths of a Foot
Table 7-5

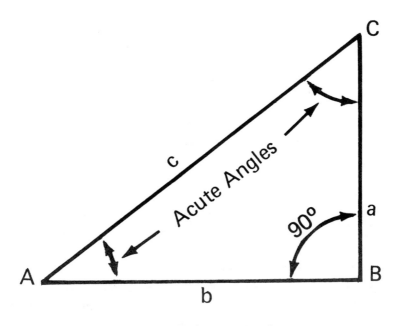

Description of Acute Angles
Figure 7-5A

$$(Sine). \ldots \ldots \sin A = \frac{a}{c}$$

$$(Cosine). \ldots \ldots \cos A = \frac{b}{c}$$

$$(Tangent). \ldots \ldots \tan A = \frac{a}{b}$$

By knowing any two values of the above equations, the third value can be found. Example:

$$\tan A = \frac{a}{b}$$

$$a = \tan A \times b$$

$$b = \frac{a}{\tan A}$$

An easy way to remember these solutions is to substitute the numbers 5 for tan A, 15 for a, and 3 for b. Example:

$$\tan A \ (5) = \frac{a \ (15)}{b \ (\ 3)} \quad or \ (5 = \frac{15}{3})$$

$$a \ (15) = \tan A \ (5) \times b \ (3)$$

$$b \ (3) = \frac{a \ (15)}{\tan A \ (5)}$$

In Figure 7-6 the foundation dimensions are 40'-0'' x 30'-0'' and the acute angle *A* (angle *BAC*) is 36°-52'-12''. Given the value of a (30'-0'') and b (40'-0''), the angle was computed by using the following equation.

$$\tan A = \frac{a}{b} = \tan A = \frac{30}{40}$$

$$\tan A = .75000$$

$$\text{arc tan (angle)} \quad A = 36.870° \ (36° \ 52' \ 12'')$$

The values of sin, cos and tan, as well as the arc sin (sin $^{-1}$), arc cos (cos $^{-1}$) and arc tan (tan $^{-1}$) are preprogrammed in the scientific calculator. The solution to any of these equations takes only seconds. Every manufacture furnishes directions for the proper use of its equipment, but all scientific calculators are similar in the solution of any of these problems.

To change degrees and decimals to degrees, minutes and seconds, do the following:

1. Multiply the decimal equivalent in degrees (°) by 60 to get minutes (') and decimal equivalents in minutes.

2. Multiply the decimal equivalent in minutes (') by 60 to get seconds ('').

Example: In the above problem the arc tan of .75000 is 36.870°.

1. .870° x 60 = 52.200 minutes (').

2. .200 x 60 = 12.000 seconds (''), 36.870° = 36° 52' 12''.

To change degrees, minutes and seconds to degrees and decimal equivalents, do the following:

1. Divide the whole number of seconds ('') plus the decimal equivalent by 60 to get the decimal equivalent in minutes (').

2. Add the whole number of minutes (') to the decimal equivalent in minutes and divide by 60 to get the decimal equivalent in degrees (°).

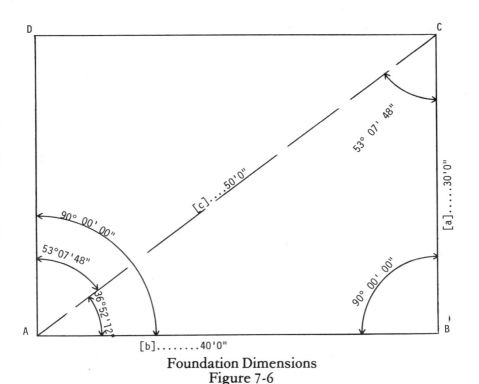

Foundation Dimensions
Figure 7-6

3. Add the whole number of degrees (°) to the decimal equivalent in degrees to get degrees and decimal equivalents.

Example: Convert 36° 52' 12'' to degrees and decimal equivalents.

1. 12'' ÷ 60 = .200 minutes (').

2. 52' + .200' = 52.200' (52.200' ÷ 60 = .870 degrees [°]).

3. 36° + .870° = 36.870°.

Another method of solving the diagonal distance *AC* (as

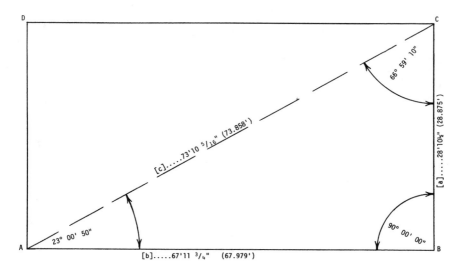

Acute Angle
Figure 7-7

shown in Figure 7-6) without using the Pythagorean theorem is to use the equation $\sin A = \dfrac{a}{c}$ or $\cos A = \dfrac{b}{c}$. Using the equation $\sin A = \dfrac{a}{c}$ the solution is:

$$c = \frac{a}{\sin A}$$

$$c = \frac{30'}{.60000 \ (\sin 36.870°)}$$

$$c = 50'\text{-}0''$$

In Figure 7-7 the acute angle A is found by the following equation:

$$\tan A = \frac{a}{b}$$

$$\tan A = \frac{28.875'}{67.979'}$$

$$\tan A = .42476$$

$$\text{arc tan (angle)} = 23.014° \ (23° \ 00' \ 50'')$$

Acute angle C can be found by subtracting acute angle A from 90°. In the above example 90.00° (or 89° 59' 60'') minus 23° 00' 50'' = 66° 59' 10''. The three angles in any triangle always add up to 180°. To prove the computations, always add the three angles to verify the accuracy of your calculations. In the above problem the angles are:

Angle A = 23° 00 50''

Angle B = 90° 00' 00''

Angle C $= \dfrac{66° \ \ 59' \ \ 10''}{179° \ \ 59' \ \ 60''}$ or 180° 00' 00''

Knowing the angle A (23.014° in the above example) and side a (28.875'), the diagonal distance AC can be found by the following equation:

$$c = \frac{a}{\sin A} = c = \frac{28.875'}{.39096} \ (\sin \ 23.014°)$$

$$c = 73.858' \ (73'\text{-}10\text{-}5/16'')$$

Diagonals And Accurate Foundation Layouts

It has long been known that any corner can be checked to see if it is square by measuring 3'-0'' along one side and 4'-0'' on the other side. If the diagonal distance (hypothenuse) between these two points measures 5'-0'', the corner is square. These measurements can also be multiples of 3'-0'', 4'-0'' and 5'-0'', such as 6'-0'', 8'-0'' and 10'-0'' or 9'-0'', 12'-0'' and 15'-0''. Diagonals are calculated to check the whole foundation for square. If the diagonal distances between opposite corners of a rectangular foundation measure the same, the foundation is square. If they do not measure the same, the foundation is not square.

If the diagonal distances between these opposite corners are computed beforehand to the nearest sixteenth of an inch, the corner that is not square can be found easily. But not knowing in advance what the diagonal distances between opposite corners should measure when they are not the same means that you must recheck the entire foundation, thus adding to the time and costs.

In Figure 7-8 the foundation dimensions are 48'-8'' (48.67') x 28'-4'' (28.33'). The solution to the diagonal distance A-C is:

$$AC = \sqrt{BC^2 + AB^2}$$

$$AC = \sqrt{28.33^2 + 48.67^2}$$

$$AC = \sqrt{802.59 + 2368.77}$$

$$AC = \sqrt{3171.36}$$

$$AC = 56.31' \ (56'\text{-}3\tfrac{3}{4}'')$$

Where equal diagonal distances have been calculated and used to check foundations for square, you can save time by using them to lay out offsets in foundations rather than setup the transit again and again. Figure 7-9 shows a foundation with two offsets (*G-H-I-J*) and (*C-D-E-EE*). By using diagonals to lay out these offsets, two setups of the transit can be eliminated.

1. In *G-H-I-J* the two corners *H* and *I* can be located after *G* and *J* are located by calculating the diagonal distance *J-H* as follows:

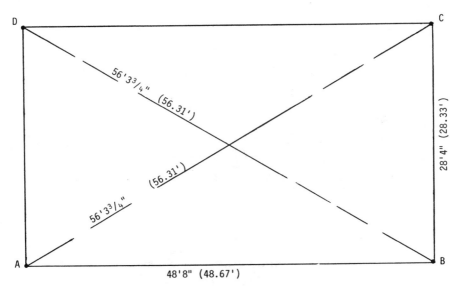

Foundation Dimensions
Figure 7-8

$$JH = \sqrt{GH^2 + IH^2}$$

$$JH = \sqrt{4.0^2 + 10.0^2}$$

$$JH = \sqrt{16 + 100}$$

$$JH = \sqrt{116}$$

$$JH = 10.77' \ (10'\text{-}9\tfrac{1}{4}'')$$

(a) To locate *H*, measure 4'-0'' from *G* and 10'-9¼'' from *J*. The point where the two measurements intersect is *H*.

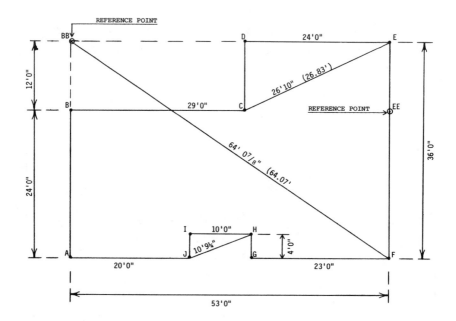

Foundation With Two Offsets
Figure 7-9

    (b) To locate *I*, measure 4'-0'' from *J* and 10'-9¼'' from *G*.

The point where these two measurements intersect is *I*.

    2. In *C-D-E-EE* the two corners *D* and *E* can be located after *C* and *EE* are located by calculating the diagonal distance *C-E* as follows:

$$CE = \sqrt{E\text{-}EE^2 + DE^2}$$

$$CE = \sqrt{12.0^2 + 24.0^2}$$

$$CE = \sqrt{144 + 576}$$

$$CE = \sqrt{720}$$

$$CE = 26.83' \quad (26'\text{-}10'')$$

(a) To locate E, measure 12'-0'' from EE and 26'-10'' from C. The point where the two measurement intersect is E.

(b) To locate D, measure 12'-0'' from C and 26'-10'' from EE. This intersecting point is D.

For a further check of the foundation, a reference point at BB can be established (if it has not already been done), and the diagonal distance A-E can be calculated as follows:

$$AE = \sqrt{FE^2 + AF^2}$$

$$AE = \sqrt{36.0^2 + 53.0^2}$$

$$AE = \sqrt{1296 + 2809}$$

$$AE = \sqrt{4105}$$

$$AE = 64.07' \quad (64'\text{-}0\text{-}7/8'')$$

If the diagonal distances A-E and BB-F each measure 64'-0-7/8'', the foundation is perfectly square. If they do not (allowing for any slack in the steel tape) an error has been made and you should recheck. If necessary, these corners can be checked with the transit. If you setup the instrument at A, points B and BB should fall directly in the vertical crosshair. Turning 90° toward F, points J, G and F should line up in the vertical crosshair. If these points are correct, EE and E can be verified by setting up the transit at F and repeating the above steps.

A builder who uses diagonals increases the speed and

accuracy of all of his foundation layouts. Using both diagonals and a transit is a safeguard against human error. But faulty vernier readings and setting up the transit incorrectly are both common contributors to off-square buildings and costly foundation mistakes. Use good measurement techniques and correct calculations to keep these human errors to a minimum. In using diagonals, remember especially that the steel tape must be taut when measurements are taken.

Laying Out The Foundation

Laying out the building foundation is the most critical part of the construction program. An accurate layout makes the later work much easier. A foundation that is out of square and not properly laid out requires either very costly corrective work later or results in a faulty building that stands — like it or not — as representative of your skills.

Figure 7-10 shows a foundation layout with dimensions of 90'-0'' x 36'-8''. The front setback from the street is 50'-0''. The setback from the side line is 10'-0''. To lay out this foundation, proceed as follows:

1. Setup the transit at either lot corner 1 or 2. Here, it is setup at 1 and sighted on the tack in the stake at lot corner 3. Along this line the setback distance (50'-0'') is measured and a reference stake *a* is placed with a tack marking the exact 50' point. This stake should be placed firmly as it will be needed again.

2. Move the transit to stake *a* and again setup. From stake *a* sight on the tack at lot corner 1 and turn an angle of 90° toward the foundation building line *A-B*.

3. After turning 90° from lot corner 1, measure the sideline

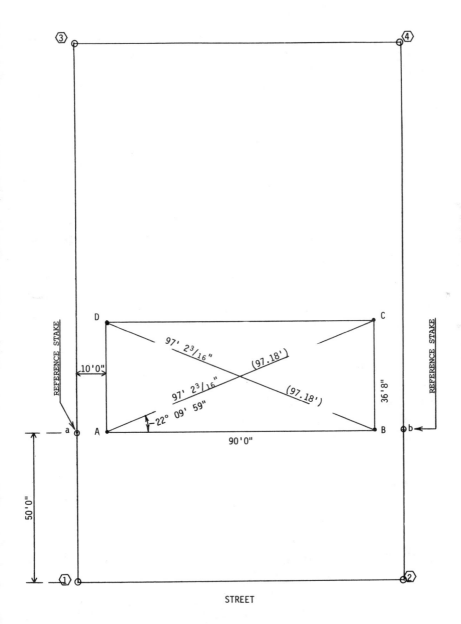

Foundation Layout With Dimensions
Figure 7-10

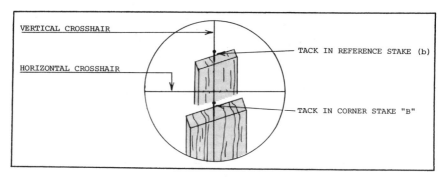

Reference Point Viewed Through Transit Eyepiece
Figure 7-11

setback (10'-0'') along this line and place stake *A*. The left front corner of the foundation is now established. Along this same line of sight, with the transit remaining at reference stake *a*, measure the dimensions from *A* to *B* (90'-0'') and place stake *B*. Foundation corners *A* and *B* are now located. While the instrument is still at *a*, reference point *b* can be located. In the line of sight with *A — B* place reference stake *b* with a tack at this point. This stake should be on property line 2-4. Figure 7-11 shows how the reference point *b* should be viewed through the eyepiece of the transit when setup at *a* and sighted on *B* and *b*.

4. Move the transit to *A* and again setup. From *A* sight on the tack at *B* and turn a 90° angle toward *D*. Along this line (*A-D*) measure the required distance from *A* to *D* (36'-8'') and place stake *D*.

Foundation corners *A, B* and *D* are now located. To locate corner *C*, either of the following two options may be used:

Option 1

Move the transit from *A* to *D* and setup. From *D* sight on the tack at *A* and turn 90° toward *C*. Sighting through the transit along line *D-C*, measure the required distance from *D* to *C*

(90'-0'') and place stake *C*. Corners *A-B-C-D* are now established. Check all measurements for accuracy.

Option 2

If you have a transit or theodolite that gives horizontal readings in seconds (''), locate corner *C* from the original position at *A* by calculating the acute angle *BAC*, as explained earlier in the chapter. In Figure 7-10, the angle is 22° 09' 59''. With the instrument still at *A*, sight on the tack in stake *B* and turn an angle of 22° 09' 59'' toward *C*. From *B* measure the required distance from *B* to *C* (36'-8''). At the point where the line of sight from *A* to *C* coincides with the measurement from *B* to *C* place a stake. Corner *C* is now established.

You can use option 2 on any foundation, regardless of the number of corners (as long as they are 90°, and all corners are visible). You can lay out all corners from one central location with the proper transit or theodolite. This saves time by eliminating additional setups and batterboards. It also cuts down on human error and is both fast and accurate.

Regardless of which option is used, calculate the diagonal distance *A-C* and *B-D* and check the foundation for errors. Here, the diagonal distance *A-C* and *B-D* is 97'-2-3/16''. If the measurement from *A* to *C* and *B* to *D* is 97'-2-3/16'' (allowing for any slack in the steel tape), the foundation is accurate.

When the foundation is other than a rectangle, the procedure for locating each corner is the same as that for Figure 7-10, except that more corners have to be located and more errors are likely to occur. It is advisable in these cases to start with a layout of a single large rectangle that will comprise the entire foundation or the greater part of it. This is shown in Figure 7-12 as that enclosed by *A-BB-E-F*. Once this is done and the accuracy proven, the

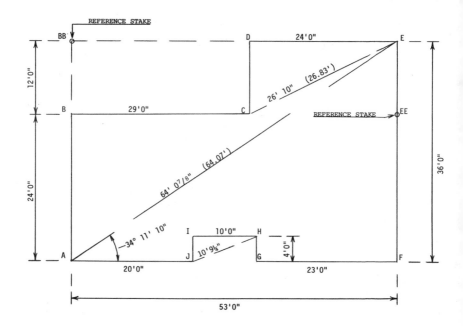

Foundation Consisting of Small Rectangles
Figure 7-12

remaining parts of the foundation will consist of small rectangles which can be laid out and checked. See Figures 7-13 and 7-14, which are details taken from Figure 7-12.

After corners A and F are located and the transit is set up at A, all the remaining corners can be found from this single location if the instrument reads angles to ten seconds (10″) or better, *as explained in Option 2 below.*

Option 1

1. J and G can be located from A by sighting the instrument along line A-F and measuring the required distance from A to J (20'-0″) and 30'-0″ from A to G.

2. H and I can be located by calculating the diagonal distance

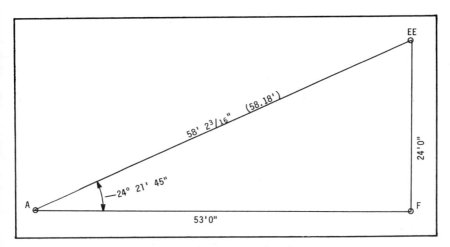

Computing Acute Angles
Figure 7-13

J-H and *G-I* (10'-9¼''). To locate *H*, measure from *G* 4'-0'' and from *J* 10'-9¼''. The point where these two measurements intersect is *H*. To locate *I*, measure 4'-0'' from *J* and 10'-9¼'' from *G*. The point where these measurements intersect is *I*. Check all measurements for accuracy.

3. With the instruments setup at *A* and sighted on the tack at *F*, turn 90° toward *B* and *BB*(the reference stake). Along this line measure the required distance from *A* to *B* (24'-0'') and from *A* to *BB* (36'-0''). *B* and *BB* are now located.

4. Move the instrument to *B* and setup to locate *C* and *EE* (the reference stake). From *B* sight on the tack at stake *A* and turn 90° toward *C*. Along line *B-C* measure the required distance from *B* to *C* (29'-0'') to locate *C*, and measure the required distance from *B* to *EE* (53'-0'' [29'-0'' + 24'-0'']) to locate *EE*.

Setup the instrument at *BB* to locate *D* and *E*. Sight on the tacks at *B* and *A* with the instrument and turn 90° towards *D* and *E*. Along line *BB-E*, measure the required distance from *BB* to *D*

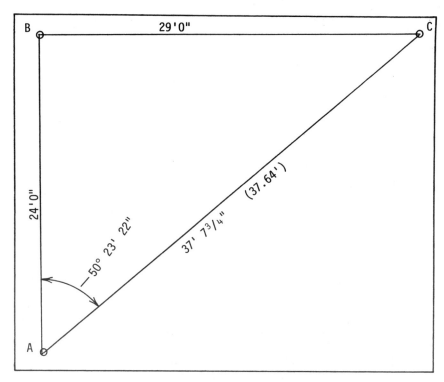

Computing Acute Angles
Figure 7-14

(29'-0'') and place stake *D*. Measure the distance from *BB* to *E* (53'-0'') and place stake *E*. All corners of the foundation are now located, including the large rectangle that encloses the entire foundation (*A-BB-E-F*). The accuracy of the foundation layout can now be checked by calculating the diagonal distance *A-E* and *F-BB* (64'-0-7/8''), and the diagonal distance *C-E* and *D-EE* (26'-10''). If these diagonals check, the foundation is accurate.

Option 2
1. To locate *E* with the instrument setup at *A*, compute the acute angle *FAE* (34° 11' 10''). With the instrument sighted on *F*

turn an angle of 34° 11' 10'' toward *E*. Measure the required distance from *F* to *E* (36'-0''). Where the line of sight *A-E* coincides with the correct tape reading from *F*, place a stake. Point *E* is now located.

2. *B* and *BB* are located from *A* the same as explained in Option 1, number 3 above.

3. *I* and *H* are located the same as explained in Option 1, number 2 above.

4. To locate *EE* from *A*, compute the acute angle *F-A-EE* (24° 21' 45'') as shown in Figure 7-13. With the instrument setup at *A*, sight on the tack at *F* and turn an angle of 24° 21' 45'' toward *EE*. Measure the required distance from *F* to *EE* (24'-0''). Where this measurement coincides with the line of sight *A-EE*, place a stake. Reference point *EE* is located. A check for accuracy can be made by calculating the diagonal distance *A-EE* (58'-2-3/16''). If the distance *A-EE* measures 58'-2-3/16'', reference stake *EE* is accurate.

5. To locate *C* from *A*, compute the acute angle *BAC* (50° 23' 22'') as shown in Figure 7-14. With the instrument setup at *A* and sighted on the tack at *B*, turn an angle of 50° 23' 22'' toward *C*. Measure the required distance from *B* to *C* (29'-0''). Where this measurement coincides with the line of sight *A-C* place a stake. Point *C* is now located. (Note this procedure on an instrument that reads directly to ten seconds (10''). To read 22'' on the micrometer scale, first set the scale on 20'' and estimate the additional 02''. The chart in Figure 7-15 shows that any error in this estimate will be so small that it easily falls within allowable limits.) Calculate the diagonal distance *A-C* (37'-7¾''). If the distance *A* to *C* measures 37'-7¾'', corner *C* is accurate. The accuracy of the entire foundation can now be checked. *A-B* should measure 24'-0'', *B-C* 29'-0'', *C-D* 12'-0'', *D-E* 24'-0'', *E-F* 36'-0''

ANGULAR ERROR	LINEAR ERROR IN 100 FEET	
1° 00' 00"	1' 8$^{15}/_{16}$"	(1.7455')
0° 30' 00"	0' 10$\frac{1}{2}$"	(0.8727')
0° 15' 00"	0' 5$\frac{1}{4}$"	(0.4363')
0° 10' 00"	0' 3$\frac{1}{2}$"	(0.2909')
0° 05' 00"	0' 1$^3/_4$"	(0.1454')
0° 01' 00"	0' 0$^3/_8$"	(0.0291')
0° 00' 30"	0' 0$^3/_{16}$"	(0.0145')
0° 00' 20"	0' 0$^1/_8$"	(0.0097')
0° 00' 10"	0' 0$^1/_{16}$"	(0.0048')
0° 00' 05"	0' 0$^1/_{32}$"	(0.0024')
0° 00' 01"	0' 0$^1/_{200}$"	(0.00048')

One Circle = 360° (Degrees)

One Degree = 60' (Minutes)

One Minute = 60" (Seconds)

One Circle = 360° or 21,600' or 1,296,000"

Linear Error in 100 Feet
Table 7-15

and *F-A* 53'-0''. In the offset *J-G-H-I,* the building line J-I and *G-H* should measure 4'-0'', and *J-G* and *I-H* should be 10'-0''. If the instrument was properly setup (and not out of adjustment), and all instrument readings and tape measurements were read correctly, *these dimensions will be perfect.* Should there be an error (that does not fall within an allowable tolerance), recheck each small rectangle within the foundation layout until the error is found and corrected.

Foundations are relatively easy to layout on level lots. But when the lot has a steep slope or is on a hillside, the problems multiply and the chances for error are many. It often becomes necessary to change from one option to the other. Sometimes it is necessary to use both options on the same foundation, depending upon the terrain. Frequently there will be a difference between the transit readings and the actual measurements. Refer to Table 7-15 to determine how large an error exists when the foundation layout does not check. This chart shows the linear error in 100 feet as it relates to angular errors from one degree (1°) down to one second (0° 00' 01''). Thus, if a building is 100'-0'' in length and one corner is off 0' 10½'', the chart shows the angular error to be 0° 30'. If the measurements have been properly taken, it is evident that the error is caused by one of the following:

1. The instrument is out of adjustment.

2. The instrument was not level and was not properly centered over the point where the angle was read.

3. An error was made in reading the horizontal circle and vernier (or micrometer scale).

If an error has been made in laying out the foundation and the source of the error is known, the solution to the problem is easier.

If there is still an error that does not fall within the allowable tolerance after rechecking all measurements and the angular readings from the transit, the work must be repeated until it is correct. If the error *does* fall within the allowable tolerance, and there is a small difference between the angular reading of the transit and the actual measurement, *accept the measurement reading as it must be correct.*

Chapter 8

Calculating Elevations For Footers And Forms

Accurate floor elevations require accurate footer elevations. If footer elevations are not correct, all of your floor level calculations will be wrong unless structural changes are made in the building. Constructing footers to designated elevations is not difficult, but it requires attention to detail. This chapter shows you how to calculate footer elevations, set and level the forms, construct stepped footers for hillside sites, and estimate footer costs. The procedure recommended here for calculating elevations can also be used to establish the correct grade, foundation and other elevations on the site.

Figure 8-1 shows the wall section of a bi-level house. The bench mark (not shown) was assigned an elevation of 100.0'. The floor elevation is to be 110.73'. The wall section of the blueprints shows the height of the lower level to be 8'-1½'' from the concrete floor to the bottom of the floor joists, and 9'-0'' from the finished floor to the concrete basement floor. The plans call for a 4'' concrete floor to be poured over a 4'' layer of crushed stone. The footer elevation is calculated as follows:

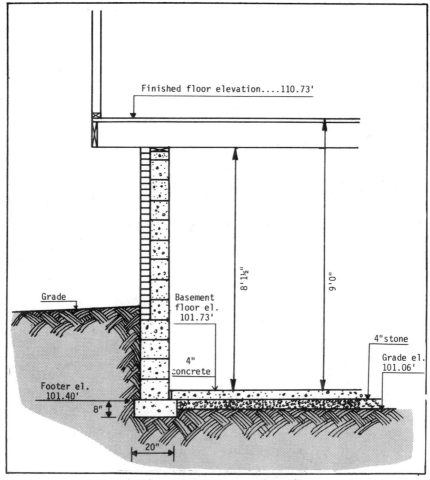

Calculating The Footer Elevation
Figure 8-1

1. Determine the basement floor elevation by subtracting the height of the finished floor above the basement floor (9'-0'' in this example) from the finished floor elevation. The elevation of the basement floor in Figure 8-1 is 101.73' (110.73' less 9.0').

2. The plans call for the footers to be 4'' below the concrete

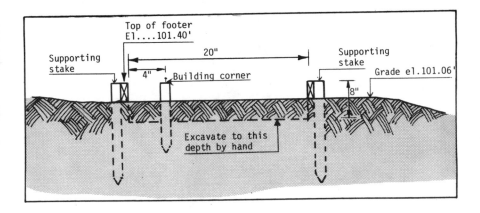

Forming In The Footer To Elevation
Figure 8-2

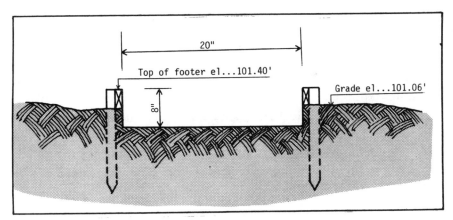

Completed Formwork For Footers
Figure 8-3

floor. Subtracting 4'' (.33') from the basement floor elevation gives the elevation of the footers: 101.40' (101.73' less .33').

From the plans we know that the grade elevation in the basement area is 8'' below the basement floor (4'' of stone plus 4'' of concrete). Therefore, the grade elevation is 101.06' (101.73'

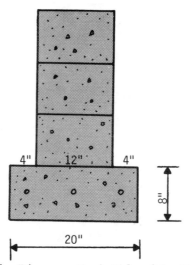

Determine The Distance Each Side of the Footer Should
Extend Beyond the Foundation Wall
Figure 8-4

less .67 [8"]). When the excavation begins, make sure the
equipment operator stays as close to this elevation as possible. A
little care during excavation saves time and money later.

After the excavation is completed, the footers are formed as
shown in Figure 8-2 and 8-3. The correct footer elevation can be
established as follows:

1. Locate all corners of the building and place a stake with a
tack in it at each corner (Figure 8-2).

2. From the wall section of the plans determine the wall
thickness (12") and the size of the footers (20" wide and 8" deep
in this example). Subtract the thickness of the wall from the width
of the footers and divide by 2 to determine the distance each side
of the footers will extend beyond the foundation wall. (20" less
12" = 8" ÷ 2 = 4"). See Figure 8-4.

3. At each corner of the building establish a line 4'' outside and parallel to the building line. Place the inside of 2'' x 4'' forms on these lines. On the outside of this form place a support stake as shown in Figure 8-2. Do not nail the 2'' x 4'' form to the support stake at this time. This should be done only after the correct elevation is established.

4. Setup the builder's level at a central location where a rod reading can be taken on the bench mark and all footer forms without moving the instrument. *Note:* If the bench mark can not be seen from this central point, sight on any other point of known elevation to find the H.I. reading.

5. Add the rod reading at the bench mark to the elevation of the bench mark for the H.I. reading. See Figure 8-5A. In our example the elevation of the B.M. is 100.0'. Assume that the rod reading is 5.65'. The H.I. is then 105.65' (100.0' + 5.65').

6. Subtract the calculated footer elevation from the H.I. to determine the rod reading for the footers. In this example it is 4.25' (105.65' less 101.40').

7. Set the target on the level rod at 4.25'. Hold the level rod on top of the 2'' x 4'' form you set at the building corners. At each supporting stake raise or lower the form until the horizontal crosshair of the instrument bisects the target where it is set at 4.25' on the level rod. See Figure 8-5B. The form can be nailed to the supporting stake when it is at the right elevation.

The footer forms between the corners should be aligned precisely by the following procedure. See Figure 8-6.

1. First set the forms at each corner of the building as described previously.

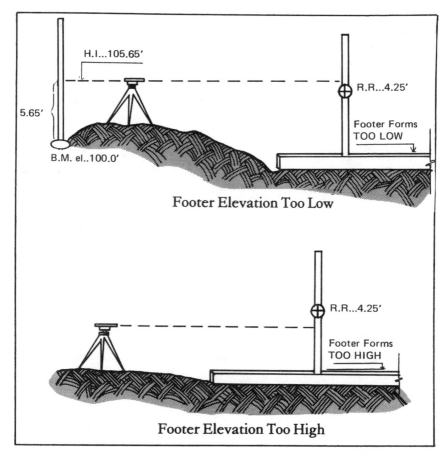

H.I...105.65'

5.65'

B.M. el..100.0'

R.R...4.25'

**Footer Forms
TOO LOW**

Footer Elevation Too Low

R.R...4.25'

**Footer Forms
TOO HIGH**

Footer Elevation Too High

Figure 8-5A

2. At opposite corners along one wall temporarily tack small blocks on the inside of the footer corner forms. These blocks must be the same thickness, such as two pieces of ¾'' plywood. These are shown at *a* and *b* in Figure 8-6.

3. Run a nylon line between the two corners and at the same distance below the top of the form over the two small blocks. Draw it and secure it taut. Place the footer forms in approximate

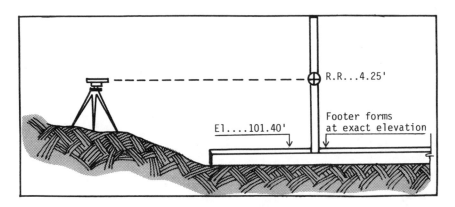

Footer Elevation Exact
Figure 8-5B

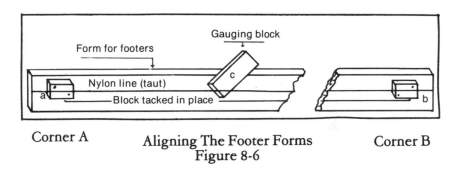

Corner A   Aligning The Footer Forms   Corner B
Figure 8-6

position along this line between the two corners.

4. Insert a gauging block between the line and the footer form
at either corner. This block should be the same thickness
(preferably cut from the same material) as the two blocks
temporarily tacked at the corners. Mark the gauging block or
place small nails at or on the line where the block rests under
string and where the top of the form crosses the block on the other
side of the block. Then adjust the footer forms between the
corners until the gauging block can slide between the nylon line
and the form with a minimum of clearance (as shown in *c*, Figure

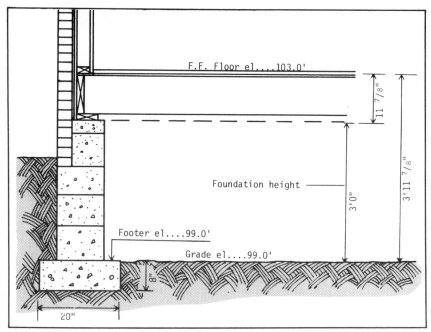

F.F. Floor el....103.0'

11 7/8"

Foundation height

3'0"

3'11 7/8"

Footer el....99.0'

Grade el....99.0'

8"

20"

Determining Crawl Space Grade Elevations
Figure 8-7

8-6) and the lines on the block fall on the string and the top of the form. As each position along the form is aligned and leveled, nail the form to a supporting stake.

After the forms have been nailed in place at the proper elevation and checked once again, finish excavation for the footers by hand. Excavating by hand insures that the dimensions of the footers are maintained true throughout the perimeter of the foundation. It also prevents waste of concrete.

If the foundation encloses only a crawl space rather than a basement, the grade elevation can be determined by subtracting the foundation height plus the floor system height from the height of the finished floor. In Figure 8-7, this is 3'-0" + 11-7/8" =

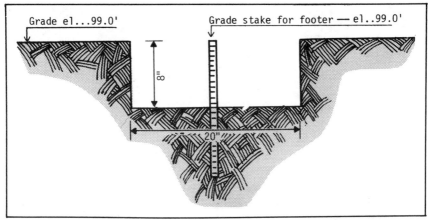

No Formwork Needed For Footers At or Below Grade
Figure 8-8

3'-11-7/8'' (or 4'-0''). The grade elevation in Figure 8-7 is 99.0' (floor height of 103.0' less 4.0'). If the top of the footers is to be at the same elevation as the grade, the footer elevation will also be 99.0'.

If the elevation of the footers is at or below the grade elevation, no formwork will be necessary. See Figure 8-8. The depth of the footers will have to be excavated by hand or machine, and screeds or grade stakes installed for the desired elevation.

To yield an effective bearing area, the bottom of the footers should be at least the same width as the top, and the corners should be cut square. See Figure 8-9. Footers should never be less than the dimensions specified on the blueprints.

Once the correct footer elevation has been established and the grade stake or forms are in place, it may be more convenient to move the builder's level to another location to level the remaining stakes. This can be done easily by this method:

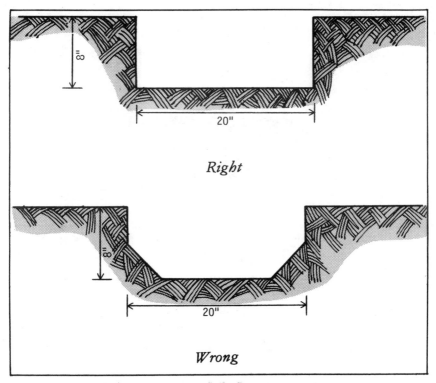

Right and Wrong Footer Excavation
Figure 8-9

1. Set up the instrument at the desired location.

2. Take a rod reading on one of the grade stakes or forms that has already been set to the desired elevation.

3. Hold the level rod on each new grade stake. Where the horizontal crosshair of the instrument bisects the rod reading (as in 2 above) the stake or form is level. This is just like the method shown in Figure 8-5B except that some of the stakes have already been set to the desired elevation. The balance of the grade stakes are leveled from those already set.

Stepped Footers

When the lot is sloping or on a hillside, or if the building is to have a partial basement, crawl space or garage within one foundation, stepped footings will probably be required. In stepped footings, each step must be in multiples of 8" (8", 16", 24", 32", 40", etc.) above or below the baseline or starting point throughout the entire foundation. The base line should always be where the elevation of the footers has been assigned. See Figure 8-1.

After the rough excavation for the footers has been completed, prepare the footers in the base line area with the proper forms or grade stakes set to the assigned elevation as explained earlier in this chapter. After this section is finished, the stepped footers are formed in multiples of 8" above or below this base line. The height of the stepped footing is dictated by the terrain of the land. Set the vertical rise for each step in multiples of 8" and at points that require the least amount of finished excavation and the least amount of concrete beyond the required depth.

In Figure 8-10 the assigned elevation of the footers is 101.40'. The right side stepped footer is 8" above this base line. The left side stepped footer is 24" below it. After each step has been formed and is ready for concrete, repeat this procedure until the footers for the entire perimeter of the foundation have been completed.

There are other guidelines you must follow in constructing stepped footings. These are illustrated in Figure 8-11.

1. The vertical step *a* should not exceed ¾ of the horizontal step *b*. For example, if the horizontal step is 24", the vertical step should not exceed 16".

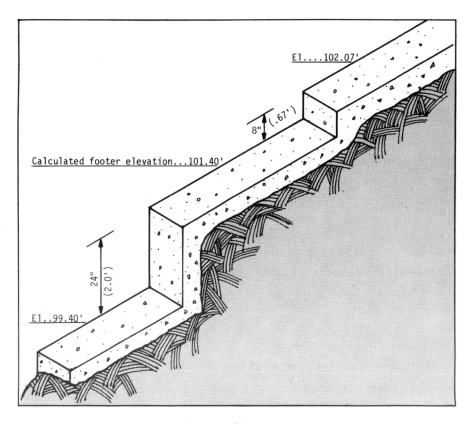

El....102.07'

8" (.67')

Calculated footer elevation...101.40'

24" (2.0')

El..99.40'

Stepped Footer
Figure 8-10

2. Horizontal distance *b* between steps must not be less than two feet.

3. Horizontal steps and vertical steps must form a 90° angle and must be poured monolithically (as a single unit without joints).

4. Vertical step *a* must be the same width as the footing *c* and not less than 6'' in thickness *d*.

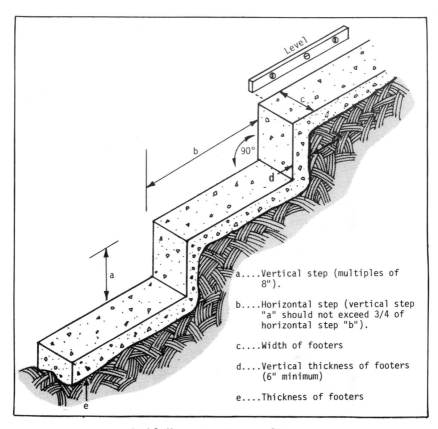

a....Vertical step (multiples of 8").

b....Horizontal step (vertical step "a" should not exceed 3/4 of horizontal step "b").

c....Width of footers

d....Vertical thickness of footers (6" minimum)

e....Thickness of footers

Guidelines For Stepped Footers
Figure 8-11

5. All horizontal steps *b* must be level.

When the grade stake or forms are in place at the base line and are set to the assigned elevation, the stepped footing forms can be constructed as follows. See Figure 8-12.

1. If grade stakes are used (½'' reinforcing rods cut in lengths of about 20'' are suitable), drive them firmly in the ground so they will not be easily knocked out of level.

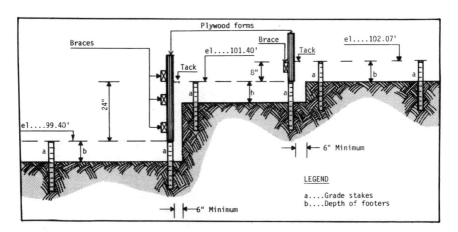

Constructing Stepped Footer Forms
Figure 8-12

2. From the grade stakes at the base line (at 101.40' here), set the grade stake for the first step at a height in a multiple of 8" above or below the base line. Place the step at the point which will reduce the finish excavation required and minimize the amount of wasted concrete. In Figure 8-12 the first stepped footer above the base line is 8". The elevation of the horizontal step will be 102.07'.

3. Cut a piece of plywood for the form (½" or more in thickness) long enough to extend above the step. Set the piece of plywood on top of the lower grade stake whose elevation is 101.40'. Brace the plywood adequately. See Figure 8-12.

4. Set a tack in this form 8" above the top of the grade stake. From this tack, level all grade stakes at elevation 102.07 (101.40' + .67'). Use an alignment instrument as shown in Figures 8-5B and 8-6.

5. Excavate by hand to the correct footer depth. If needed,

excavate the vertical rise for a 6'' minimum thickness of concrete as shown in *d*, Figure 8-11.

6. Because the terrain slopes both up and down from the base line, another step is needed below this base line. In Figure 8-12 a 24'' step is used. From the grade stake at the base line (el. 101.40'), measure down 24'' to the top of a grade stake set firmly in place. On top of this lower grade stake (el. 99.40') set a plywood form and brace it. Place a tack in this form at the base line elevation of 101.40'. Here, the distance from this tack down to the top of the lower grade stake is 24''.

7. Level all grade stakes at elevation 99.40' from the grade stake the plywood form sits on.

8. Excavate by hand as needed for the correct footer thickness in the horizontal and vertical steps, as explained in 5 above.

9. Repeat these steps as many times as required until the footers for the entire foundation have been formed and are ready for concrete.

10. Check all forms for accuracy before pouring the concrete footers. (See the checklist later in this chapter.)

Be sure that all vertical steps in stepped footings are in multiples of 8''. Masonry blocks courses are normally 8'' high after they are laid with a mortar joint. If the vertical steps in the stepped footing deviate from these dimensions, the mason laying the blocks will have to either cut the blocks or build them up to make the courses correspond with the vertical steps. This can be very costly, and it can be a major problem in leveling the top of the foundation. Figure 8-13 shows how the masonry block courses should fall on all stepped footers.

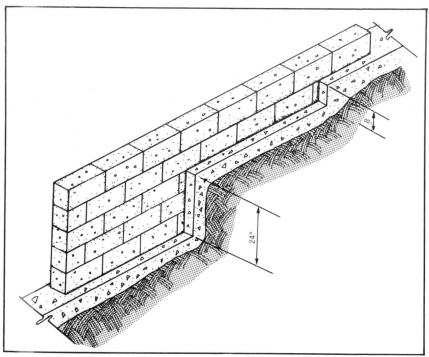

Masonry Block Courses and Stepped Footers
Figure 8-13

You can expect some shrinkage in concrete while it is curing. This will cause changes in the footer level and variations in the height of each stepped footer. See Figure 8-14. This variation may be ± ¼ inch in ten feet. Fortunately, these variations caused by shrinkage can be corrected easily if detected in time. The major cause of concrete shrinkage during the cure is water loss. Normally, there are 30-40 gallons of water in each cubic yard of concrete. This amounts to between four and five cubic feet, or 15-19% of the volume of the concrete. When this water is lost, the volume of the concrete is reduced by that amount. If foundation blocks are laid on the footer before the concrete has cured

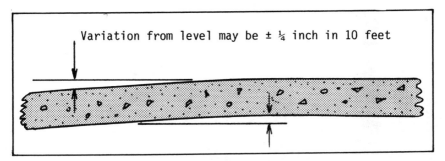

Concrete Shrinkage
Figure 8-14

sufficiently, the top of the foundation may be out of level and the walls out of plumb, in spite of precautions taken to insure a level and true foundation. This can also happen with column posts and piers. If they are set in place before the column footers have cured sufficiently, they may be out of plumb later after shrinkage of the concrete.

Column footers support piers and steel column posts. Although they are not directly connected to the main footers, they should be poured at the same elevation or in multiples of 8" below them. Figure 8-15 shows column footers 24" below the main footers in a basement area. Use solid masonry blocks to build this footer up to the same level as the main foundation footing. This saves money by eliminating the formwork that would be required to raise the column footers to the same level as the main footers. The column posts rest on these solid masonry blocks. Their lengths are uniform and can be calculated in advance from the foundation height.

Figure 8-16 shows a column footer in a crawl space area that supports a masonry block pier. It is poured 16" below the main

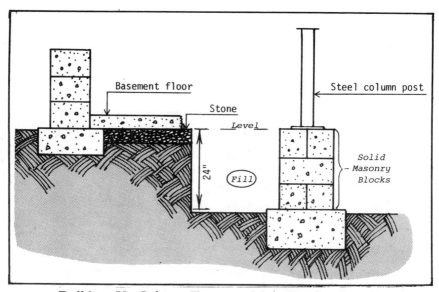

Building Up Column Footer to Main Footing Level
Figure 8-15

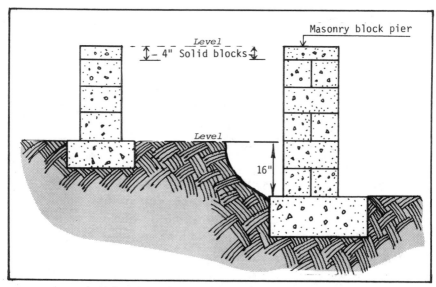

Building Up Column Footer in Crawl Space
Figure 8-16

footers. Here two courses of block bring the column footer up to the same level as the main footing. From this elevation the blocks for the pier can all be the same level as the corresponding blocks in the foundation wall. The top of the pier will be level with the top of the foundation without making any adjustment in the blocks.

Before pouring the concrete for the footers, make an inspection to check for the following:

1. Is the excavation down to solid earth?

2. Are all dimensions correct?

3. Are all drain pipes, plumbing and underground conduit pipes for the utility lines in place?

4. Are all forms for the stepped footing adequately braced?

5. Are all reinforcing rods in place as specified?

6. Can the ready-mix concrete truck get to the construction site without any unnecessary delay?

7. In cold weather, have all precautions been taken to protect the concrete from freezing?

Estimating Footer Costs

Figure 8-17 is a worksheet for estimating the cost of footers on a residential job. Figure 8-18 is a sample estimate filled out to show actual figures. On lines *a* through *l* you list the required materials and their current costs. The bottom section of the worksheet is the step-by-step calculation of footer costs.

COST ESTIMATE SHEET FOR FOOTERS

(a) Footer size:____width x ____depth x ____length = ____ ÷ 27 = _____ cu. yds.
Column footers: Number____.
Size:____w x ____d x ____l = ____ ÷ 27 = ____ x ____(no.) =_____ cu. yds.
(b) Cubic yards of concrete required   _____
(c) Cost of concrete per cubic yard (test:____psi) $_____
* (d) Linear feet of reinforcing rods required   _____
(e) Cost of reinforcing rods (size:____) $_____
(f) Number of stepped footers required   _____
(g) Average height of stepped footers   _____
(h) Cost of plywood forms (quantity and size:_____). $_____
(i) Cost of framing lumber (quantity and size:_____). $_____
(j) Cost of other material (specify:_____). $_____
(k) Estimated cost of footer excavation $_____
(l) Estimated cost to form and pour footers $_____

   * *If grade stakes are cut from reinforcing rods 20" in length*
   allow 12 stakes for each 20' piece of reinforcing rod.

(b)_____ x (c)_____ = $_____ cost of concrete
(d)_____ x (e)_____ = _____ cost of reinforcing rods
         Add (h)   _____
         Add (i)   _____
         Add (j)   _____
                    ======

         $_____ sub total
         _____ sales tax (____%)
         $_____ cost of material
Add (k) _____
Add (l) _____
         ======

         $_____ Cost Of Footers

Cost Estimate Sheet For Footers
Figure 8-17

COST ESTIMATE SHEET FOR FOOTERS

(a) Footer size: __24"__ width x __8"__ depth x __250'__ length = __333.33__ ÷ 27 = __12.35__ cu. yds.
Column footers: Number __6__ .
Size: __24"__ w x __12"__ d x __24"__ l = __4.00__ ÷ 27 = __.15__ x __6__ (no.) = __.89__ cu. yds.

(b) Cubic yards of concrete required .... __13.24__

(c) Cost of concrete per cubic yard (test: __3000__ psi) .... $ __39.00__

* (d) Linear feet of reinforcing rods required .... __820'__

(e) Cost of reinforcing rods (size: __½"__) .... $ __13.50ᶜ__

(f) Number of stepped footers required .... __6__

(g) Average height of stepped footers .... __16"__

(h) Cost of plywood forms (quantity and size: __2 pcs ½x4'x8'__). $ __19.80__

(i) Cost of framing lumber (quantity and size: __10 pc. 2"x4"x12'__). $ __26.00__

(j) Cost of other material (specify: __allow for nails__). $ __5.00__

(k) Estimated cost of footer excavation .... $ __200.00__

(l) Estimated cost to form and pour footers .... $ __500.00__

  * *If grade stakes are cut from reinforcing rods 20" in length
  allow 12 stakes for each 20' piece of reinforcing rod.*

(b) __13½__ x (c) __39⁰⁰__ = $ __526.50__ cost of concrete
(d) __820__ x (e) __13.50c__ = __110.70__ cost of reinforcing rods
            Add (h)   __19.80__
            Add (i)   __26.00__
            Add (j)   __5.00__

            $ __668.00__ sub total
              __27.52__ sales tax (__4__ %)
            $ __715.52__ cost of material
            Add (k)   __200.00__
            Add (l)   __500.00__

            $ __1415.52__ Cost Of Footers

Cost Estimate Sheet For Footers
Figure 8-18

(a) The size of the footers. The calculations to determine the cubic yards must be made in feet and decimal equivalents, not in inches. For example, from the sample calculation sheet (Figure 8-18) the footers are 24'' wide and 8'' deep. The total length of all footers is 250'. The decimal equivalent in feet for 24'' is 2.0'; for 8'' it is .67'. The calculation is then 2.0' x .67' x 250' = 333.33 ÷ 27 = 12.35 cubic yards. *

(b) The total amount of concrete required for the main footers plus the column footers. If additional concrete will be needed, add the amount to this total.

(c) The current cost of the concrete as quoted from the supplier.

(d) The total linear feet of reinforcing rod required, including the grade stakes if they are used and are made from these rods.

(e) The current cost of the reinforcing rods. They may be quoted in price per one hundred linear feet.

(f) and (g) You must know this information to estimate the material and labor required to construct the forms for the stepped footers.

(h), (i) and (j) Calculate the quantity and unit cost of each separately and enter the total cost on the appropriate line.

(k) This can be either the estimated cost or a firm contract price for excavating the footers.

---

*These calculations were made using the full decimal equivalent of a foot for 8'' (example, using .666667' rather than two decimal places [.67'] as shown). Hence there is a slight difference in the totals.

(l) This cost is an estimate of the labor to level, form, do the finish excavation for the required depth of the footers, pour the concrete and strip the forms from the concrete after it has cured.

Chapter 9

Foundation Construction And Leveling

Batter boards are horizontal boards nailed to upright stakes a few feet outside the foundation line. They are used as reference points for relocating the corners of the proposed building after excavation has been completed and the original corner stakes of the building have been removed. They are usually set at right angles to one another at each corner of the building.

Batter boards must be erected with the following considerations in mind if they are to be effective.

1. They must remain rigid and in position as long as needed.

2. They must be set back far enough from the building line so they will not be disturbed during excavation. This distance should be three or four feet.

3. They must be parallel to the building lines.

4. All batter boards must be at the same level. Level the batter boards with a transit-level or builder's level. The top of the

batter boards may be set at a predetermined elevation, such as the floor elevation or the top of the foundation elevation. From the top of the batter boards the depth of the excavation can be measured. For example, assume the following elevations:

Floor elevation . . . . 106.23'

Excavation grade elevation . . . . 101.10'

Footer excavation elevation . . . . 100.77'

From the bench mark or other point of known elevation, set all batter boards to the floor elevation of 106.23'. Measure from the top of the batter boards down to the excavation a distance of 5.13' (106.23' *less* 101.10', or 5'-1-5/8'') to reach the correct graae elevation of 101.10'. Use a nylon line stretched taut between the batter boards for a center measurement. For the correct depth of the footer excavation, measure down from the batter boards 5.46', or 5'-5½''. This figure is the result of subtracting the elevation of the footer depth (100.77') from the floor elevation (106.23').

There are two advantages to using batter boards: the corners of the proposed building can be relocated easily after the excavation has been completed. Second, when batter boards are set to a predetermined elevation, an approximate depth of the excavation can be found from the top of the board.

But using batter boards has its disadvantages. They are expensive to build; they are also easily knocked out of alignment. This means rebuilding them, thus adding to construction time and cost. Batter boards may be impractical on the lower elevations on a sloping lot with stepped footers because you must build them up to the same elevation as the batter boards on the upper side of the slope. The final disadvantage is that they must be checked continually for accuracy. The level and measurements of the building corners require a constant batter board location. Check the boards after each phase of footer construction and before the foundation blocks are laid.

You can avoid using batter boards by laying out the foundation for the footers three times—before the excavation begins, after it has been completed, and again after the footers have been poured. Use 1" concrete nails driven into the concrete footers to mark the permanent corners of the building. This is a more accurate method. Even though it requires that the building be laid out two additional times, it can be cheaper than using batter boards if the batter boards have to be rebuilt several times because they were knocked out of alignment. But it still requires two additional layouts of the foundation. This can take extra time, and can even result in construction delays if the person responsible for the layout work is not available when needed. You have to decide on each job which method is best, batter boards or additional layouts.

The Masonry Contractor's Checklist

Assume that the footers have been poured and a masonry contractor is ready to start the foundation wall. It is good policy to go over construction details with him before he begins laying the blocks. Mistakes are common and costly. Most mistakes can be prevented with proper caution and a little foresight. Here is a checklist of some of the details that should be reviewed with the masonry contractor prior to foundation construction:

1. Check the location of all corners and their dimensions and the size of the blocks at each section of the foundation. These dimensions should be verified for accuracy before the blocks are laid.

2. Verify all dimensions and locations of windows, vents and doors in the foundation wall. A window that is 3'-2" wide can easily be misread as 32". If not caught in time, these errors must be corrected later.

3. Go over the locations and sizes of all other openings in the foundation wall: access doors, dryer vents and the notches in the wall to receive the beams, girders, or floor joists.

4. Check the location, size, and height of all piers. Verify how they are to be constructed.

5. Know where solid masonry blocks are to be used.

6. Agree on how the foundation wall is to be leveled. If a story pole is to be used, who will be responsible for laying it out, and how is this to be done? Verify the height of the foundation wall.

7. Verify on what course of blocks the brick begins.

8. Know where the anchor bolts are and how far apart they are to be spaced.

9. Verify the location of wall ties and how they are to be spaced.

10. Know where and how mortar joints are to be tooled.

11. Check the correct mix for the mortar.

12. In cold weather, ask about the precautions the masonry contractor will take to prevent the mortar from freezing.

The time you spend going over these items with the masonry

contractor will be small compared to the time and money that may be required to correct the mistakes later. The old saying that an ounce of prevention is worth a pound of cure is certainly true with foundation construction.

Leveling The Foundation Wall

Leveling the foundation wall is one of the most important parts of any construction project. This task is often taken too lightly and the error is noticeable as long as the building stands. Leveling a foundation wall is the responsibility of the builder and not the masonry or concrete contractor.

It is common practice to level a foundation wall by laying out each block course from the footers to the top of the foundation with a measuring rod called a story (or storey) pole. This is an excellent method, but the story pole should never be laid out from the footers. Concrete shrinks, as explained in Chapter 8. Regardless of how accurate the footers were formed and poured, shrinkage and slump will cause some variation in the footers. Use the story pole as follows: First, use a builder's level to establish level points around the perimeter at each corner of the foundation wall. If the foundation is for a basement, a convenient height for the level points is approximately the mid-point in the foundation height. This gives the mason enough space to make his corrections in the height of each block course without it being noticeable. Establish these level points early enough in construction to avoid unnecessary leveling once the foundation wall is up.

Figure 9-1 shows a foundation wall made of 11 courses of regular blocks plus a 4'' solid cap course. The level points were marked around the perimeter of the foundation on the 6th course. See Figure 9-2. A nail was driven in the mortar joint on top of the

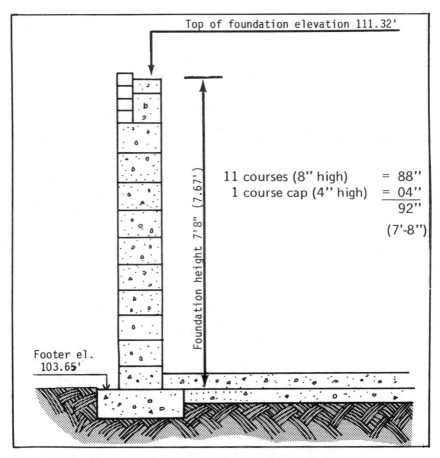

Top of foundation elevation 111.32'

Foundation height 7'8" (7.67')

11 courses (8" high)   = 88"
1 course cap (4" high) = 04"
                          92"
                        (7'-8")

Footer el.
103.65'

Foundation Wall
Figure 9-1

6th block course and all succeeding level points were taken from
this point. If the foundation is not fairly level, the succeeding level
points will vary from the top of the sixth course by the amount
that course is out of level. This is shown at level point *b* in Figure
9-3.

After all level points around the perimeter of the foundation

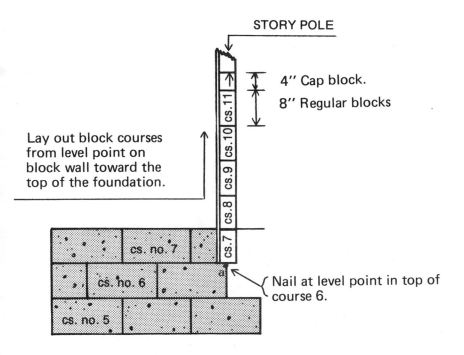

STORY POLE

4″ Cap block.

8″ Regular blocks

cs.11

cs.10

cs.9

cs.8

cs.7

Lay out block courses from level point on block wall toward the top of the foundation.

cs. no. 7

cs. no. 6

cs. no. 5

a

Nail at level point in top of course 6.

Using The Story Pole
Figure 9-2

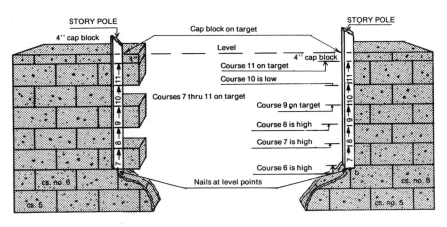

STORY POLE

4″ cap block

Cap block on target

Level

Course 11 on target

Course 10 is low

Courses 7 thru 11 on target

Course 9 on target

Course 8 is high

Course 7 is high

Course 6 is high

Nails at level points

STORY POLE

4″ cap block

cs. no. 6

cs. 5

cs. no. 6

cs. no. 5

b

Foundation At Right Not Level
Figure 9-3

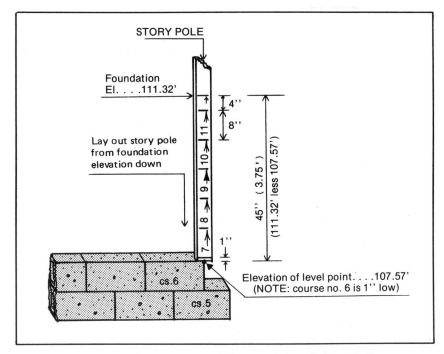

Laying Out The Remaining Height of The Wall
Working to a Designated Elevation
Figure 9-4

have been established, a story pole can now be marked off. Lay off from the first level point the remaining courses of blocks in the foundation wall. These courses should be laid off from level point *a* toward the top of the foundation, as shown in Figure 9-2. All level point nails in the foundation should be firm and left long enough so that the story pole can rest on the body of the nail between the nail head and the wall. The story pole must not rest on the nail head.

Many masonry contractors use another method of course leveling. They measure the height of each block course from the central leveling points. If the measurements from each level point

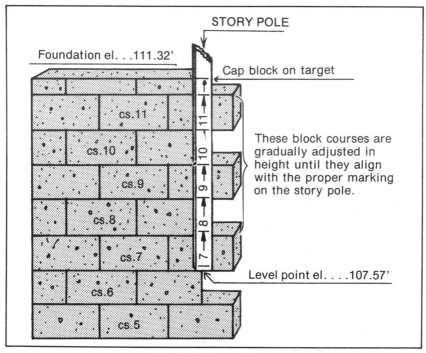

STORY POLE

Foundation el. . . .111.32'

Cap block on target

cs.11

cs.10

cs.9

These block courses are
gradually adjusted in
height until they align
with the proper marking
on the story pole.

cs.8

cs.7

Level point el. . . .107.57'

cs.6

cs.5

Aligning Block Courses
Figure 9-5

to the top of the foundation wall are identical the foundation is level. The height of each course of blocks is measured from the level points, and gradual adjustments are made as needed until all blocks courses measure the same height. This method is common but often results in errors. The most accurate method is the story pole.

If care is taken, the foundation will be level by using either of these two methods. But a further check on leveling the foundation wall should be made with the builder's level as the cap block at each corner is laid. This is shown in Figure 9-6. Setup and level the instrument. After the first cap block has been laid, take a rod reading on it and set the target on the level rod at this reading. In

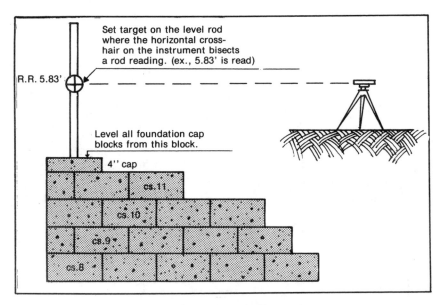

Set target on the level rod where the horizontal cross-hair on the instrument bisects a rod reading. (ex., 5.83' is read)

R.R. 5.83'

Level all foundation cap blocks from this block.

4" cap

cs.11

cs.10

cs.9

cs.8

Checking The Wall Level
Figure 9-6

Figure 9-6 the rod reading (R.R.) is 5.83' and the target is set on the rod at 5.83'. Bring all succeeding cap blocks to this reading, as shown in Figure 9-7. If a foundation has more than one level, such as a tri-level house, level each section separately as explained above.

This is extremely precise leveling. There are few times in ordinary residential construction when the foundation elevation must be this precise. Most foundations for residential houses can deviate slightly from the assigned elevation, and you do not need to use this method. But there are occasions when you have to construct the foundation wall exactly to the assigned elevation. Where a new addition is joined to an existing building, the floor in the addition must align precisely with the floor in the old building. See Chapter 5. You can accomplish this in the following way.

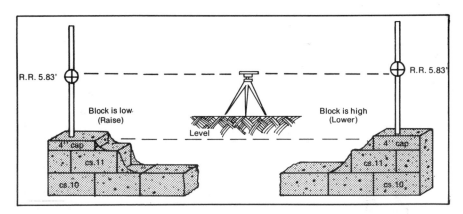

Checking The Cap Blocks For Level
Figure 9-7

1. Construct the footers to the assigned elevation, as explained in Chapter 8.

2. After the foundation blocks have been started, establish level points around the foundation wall with a story pole. as explained previously in this chapter. See also Figures 9-2 and 9-3.

3. Setup the instrument where it can be sighted on a point of known elevation. Find the H.I. reading (see Chapter 4) and the starting level point (for example, level point *a* in Figure 9-2). Calculate the elevation of level point *a*. In Figure 9-4 the elevation of the level points is calculated to be 107.57'.

4. Subtract the elevation of the level points from the assigned foundation elevation for the height of the remaining block courses to be laid. For example, the assigned foundation elevation in Figure 9-1 is 111.32' and the calculated elevation of the level points on the foundation wall is 107.57'. The remaining height of the foundation wall must be 3.75', or 45''. This is 111.32' less 107.57'.

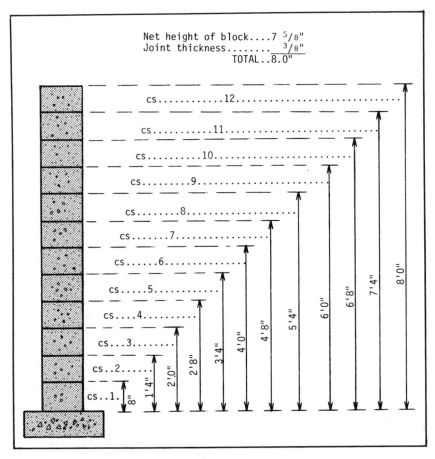

Height of Concrete Block Walls by Courses
Figure 9-8

5. Lay out this remaining height on a story pole as shown in Figure 9-4. Be sure to lay out the story pole from the foundation elevation down to the level point on the foundation wall. If the foundation block courses are running above or below the desired level, it will show up in the last measurement on the story pole. See Figure 9-4 where the sixth course is 1'' low.

COST ESTIMATE SHEET FOR FOUNDATIONS

12" x 8" x 16" concrete blocks	$_____each
8" x 8" x 16" concrete blocks	_____each
4" x 8" x 16" concrete blocks	_____each
Mortar	_____bag
Sand	_____ton
Anchor bolts (size_____" x _____")	_____each
Foundation vents (size_____" x _____")	_____each
Basement windows (size_____ x _____)	_____each
Lintels (Type:____block____steel, size_____)	_____each
Wall ties	_____M
Polyethylene (size_____ x _____)	_____roll
Other material (specify_____)	_____
Other material (specify_____)	_____
Labor	_____block/hr.

_____12" x 8" x 16" concrete blocks @ _____ = $_____

_____ 8" x 8" x 16" concrete blocks @ _____ = $_____

_____ 4" x 8" x 16" concrete blocks @ _____ = $_____

_____Total concrete blocks

_____Bags mortar @_____ =   _____

_____Tons sand @_____ =   _____

_____Anchor bolts @_____ =   _____

_____Foundation vents @_____ =   _____

_____Basement windows @_____ =   _____

_____Wall ties @_____ =   _____

_____Lintels @_____ =   _____

_____Polyethylene @_____ =   _____

_____(Specify item_____) @ _____ =   _____

_____(Specify item_____) @ _____ =   _____

Cost of material $ _____

Sales tax (____%).   _____

Total cost of material $_____

Labor:_____ blocks @ _____ =   _____

Cost Of Foundation $_____

Cost Estimate Sheet for Foundations
Figure 9-9

COST ESTIMATE SHEET FOR FOUNDATIONS

12" x 8" x 16" concrete blocks $ __.74½¢__ each
 8" x 8" x 16" concrete blocks   __.50__ each
 4" x 8" x 16" concrete blocks   *solid*   __.39__ each
Mortar   __2.75__ bag
Sand   __9.25__ ton
Anchor bolts (size __½__ " x __12__ ")   __.37__ each
Foundation vents (size __8__ " x __16__ ")   __4.52__ each
Basement windows (size __15"__ x __20"__)   __7.30__ each
Lintels (Type: ___ block __x__ steel, size __8"x5' 0"__)   __4.45__ each
Wall ties   __11.50__ M
Polyethylene (size __12'__ x __100'__)   __12.85__ roll
Other material (specify __3/0 x 6/8 of door frame__)   __33.85__ each
Other material (specify ___*none*___)   __- 0 -__
Labor   __70__ block/hr.

__1200__ 12" x 8" x 16" concrete blocks @ __.74½¢__ = $ __894.00__
  __600__ 8" x 8" x 16" concrete blocks @ __.50¢__ = $ __300.00__
  __205__ 4" x 8" x 16" concrete blocks @ __.39¢__ = $ __79.95__
__2005__ Total concrete blocks
  __65__ Bags mortar @ $__2.75__ =   __178.75__
  __15__ Tons sand @ $__9.25__ =   __138.75__
  __30__ Anchor bolts @ __37¢__ =   __11.10__
   __3__ Foundation vents @ $__4.52__ =   __13.56__
   __4__ Basement windows @ $__7.30__ =   __29.20__
__1000__ Wall ties @ __11.50/M__ =   __11.50__
   __5__ Lintels @ __445__ =   __22.25__
__1 roll__ Polyethylene @ __12.85__   __12.85__
   __1__ (Specify item __3/0 x 6/8 of door fr.__) @ 33.85 = __33.85__
  _____ (Specify item _____) @ _____ =
         Cost of material $ __1725.76__
         Sales tax (__4__ %).   __69.03__
         Total cost of material $ __1794.79__
         Labor: __2005__ blocks @ __70¢__ = __1403.50__
         Cost Of Foundation $ __3198.29__

Cost Estimate Sheet For Foundations
Figure 9-10

6. Figure 9-5 shows how each succeeding block course can be adjusted in height until the cap block makes a perfect alignment with the proper marking on the story pole.

7. Check the cap blocks at each corner of the foundation as they are laid. The method for checking this elevation is identical to the method for checking the level of the foundation as explained above (Figure 9-6 and 9-7), except that the rod reading must first be calculated for the assigned elevation. This is explained in Chapter 8 and shown in Figure 8-5.

Figure 9-8 is a chart showing the height of concrete blocks by courses. It can be used for a quick reference in laying out the story pole.

Estimating Foundation Costs

Figure 9-9 is a guideline for estimating residential foundation costs. It is only a guideline as foundation designs vary. But this estimate sheet should be sufficient for most residential construction jobs. The upper section of the estimate sheet lists the material needed and the latest unit cost for each. The lower section has the step-by-step calculations to arrive at the total cost of the foundation. Figure 9-10 is an estimate sheet which has been filled out with sample figures.

Chapter 10

Circular Stair Layout

Circular stairs are a luxury usually found only in more expensive homes. But where they are designed into more modest plans they can enhance the aesthetics, salability and value of the house. Prefabricated spiral stairs that wind around a center pole use little space. They usually serve as auxiliary stairs. But circular stairs are usually the primary stairs for the house and require more space than conventional straight stairs. Ideally, the house should be designed to include the circular stair case. An experienced stair builder should be able to lay out and frame circular stairs at the jobsite.

Determine the number of risers in the flight of stairs you are laying out. The number of treads will be one less. For example, for 14 risers there will be 13 treads. This is true for any stair design, whether it is for straight stairs, winders, circular or spiral stairs. The width of the treads varies depending on the run (or the *arc* in circular stairs). There are several popular guidelines for calculating the proper relationship between the width of the stair tread and the height of the stair riser. These guidelines are necessary to prevent the stairs from being dangerous and difficult to use. The rule recommended here is that: (1) each riser in the

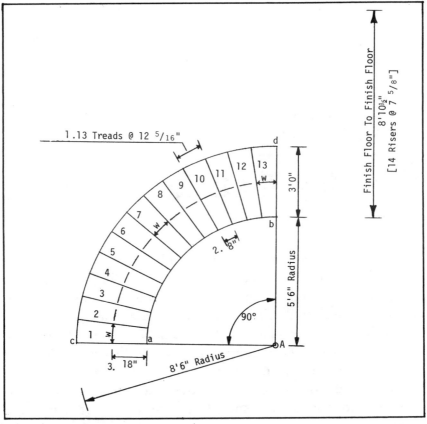

1. Length of arc *c-d* for the 8'-6'' radius = 13'-4¼'' [13.35'].
(13 treads @ 12-5/16'')

2. Length or arc *a-b* for the 5'-6'' radius = 8'-7-11/16''
[8.64']. (13 treads @ 8'')

3. The width of each tread 18'' from the short radius as at *w*
plus the height of one riser should be not less than 17'' or more
than 19'' in total rise and run for one riser and one tread.

Calculating Tread Width For Each Arc
Figure 10-1

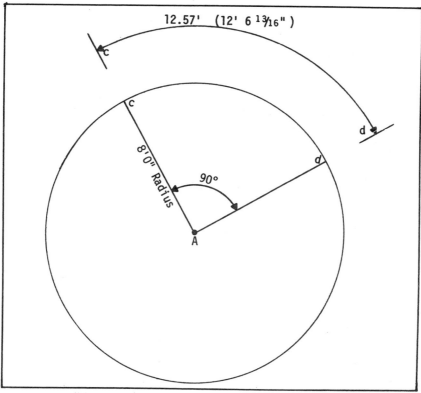

Arc *c-d* = 12.57' (150.84") . . . . 13 Treads @ 11-5/8"
Arc *a-b* (not shown) = 7.85' (94.20") . . . 13 Treads @ 7-1/4"

Average tread width   =   9-7/16" (*)
Riser height   =   7-5/8"
Average of one riser plus one tread   =   17-1/16" (*)
(*) The projection of the tread nosing is to be added to this figure.

Figure 10-2

main stairs is never more than 8¼", and (2) the height of one riser plus the width of one tread is never less than 17" or more than 19". All riser heights must be the same in any one flight of stairs. Following these rules should result in stairs that comply

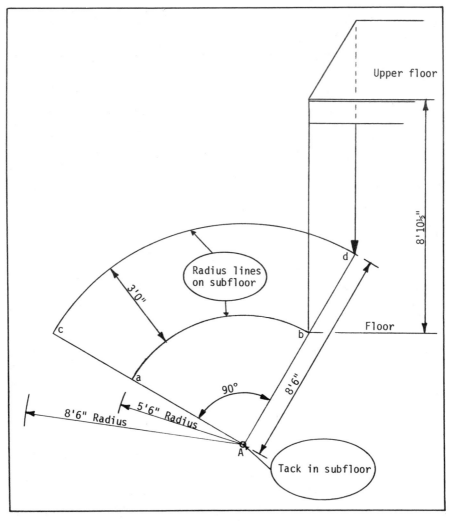

Calculating The Radii of Long and Short Arcs
Figure 10-3

with most building codes.

It is beyond the scope of this book to include construction details or tables or rise and run dimensions. A book entitled *Stair*

Builders Handbook is available from Craftsman Book Company (6058 Corte Del Cedro, Carlsbad, California 92009) for $15.50. This book includes both complete stair tables and construction details.

To calculate the width of each tread in a straight flight of stairs, divide the number of treads to be used into the total run in inches. Then check to see if the riser height and the width of the tread are acceptable. Calculating dimensions for circular stairs requires that you use two different arcs. The tread width must be calculated separately for each arc. See Figure 10-1.

Circular stairs are based on arcs whose radii should be indicated by the designer on the blueprints. In Figures 10-1 and 10-2 the long radius is arc *c-d* and the short radius is arc *a-b*. The short radius is the long radius less the width of the stairs. For example, in Figure 10-3 the long radius is 8'-6'' and the width of the stairs is 3'-0''. The short radius is 5'-6'' [8'-6'' *less* 3'-0'']). To simplify explanations, all references in this chapter to arc *c-d* will mean the long radius and all references to arc *a-b* will mean the short radius.

There is a direct relationship between the angle *d-A-c* (angle in Figure 10-3) and the length of the long and short radii. Angle *A* should always be approximately 90°, and the long radius *c-d* should be approximately the floor-to-floor height. When angle *A* deviates too much from 90°, arcs *c-d* and *a-b* are lengthened or shortened and the treads may become too wide or too narrow.

Figure 10-4 shows a circle with angle *A* and the long radius of 8'-6''. Arc *c-d* is the *run* of the long side of the circular stairs. The length of this arc (in inches) must be known to calculate the correct tread width for arc *c-d*. Before you calculate the length of arc *c-d* you must first find the circumference of the circle. The formula for finding the circumference of any circle is:

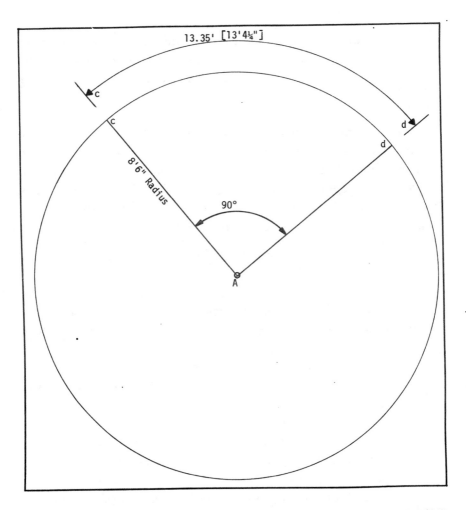

Circumference = π2R . . . . Circumference = 53.41' (53'-4-7/8")

$$\text{Arc } c\text{-}d = \frac{\text{Angle } A}{360°} \times \text{Circumference} . . \text{Arc } c\text{-}d = 13.35' (13'\text{-}4\frac{1}{4}")$$

Finding The Circumference of the Circle
Figure 10-4

$$\text{Circumference} = \pi\, 2R$$
$$\text{Whereas: } \pi = 3.1416$$
$$R = 8\text{'}\text{-}6\text{''} \ (8.5\text{'})$$

$$\text{Circumference} = 3.1416 \times 2 \times 8.5\text{'}$$
$$\text{Circumference} = 53.41\text{'} \ (53\text{'}\text{-}4\text{-}7/8\text{''})$$

The arc length of a circle has the same proportion to its circumference as the central angle *A* has to 360°. For example, if angle *A* is 90°, it is 25% of 360° (90° divided by 360° = .25) and the length of the arc is 25% of the length of the circumference (53.41' x .25 = 13.35'). The formula for finding the length of the arc of a circle is:

$$\text{Arc} = \frac{\text{Angle } A}{360°} \times \text{Circumference}$$

$$\text{Arc} = \frac{90°}{360°} \times 53.41\text{'}$$

$$\text{Arc} = .25 \times 53.41\text{'}$$

$$\text{Arc} = 13.35\text{'} \ (13\text{'}\text{-}4\tfrac{1}{4}\text{''})$$

As mentioned above, there is a direct relationship between the central angle *A* and the radius. The preferred circular stair layout keeps the length of the long radius approximately equal to the floor-to-floor height and the central angle *A* close to 90°. But this is not always possible because of space limitations. You can have some deviation in the central angle *A* and the length of the radius and still have a well balanced flight of circular stairs.

Figure 10-3 shows how the line between points *d* and *b* is perpendicular to the part on the upper floor where the stairs are to be attached. Points *d* and *b*, point *c* on arc *c-d* and point *a* on arc *a-b*

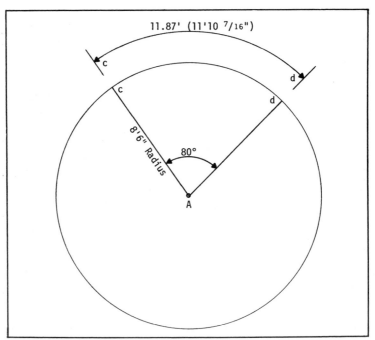

Arc *c-d* = 11.87' (142.42") . . . . . . 13 Treads @ 10-15/16"
Arc *a-b* (not shown) = 7.68' (92.15") . . 13 Treads @ 7-1/16"

Average tread width = 9" (*)
Riser height = 7-5/8"
Average of one riser plus one tread = 16-5/8" (*)

(*) The projection of the tread nosing is to be added to this figure.

Figure 10-5

are determined by the space limitations. Assume that there is a door nearby that will prohibit using the calculated radius (here, 8'-6'') and still maintaining a central angle of 90° at *A*. The long radius may be reduced in length as shown in Figure 10-2, keeping angle *A* at 90°. Angle *A* may also be reduced while the calculated radius (8'-6'') is held constant, as shown in Figure 10-5.

Each circular stair tread varies in width from the long radius to the short radius, as shown in Figure 10-1. The wider the stairs, the narrower the tread will be at the short radius. If the stairs are too wide, the step at the short radius will be dangerously narrow. A rule of thumb to follow in laying out circular stairs is illustrated in Figure 10-1. The width of the tread 18" from the short radius plus the height of one riser should not be less than 17" or more than 19". The projection of the tread nosing can be added to the tread width of the stair stringer (or *horse*) in applying this 17" to 19" guideline.

Figure 10-2 shows how the long radius can be reduced when some deviation in the radius becomes necessary. Figures 10-1 and 10-3 show the finish-floor-to-finish-floor height to be 8'-10½". Stair computation tables or calculation show that either 13 or 14 risers may be used. Assume that you select fourteen risers at 7-5/8" each. Thus 13 treads will be required. The calculations are as follows:

Arc *c-d* = 150.84" (12.57' x 12 = 150.84")
Tread width at arc *c-d* = 11-5/8" (150.84") divided by 13 = 11-5/8")

Arc *a-b (not shown)* = 7.85' (94.20")
Tread width at arc *a-b* = 7¼" (94.20" divided by 13 = 7¼")

Average tread width (18" from short radius)	=	9-7/16"
Riser height	=	7-5/8"
Average of one riser plus one tread	=	17-1/16"*

* Note that when the finished tread is installed and the projection of the nosing is considered, the tread width plus the riser height will be between 17" and 19". By maintaining a 90° angle at *A*, the long radius can be reduced in length from 8'-6" to 8'-0" and a satisfactory circular stair will result.

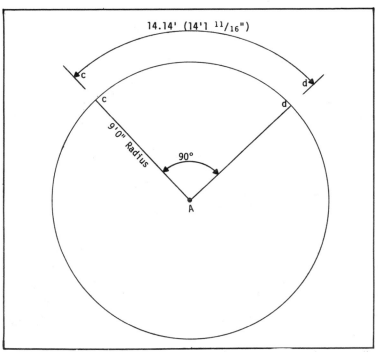

Arc *c-d* = 14.14' (169.65") . . . . . . 13 Treads @ 13-1/16"
Arc *a-b* (not shown) = 9.42' (113.10")   .   13 Treads @ 8-11/16"

Average tread width   = 10-7/8" (*)
Riser height   =   7-5/8"
Average of one riser plus one tread   = 18-1/2" (*)

(*) The projection of the tread nosing is to be added to this figure.

Long Radius Lengthened
Figure 10-6

Figure 10-6 shows the central angle *A* at 90°, but the long radius is lengthened from 8'-6" to 9'-0". The average of one riser plus one tread is 18½". Thus, when the projection of the tread nosing is added, the average width of one tread plus one riser will be more than the 19'' maximum. This violates the basic rule of stair layout.

Figure 10-5 shows the long radius maintained at 8'-6'' but the central angle *A* reduced to 80°, Note that this angle at *A* can be measured with a protractor. First lay out lines *d-A* and *c-A* on the subfloor. Place the index of the protractor at *A* with the line from the index to the 0° mark on the protractor placed directly over the mark on the subfloor from *d-A*. The angle reading that the line on the subfloor from *c-A* bisects is the angle at *A*. In this example it is 80°). The average of one tread plus one riser is calculated to be 16-5/8'', which is less than the minimum of 17'' used as a guideline. Thus, when the projection of the tread nosing is added to 16-5/8'', the average width of one tread plus one riser will fall between 17'' and 19''. Maintaining the 8'-6'' radius allows angle *A* to be reduced to 80° and still results in a satisfactory circular stairway.

Figure 10-7 shows the result of no space limitations on building circular stairs. The long radius of 8'-6'' is used, but arc *c-d* is lengthened (to provide a longer flight of stairs) by making angle *A* 100°. The average of one tread plus one riser is calculated to be 18-7/8'', close to the maximum 19'' guideline. Thus, when the projection of the tread nosing is added to this figure, the average width of one tread plus one riser reaches approximately 20'' and exceeds the 19'' maximum.

It can be seen in the examples above that some deviation can be allowed in the length of the radius and the size of the central angle *A*. Make the calculations as explained above and in Figures 10-1 through 10-7 before actual stair construction begins. This way, you know in advance that the risers and treads will fall within the guideline and result in a safe stairway.

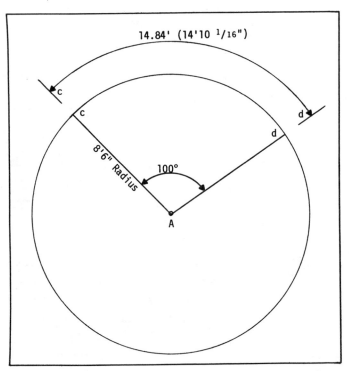

14.84' (14'10 1/16")

8'6" Radius

100°

A

Arc *c-d* = 14.84' (178.02") . . . . . .   13 Treads @ 13-11/16"
Arc *a-b* (not shown) = 9.60' (115.19")   .   13 Treads @ 8- 7/8"

Average tread width   = 11-1/4" (*)
Riser height   =   7-5/8"
Average of one riser plus one tread   = 18-7/8" (*)

(*) The projection of the tread nosing is to be added to this figure.

Stairs Calculated For Space Limitations
Figure 10-7

Building Circular Stairs

Circular stairs serve the same purpose as any other type of stairs: they should provide a safe and easy way for ascending and descending from one floor elevation to another. Because circular stair treads are not parallel to each other, they have to be planned and built with more care and precision than straight stairs. Building stairs is work carpenters and builders often leave to specialists. Many circular stairs are fabricated in a mill, but any good craftsman should be able to lay out and frame circular stairs if the building is designed for them or if space is available.

After the house has been framed in and before the wall finish applied, begin by laying out the stairs on the subfloor as shown in Figure 10-1. Be sure the subfloor is adequately supported to carry the stairs and the loads the stairs will bear. Assume that you have calculated or read off the plans the following dimensions:

Long radius, arc *c-d* = 8'-6''
   Width of stairs = 3'-0''
Short radius, arc *a-b* = 5'-6'' (long radius less width of stairs)
      Angle *A* = 90°
Floor-to floor height = 8'-10½''

Proceed as follows:

1. From the upper floor where the stairs will be attached, drop a plumb bob down to the lower subfloor and establish points *d* and *b* as shown in Figure 10-3. These are fixed points.

2. Measure from point *d* through point *b* the length of the long radius (in this example 8'-6''), to establish point *A*. Make a mark on the subfloor from *d* to *A*.

3. Lay a framing square with the blade along line *A-d* on the subfloor. With the 90° corner at *A* lay out line *A-c*. (*Note: A*

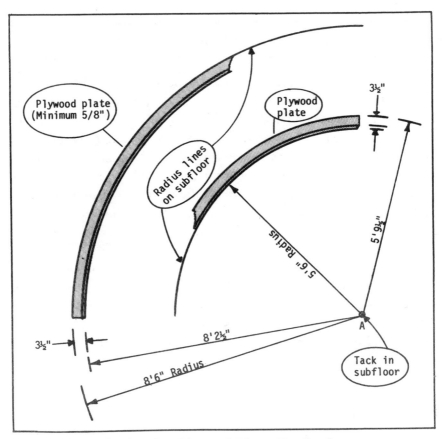

Laying Out Plywood Plates For Studs
Figure 10-8

framing square can be used here because angle A is 90°). Line A-c on Figure 10-3 is the stopping point for the circular stairs.

4. Drive a small nail in the subfloor at A. Using a steel measuring tape, place the ring of the tape at A. At the 8'-6'' mark lay out arc c-d on the subfloor.

5. Subtract the width of the stairs from radius c-d. In this example it is 8'-6'' less 3'-0''. Arc a-b = 5'-6''.

6. Check all measurements for accuracy.

Fourths	Eighths	Sixteenths	Thirty-secondths	Decimal Equivalents
			1/32	.031
		1/16	2/32	.063
			3/32	.094
	1/8	2/16	4/32	.125
			5/32	.156
		3/16	6/32	.188
			7/32	.219
1/4	2/8	4/16	8/32	.250
			9/32	.281
		5/16	10/32	.313
			11/32	.344
	3/8	6/16	12/32	.375
			13/32	.406
		7/16	14/32	.438
			15/32	.469
2/4	4/8	8/16	16/32	.500
			17/32	.531
		9/16	18/32	.563
			19/32	.594
	5/8	10/16	20/32	.625
			21/32	.656
		11/16	22/32	.688
			23/32	.719
3/4	6/8	12/16	24/32	.750
			25/32	.781
		13/16	26/32	.813
			27/32	.844
	7/8	14/16	28/32	.875
			29/32	.906
		15/16	30/32	.938
			31/32	.969

Decimal Equivalents of Fractions of an Inch
Table 10-9

Lay pieces of 5/8'' (or thicker) plywood over the radius lines on the subfloor and cut out the plates for the studs. First, lay out arc *c-d* on the plywood. If the stairs are to be open with no wall on either side as shown in Figure 10-8, deduct the stud width (3½'') from the long radius *c-d* for the width of the plate. In the example, 8'-6'' less 3½'' = 8'-2½''. If the stairs have a wall on one side (semi-housed), the long radius *c-d* may be shown to the inside of the plate. In this case, the outside of the plate would have a radius of 8'-9½'' (8'-6'' + 3½''). This information should be shown on the plans. Arc *a-b* will usually be as shown in Figure 10-8. After the plywood plates have been cut for *c-d* and *a-b*, nail them to the subfloor as shown in Figure 10-8.

Table 10-9 shows decimal equivalents for fractional parts of an inch. This will help you calculate tread widths. Chapter 7 has a detailed explanation of converting decimals of a foot to inches and fractions.

After the plywood plates are in place, verify the placement of the stair treads by laying them out on arcs *c-d* and *a-b* on the subfloor as shown in Figure 10-1. The floor-to-floor rise is 8'-10½''. A stair table or calculations as explained earlier will show that either 13 or 14 risers could be used on this stairway.

In the example, 14 risers are used. You know that 13 treads must be used with 14 risers. The height of each of the 14 riser will be 7-5/8''. The tread widths must be calculated for arcs *c-d* and *a-b*, and the width of the tread 18'' from arc *a-b* should be not less than 9-3/8'' or more than 11-3/8'' so the tread width plus the riser height falls between 17 and 19 inches. The formula for computing the tread widths for *c-d* and *a-b* is shown below.

Length of arc *c-d* = 13.35' or 160-3/16'' (13.35'' x 12 = 160.20'')
Width of each tread on arc *c-d* = 12-5/16'' (160.20'' divided by 13 = 12.32'')

Check:. . . . . Arc *c-d* = 160.20'' (160-3/16'')
                    13 treads @ 12-5/16'' = 160.06''
                              Difference = 000.14''
                    (.14'' x 8 = 1/8'' short)

Solution:. . . . . Add 1/16'' to the width of two treads.

Proof:. . . . . . 11 treads @ 12-5/16'' = 135-7/16''
                   2 treads @ 12-3/8'' = 24-12/16''
                  13 treads.. . . . . . = 159-19/16'' (160-3/16'')

Length of arc *a-b* = 8.64' or 103-11/16" (8.64' x 12 = 103.68")
Width of each tread on arc *a-b* = 8" (103.68" divided by 13 = 7.98")

Check: . . . . Arc *a-b* = 103.68" (103-11/16")
13 treads @ 8" = 104.00"
Difference = $\overline{000.32"}$
(.32" x 16 = 5/16" over run)

Solution: . . . . Subtract 1/16" from the width of five treads.

Proof: . . . . . . 8 treads @ 8" . . = 64"
5 treads @ 7-15/16" = $\underline{39\text{-}11/16"}$
$\overline{13}$ treads . . . . = $\overline{103\text{-}11/16"}$

The width of each tread 18" in from arc *a-b* is 10¼". When the projection of the tread nosing (1-1/8") is added to this figure, the average tread width will be 11-3/8". This average tread width plus the height of one riser (7-5/8") will be 19". This stair case will be safe and easy to use.

Figure 10-10 shows the plywood stringers. Two or more are laminated together for each stringer. Fourteen risers at 7-5/8" are used. The staircase will be ¼" more than the floor-to-floor rise.

Check: . . . . . Floor-to-floor rise = 106½" (8'-10½")
14 risers @ 7-5/8" = 106¾"
Difference = $\overline{000.\text{¼}"}$ (over run)

Solution: . . Subtract 1/16" from the height of four risers.

Proof: . . . . 10 risers @ 7-5/8" =   76¼"
4 risers @ 7-9/16" = $\underline{30\text{¼}"}$
$\overline{14}$ risers . . . . . = $\overline{106\text{½}"}$

The plywood stringer for arc *c-d* is cut as follows:

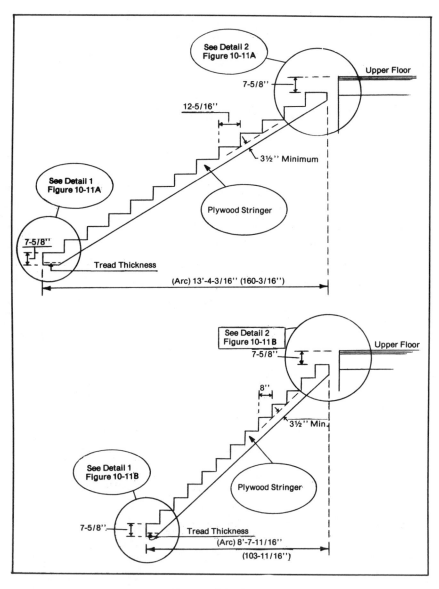

Plywood Stringers
Figure 10-10

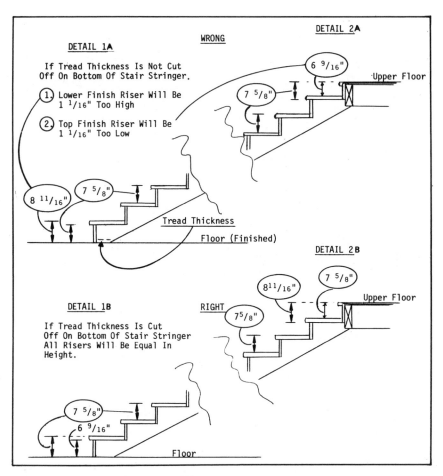

Cutting Off the Tread Thickness
Figure 10-11

14 risers   @   7-5/8"
13 treads @ 12-5/16"

The plywood stringer for arc *a-b* is cut as follows:

14 risers   @ 7-5/8"
13 treads @ 8"

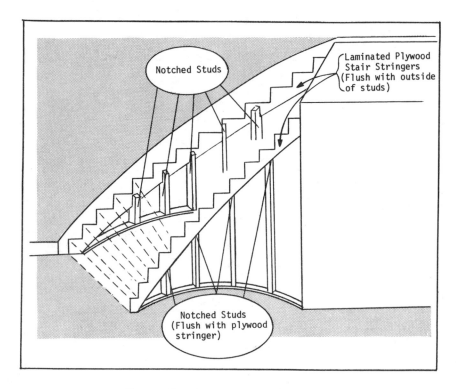

Plywood Stringers Nailed in Place
Figure 10-12

The corrections for the over run and under run are not shown here.

The thickness of the finish tread (1-1/16'') is shown by the dotted line at the bottom of each stair stringer in the figures. Each stringer is cut off this amount before securing the stringer to the studs. See Figure 10-11. Before cutting off the thickness of the finish tread, check the riser cuts by temporarily setting the stringers in place as shown in Figure 10-10 to verify the riser cuts. If all risers from finish floor to finish floor are the same, then cut off the tread thickness as shown in Figure 10-11.

Figure 10-11 shows why the tread thickness should be cut off the bottom of each stringer before securing it to the upper floor. Details 1A and 2A at the top of Figure 10-11 show what will happen if the thickness of the tread is not cut off. When the finish tread is installed the height of the lower riser will be the thickness of the tread (1-1/16'') too high and the top riser will be the thickness of the tread too low. Obviously this is unsatisfactory. If the tread thickness is cut off, all risers in the flight of stairs will be the same height. This is the right way. See Figure 10-11, Details 1B and 2B.

Figure 10-12 shows laminated plywood stringers secured to the upper floor and nailed to the studs. *Note:* If there is a wall on the long radius arc *c-d*, this plywood stringer will be on the *inside* of the studs to permit the studs to reach the upper floor for the finished wall.

Before cutting the studs on arc *c-d* and arc *a-b*, plumb and temporarily brace them. Place the plywood stringers along these studs before laminating them. Mark the studs, and cut out the notch deep enough for the two or more laminated pieces of stringer material. For example, if two pieces of 3/8'' plywood are to be laminated together, notch out each stud ¾'' so the plywood stringers will be flush with the studs.

The bullnose stair for the bottom step (shown in Figure 10-13) can be made on the job or fabricated in the mill. The finished treads, handrail, skirtboards and moulding for the circular stairs can probably be fabricated in a mill cheaper than on the job.

There are usually three stair stringers for any flight of stairs over 30'' wide, but most circular stairs have only two stringers, one for arc *c-d* and one for arc *a-b*. For this reason use support blocks to support the center of each tread. See Figure 10-14.

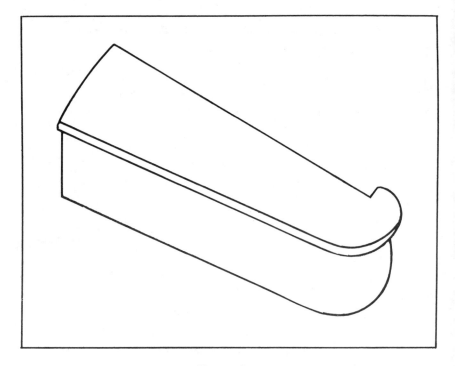

Bullnose Step
Figure 10-13

Figure 10-15 is a perspective view of how a flight of circular stairs will look with a floor-to-floor height of 8'-10½'', a long radius of 8'-6'', a stair width of 3'-0'', a central angle of 90°, with 14 risers and 13 treads.

Fabricating the handrail for the finished stairs means piecing together several sections of handrail to form the correct arc and length. See Figure 10-16. Each section is fitted together as shown in the detail. All joints should be well sanded after they are fitted together for a perfect joint. Balusters and newel posts are available at many lumber yards and can be used on conventional stairs as well as circular stairs. Extreme care should be taken in

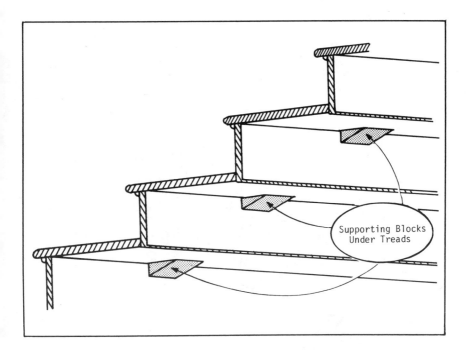

Support Blocks
Figure 10-14

drilling the mortises of the treads and handrail for the tenons of the balusters. Try for perfect alignment. The skirt board may have to be kerfed on the back to permit bending to the proper radius for the circular stairs. Fitting the treads, risers and skirt board together requires precision workmanship. Assembly of the balustrade, risers and treads must also be no less than perfect. Good planning is wasted if the workmanship is poor.

It is true that most circular stairs are fabricated in a mill. But circular stairs can be planned and built quite economically on the jobsite by an experienced stair builder. Well built circular stairs stand as a monument to the craftsman who built them.

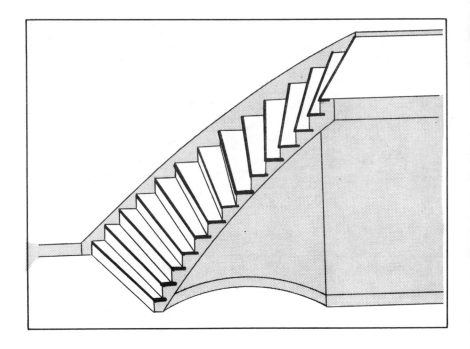

Perspective View — Finished Circular Stairs
Figure 10-15

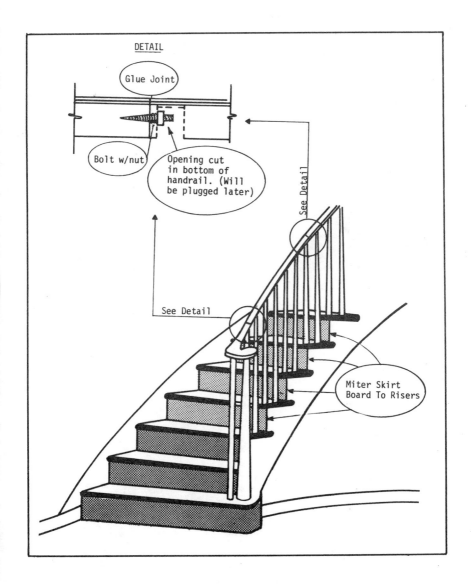

Fabricating the Handrail
Figure 10-16

Chapter 11

Other Layout Problems

Most builders are called on to build shapes other than squares and rectangles into their homes occasionally. Many otherwise qualified craftsmen are unfamiliar with the layout of rounded room corners, circles, pentagons, hexagons and octagons. The layout is fairly simple once you have mastered the basic principles.

Curved Room Corners

Curved room corners set off a room from all the other rooms in the house. They have eye appeal and they give an open invitation as a room to live in and enjoy. Curved corners are planned in some better homes to use largely wasted space to give a soft, pleasant feel to key rooms. They are not seen in many houses, but the houses that do have them create excitement among prospective buyers. Curved corners can be built in living rooms, family rooms, dining rooms, bedrooms and some foyers. They may or may not be built in every corner of a room, depending on design preference. A door or window too close to the inside corner prevents installation of a curved corner.

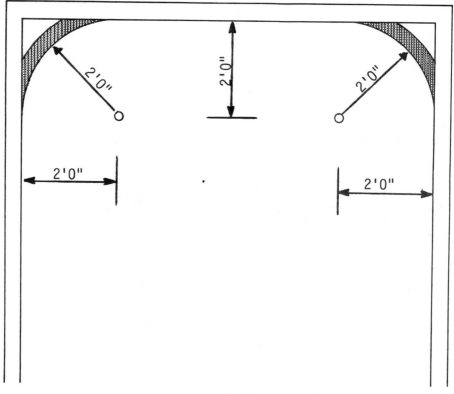

Scale.....½" = 1'0"
Radius.....2'0"

Curved Room Corners
Figure 11-1

The radius of the curve depends on the size of the room and the desired effect. Figure 11-1 shows a room with curved room corners with a radius of 2'-0''. Figure 11-2 shows a radius of 2'-6''. Figure 11-3 shows room corners with a radius of 3'-0''. The greater the radius of the curve, the more pleasing the appearance will be. But note that more room area is lost with a greater radius.

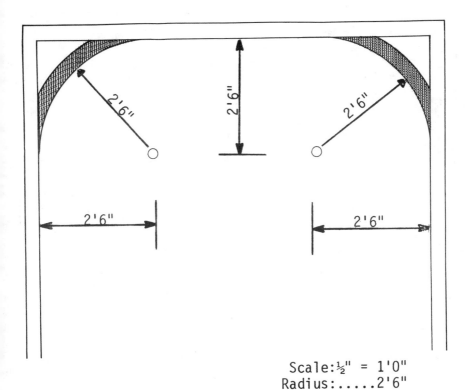

Scale:½" = 1'0"
Radius:.....2'6"

Curved Room Corners
Figure 11-2

Curved room corners are installed after the house has been framed in, before the wiring has been roughed in and the finished wall installed. Figure 11-4 shows a typical installation. The radius of the curved room corner is 3'-0" in this example. Frame in the corner as follows:

1. Lay off 3'-0" along each side of the 2" x 4" base plate and place a mark on the subfloor. Use a framing square to square the corner. Lay off 3'-0" from each of these two points on the subfloor

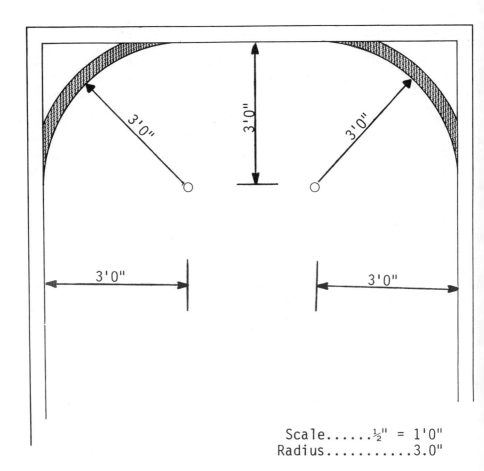

Curved Room Corners
Figure 11-3

toward *a*, as shown in Figure 11-4. Drive a small nail in the subfloor at point *a*.

2. Cut a piece of ½'' (or thicker) plywood to approximately 36'' x 36''. Lay it on the subfloor and against the two bottom plates on the inside corner.

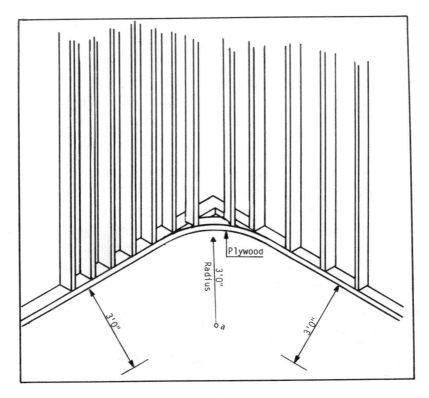

Framing The Round Corner
Figure 11-4

3. Place the ring at the end of a steel tape measure over the small nail at *a*. Hold a pencil at the 3'-0'' point and mark an arc on the plywood from plate to plate as shown in Figure 11-4. If you wish to have this plywood cut the exact width of the stud, again make an arc from point *a*, adding 3½'' to the 3'-0'' radius. The radius of the second arc is then 3'-3½'' to allow a 3½'' base for the 2'' x 4'' studs.

4. After the plywood base for the curved room corner has been cut out, use it as a pattern to cut out the remaining curved bases for the other corners.

5. Using the plywood curved base as a pattern, cut out plywood for each corner of the ceiling.

6. Nail these curved plywood bases to the subfloor and the ceiling joists at each point where the curved room corners are to be built. Make sure the ceiling bases are directly above the floor bases.

7. Cut the studs the necessary length and secure them to the curved plywood bases as shown in Figure 11-4.

8. The thickness of the wall finish around these curved corners depends on the radius of the curve. A curve with a radius of 3 feet or more will accept a stiffer wall finish material than a curve with a 2 foot radius.

Round Patios

Round patios with shrubs around the border of the concrete create a pleasant outdoor setting. They are open invitations for outdoor living. The slab forms should be both a perfect circle and level.

Construct a round patio as follows:

1. Assume the diameter of the circle is 16'-0''. See Figure 11-5. Drive a stake in the ground in the center of the circle and place a nail in it as at *a*.

2. Place the ring of a steel tape over the nail. At the 8'-0'' radius mark on the tape lay out the circumference of the circle on the ground.

3. Cut ¼ inch plywood to the desired thickness of the

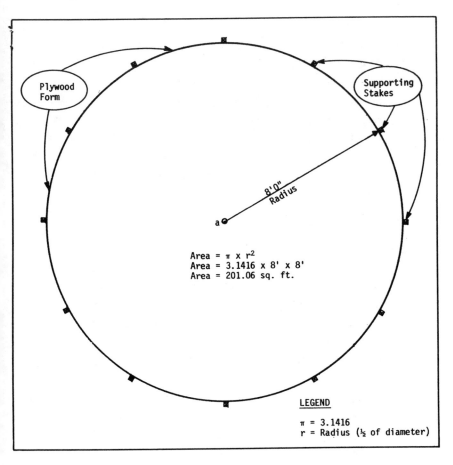

Round Patio
Diameter = 16'-0''
Figure 11-5

concrete. This plywood will be used to form the outside edge of the slab.

4. Cut enough supporting stakes (about 2'' x 2'' x 18'') to adequately brace the plywood forms.

5. With the ring of the steel tape over the nail in the stake at

a, drive a supporting stake firmly into the ground at the 8'-0'' radius mark. Nail the plywood form (with one nail only at this time) to this stake.

6. Using a builder's level, take a reading on top of the plywood form that was just nailed to the first stake. *Note:* The entire perimeter of the circle will be leveled from this reading. Drive another supporting stake firmly into the ground a short distance from the first stake along the perimeter of the circle at the 8'-0'' radius mark. Level the form with the builder's level before nailing it to the second stake. When the form is level, nail it to the stake with only one nail.

7. Continue this process until the plywood form has been installed around the perimeter of the circle. *Note:* Always check the measurements of the forms for the correct radius at each supporting stake and always level the plywood form at each stake before nailing it.

8. After the forms have been completed, check the distance each stake is from point *a*. Recheck the forms for level. Then nail the forms securely to the supporting stakes.

9. A small crown should be built into the center of the patio to prevent water from standing on it. This can be done when the screeds are built for pouring the concrete. Raise the screeds approximately ½'' higher in the center at point *a*. This gives the concrete a slight unnoticeable fall from the center of the patio to the outer perimeter.

Table 11-6 shows the square foot areas of different round patios with different diameters. Use the chart as a quick reference for calculating the quantities of concrete that will be required. A table showing the quantity of concrete for different areas is at the end of this chapter.

Diameter	Radius	Area in square feet
12'0"	6'0"	113.10
14'0"	7'0"	153.94
16'0"	8'0"	201.06
18'0"	9'0"	254.47
20'0"	10'0"	314.16
22'0"	11'0"	380.13
24'0"	12'0"	452.39
26'0"	13'0"	530.93
28'0"	14'0"	615.75
30'0"	15'0"	706.86

Square Foot Areas of Round Patios
Table 11-6

Pentagonals

A polygon of any number of sides can be formed by dividing the number of sides into 360°. This yields the degrees, minutes and seconds the center angle of each triangle in the polygon will contain. See Figure 11-7. This is a pentagon. Find the center angle at *o* in the figure, by dividing 360° by 5. This gives the number of degrees, minutes and seconds for each center angle of the pentagon. The answer is 72°. All center angles in a pentagon are 72°.

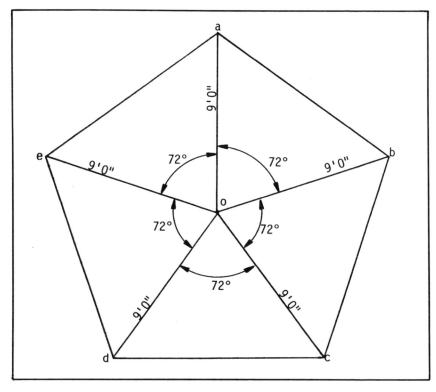

Pentagon Patio (5 Sides) Diameter 18'-0''
Figure 11-7

To layout a pentagon in the field, proceed as follows:

1. Determine the diameter of the pentagon.

2. Drive a stake firmly into the ground at the center of the pentagon and put a tack in the stake to mark the exact center. Set a transit up over the tack.

3. From this point *o*, sight on a point as at *a*. Along this line *o-a* measure the radius (½ of the diameter). In this example, the diameter of the pentagon is 18'-0'' and the radius is 9'-0''. At the

9'-0'' mark on the steel tape along line *o-a*, place a nail in the ground. Point *a* has now been established.

4. With the transit sighted on point *a*, turn an angle of 72° toward *b*. Measure the radius (9'-0'') from *o* to *b* and place a nail in the ground along the line of sight *o-b*. Point *b* has been established.

5. With a nylon line connect *a-b*. One side of the pentagon has now been laid out.

6. With the transit still at *o* and sighted on point *b*, turn an angle of 72° toward *c*. From *o* measure the radius (9'-0'') toward *c* and place a nail in the ground. Point *c* has been established. Connect line *b-c*; two sides of the pentagon have now been laid out.

7. Continue these steps until all five sides of the pentagon have been laid out. Check all measurements and angle layouts for accuracy.

After the pentagon has been laid out and checked for accuracy, you are nearly ready to cut the forms for the five sides. But first calculate the miter cut for each end of the form. The formula for the total of all interior angles of a polygon is (n-2) times 180°. (n represents the number of sides of the polygon.) This example is a pentagon. It has five sides or a total of 540° for all the interior angles ([5-2] = 3 x 180° = 540°). Each interior angle of the pentagon would then be 108° (540° divided by 5 = 108°), as shown in Figure 11-8. The form for the pentagon patio can be laid out as follows:

1. Measure the distance from *a* to *b* along one edge of the 2'' x 4'' form. If the diameter was 18'-0'', as shown in Figure 11-8 the distance *a-b* should be 10'-6-15/16''.

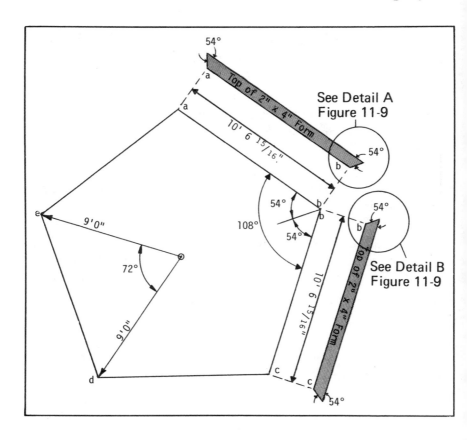

Pentagonal Patios — Calculating the Formwork Miter Cuts
Figure 11-8

2. At points *a* and *b* cut a miter of 54° (½ of 108°) as shown in Figure 11-9. All miter cuts in a pentagon will be 54° regardless of the diameter. The outside measurement of this form should be the distance from *a* to *b* plus the length of the miter cuts at each end — or in this example, 2-1/8''. See Figure 11-10. Here, the inside measurement *a-b* ror an 18 -0'' diameter pentagon is 10'-6-15/16'' and the outside measurement is 10'-9-1/16''.

3. Use the cut form as a pattern to cut the four additional

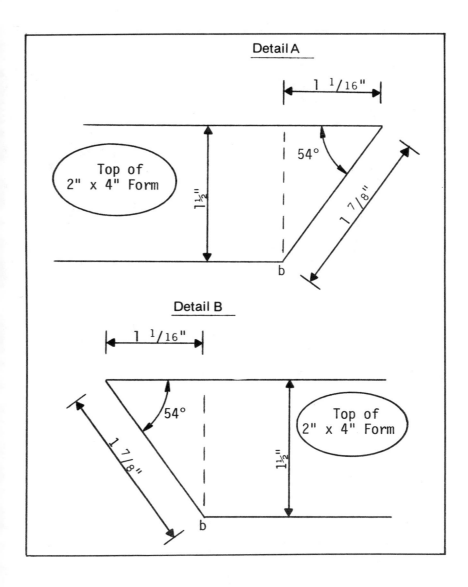

Pentagonal Patio — Formwork Miter Cut Detail
Figure 11-9

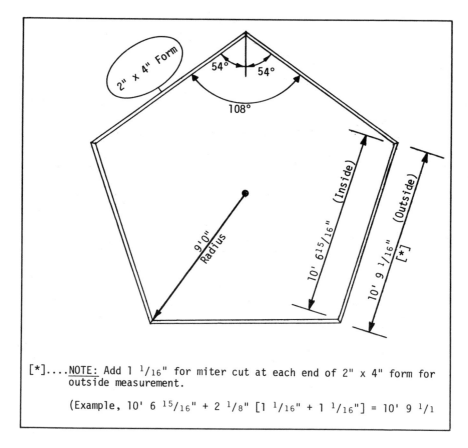

[*]....<u>NOTE:</u> Add 1 1/16" for miter cut at each end of 2" x 4" form for outside measurement.

(Example, 10' 6 15/16" + 2 1/8" [1 1/16" + 1 1/16"] = 10' 9 1/1

Inside and Outside Measurements of Pentagonal Forms
Figure 11-10

forms that will be needed. All five forms for the pentagon are now ready to be put in place.

4. Level all forms with a builder's level as they are placed. Brace them firmly with support stakes.

5. It is recommended that a small crown of about ½" be formed in the center of the patio to prevent water from standing on the concrete.

1 $^1/_{16}$" →| |←   →| |← 1 $^1/_{16}$"

54°   54°

2" x 4" Form

a   b

Diameter	Length of one side (a-b)	Area (sq. ft.)
12'0"	7' 0 $^5/_8$" (7.05')	85.54
14'0"	8' 2 $^3/_4$" (8.23')	116.57
16'0"	9' 4 $^3/_4$" (9.40')	152.07
18'0"	10' 6 $^{15}/_{16}$" (10.58')	192.64
20'0"	11' 9 $^1/_8$" (11.76')	238.01
22'0"	12' 11 $^1/_8$" (12.93')	287.73
24'0"	14' 1 $^5/_{16}$" (14.11')	342.64
26'0"	15' 3 $^3/_8$" (15.28')	401.82
28'0"	16' 5½" (16.46')	466.27
30'0"	17' 7 $^5/_8$" (17.63')	534.92

1. Length of one side (a-b) = .58779 x Diameter
   (Example, .58779 x 18'0" Diameter = 10.58' [10' 6 $^{15}/_{16}$"])

2. Area = Square of one side x 1.721
   (Example, 10.58' x 10.58' x 1.721 = 192.64')

Pentagonal Patios — Lengths of One Side and Areas
Table 11-11

Table 11-11 shows ten different diameters of pentagons, the lengths of one side and the areas of the polygon. Choosing one of the listed sizes and using the chart for planning and construction makes it unnecessary to use the transit in laying out the polygon. For example, if a pentagon patio is to be built with an 18'-0" diameter, look up the 18'-0" line in the diameter column of the figure. Note the length of one side, 10'-6-15/16" (10.58'). Mark a 2" x 4" form this length. This is the inside measurement. For the outside measurement, add the length of the miter cut (54° [1-1/16" plus 1-1/16"]) on each end. The total is 10'-9-1/16", as is shown in Figure 11-10. After this form has been laid out, checked for accuracy and cut, use it as a pattern to cut the remaining four sides. When the forms for all five sides of the pentagon have been cut, they can be installed and leveled around the central point.

Use square foot areas calculated in Table 11-11 as a quick reference in computing the amount of concrete needed. A chart showing the required quantities of concrete for different areas and thicknesses is at the end of this chapter.

Hexagonal Patios

As explained earlier, a polygon of any number of sides can be formed by dividing the number of sides into 360°. This yields the degrees, minutes and seconds each center angle of the triangle will contain. A hexagon has six sides and will then have a center angle of 60° (360° divided by 6) as shown in Figure 11-12. All center angles in a hexagon, regardless of the diameter, have 60°.

A large hexagon can be laid out by setting up a transit over a central point as at *o*. See Figure 11-12. Sight on a point as at *a* and measure the required radius from *o* to *a*. Mark the spot at *a* and turn an angle of 60° from *a* toward *b*. On line *o-b* measure the

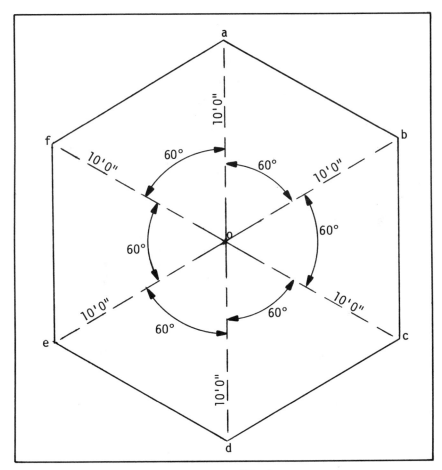

Hexagonal Patio
Figure 11-12

required radius and place a nail at point *b*. With a nylon line connect points *a* and *b*. One side of the hexagon has been laid out. With the transit still set over the central point *o* and sighted on *b*, turn an angle of 60° toward *c* and locate point *c* by measuring the correct radius from *o*. Continue the above steps until all six sides of the hexagon have been laid out. Check all measurements and angle layouts for accuracy.

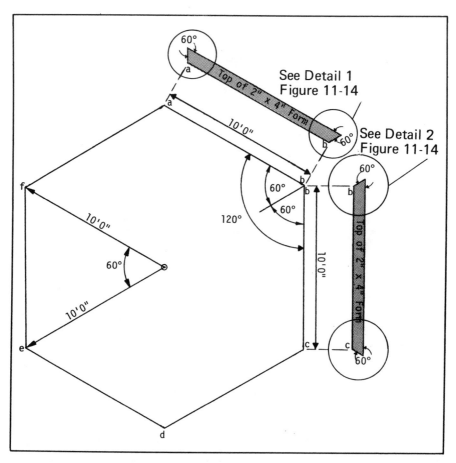

Hexagonal Patios — Calculating the Formwork Miter Cuts
Figure 11-13

The formula for the total of all interior angles of any polygon is (n−2) times 180°. (n represents the number of sides of the polygon.) A hexagon with six sides will then have a total of 720° for all interior angles ([6−2] = 4 x 180° = 720°). Each interior angle of the hexagon will be 120° (720° divided by 6 = 120°), as shown in Figure 11-13, and the miter cut for the forms will be 60° (½ of 120°) on each end. Figure 11-14 shows how a 2'' x 4'' form

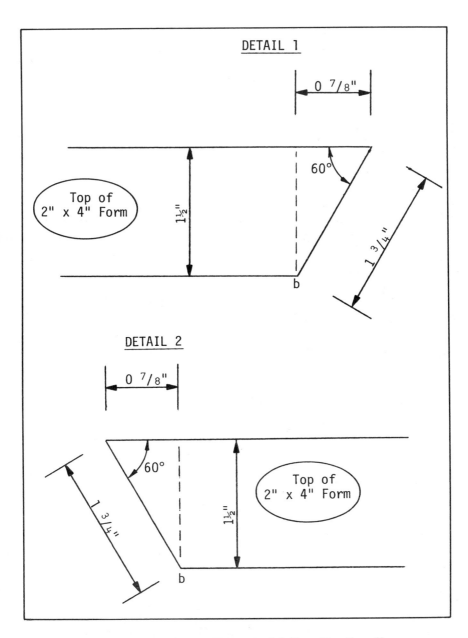

Hexagonal Patios — Formwork Miter Cut Detail
Figure 11-14

Diameter	Length of one side (a-b)	Area (sq. ft.)
12'0"	6'0" (6.0')	93.53
14'0"	7'0" (7.0')	127.30
16'0"	8'0" (8.0')	166.27
18'0"	9'0" (9.0')	210.44
20'0"	10'0" (10.0')	259.80
22'0"	11'0" (11.0')	314.36
24'0"	12'0" (12.0')	374.11
26'0"	13'0" (13.0')	439.06
28'0"	14'0" (14.0')	509.21
30'0"	15'0" (15.0')	584.55

1. Length of one side (a-b) = .50000 x Diameter
   (Example, .50000 x 20.0' = 10'0")
   NOTE: THE LENGTH OF ONE SIDE (a-b) IN ANY HEXAGON IS ALWAYS EQUAL
   TO THE RADIUS.

2. Area = Square of one side x 2.598
   (Example, 10.0' x 10.0' x 2.598 = 259.80')

Hexagonal Patios — Lengths of One Side and Area
Table 11-15

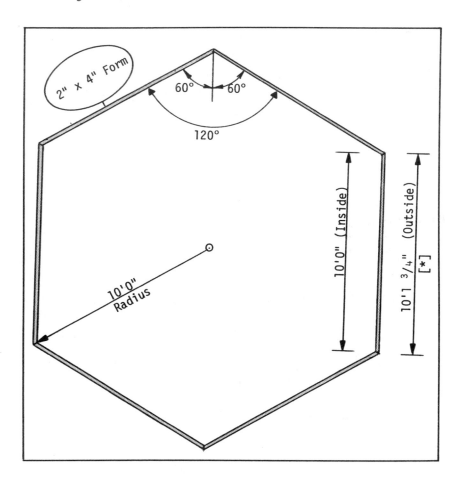

*NOTE: Add 0-7/8'' for miter cut at each end of 2'' x 4'' form for outside measurement.

(Example, 10'-0'' + 1¾'' [0-7/8'' + 0-7/8''] = 10'-1¾'')

Inside and Outside Measurements of Hexagonal Forms
Figure 11-16

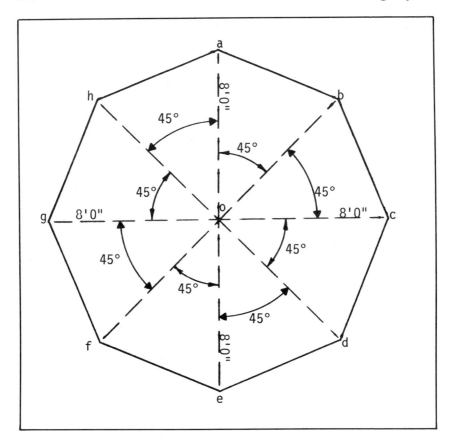

Octagonal Patio
Figure 11-17

can be cut for a 60° miter. All miter cuts for the forms in any regular hexagon will be 60°.

Table 11-15 shows the length of one side and the areas ot ten different hexagon patios. If 2'' x 4'' forms are used, the measurements to be added to each end of the form will be 0-7/8'' as shown in Figure 11-16. *Note:* The length of one side of any hexagon always equals the radius or one-half the diameter of that hexagon.

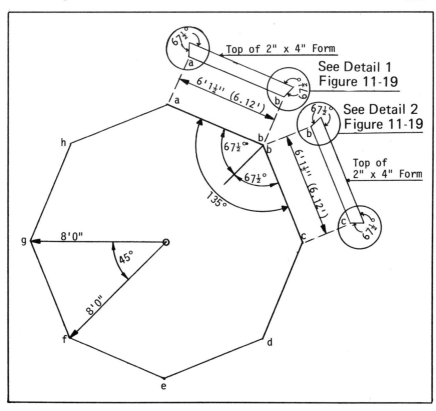

Octagonal Patio — Calculating the Formwork Miter Cuts
Figure 11-18

Octagonal Patios

The center angles of an octagon are 45°, as shown in Figure 11-17. They were computed by dividing the number of sides in an octagon into 360° (360° ÷ 8 = 45°). Regardless of the diameter of an octagon, the center angles will always be 45°

A large octagon can be laid out in the field by setting up a transit at a central point. See Figure 11-17. After sighting on point *a* the required radius from *o*, place a nail in the ground at *a*. From

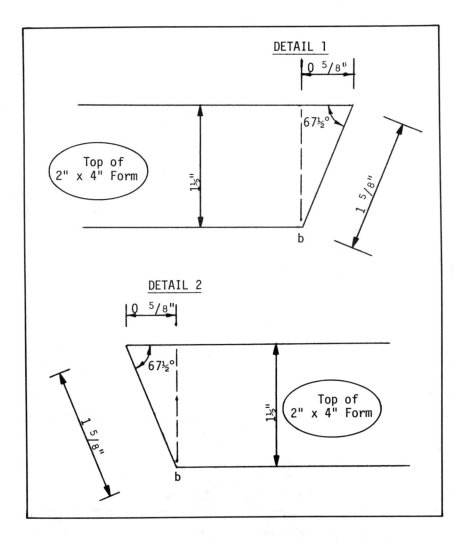

Octagonal Patio — Formwork Miter Cut Detail
Figure 11-19

—‖|←—0 $^5/_8$"   —‖|←—0 $^5/_8$"

$67\frac{1}{2}°$ $67\frac{1}{2}°$

Top of 2" x 4" Form

a   b

Diameter	Length of one side (a-b)		Area (sq. ft.)
12'0"	4'7 $^1/_8$"	(4.59')	101.72
14'0"	5'4 $^5/_{16}$"	(5.36')	138.71
16'0"	6'1½"	(6.12')	180.83
18'0"	6'10 $^5/_8$"	(6.89')	229.20
20'0"	7'7 $^7/_8$"	(7.65')	282.55
22'0"	8'5"	(8.42')	342.29
24'0"	9'2 $^3/_{16}$"	(9.18')	406.87
26'0"	9'11 $^3/_8$"	(9.95')	477.98
28'0"	10'8 $^9/_{16}$"	(10.72')	554.83
30'0"	11'5 $^3/_4$"	(11.48')	636.28

1. Length of one side (a-b) = .38268 x Diameter

   (Example, .38268 x 16'0" = 6.12' (6'1½"))

2. Area = Square of one side (a-b) x 4.828

   (Example, 6.12' x 6.12' [6'1½" x 6'1½"] x 4.828 = 180.83 sq. ft.)

Octagonal Patio — Lengths of One Side and Area
Table 11-20

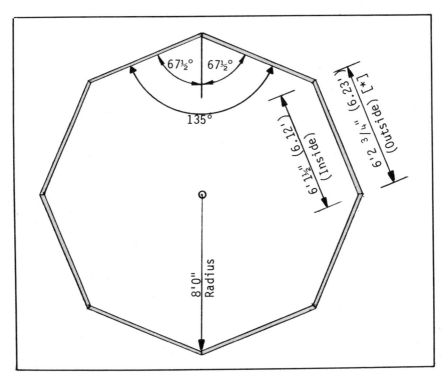

*NOTE: Add 0-5/8'' for miter cut at each end of 2'' x 4'' form for outside measurement.

(Example, 6'-1½'' + 1¼'' [0-5/8'' + 0-5/8''] = 6'2¾'').

Octagonal Patio — Formwork Inside and Outside Measurements
Figure 11-21

a turn an angle of 45° toward *b*, locate *b* the required radius from *o* and connect line *a-b*. Continue these steps until all eight sides of the octagon have been laid out. Check all measurements and angle layouts for accuracy.

The total of the interior angles is computed by the formula $(n-2) \times 180°$. (n represents the number of sides of the polygon.) An octagon with eight sides will have a total of 1080° for all the

Area In Square Feet	Thickness In Inches And Decimal Equivalents Of A Foot				
	3"	3½"	4"	4½"	5"
	.250'	.292'	.333'	.375'	.417'
05	.046	.054	.062	.069	.077
10	.093	.108	.123	.139	.154
20	.185	.216	.247	.278	.309
30	.278	.324	.370	.417	.463
40	.370	.433	.493	.556	.618
50	.463	.541	.617	.694	.772
60	.556	.649	.740	.833	.927
70	.648	.757	.863	.972	1.08
80	.741	.865	.987	1.11	1.24
90	.833	.973	1.11	1.25	1.39
100	.926	1.08	1.24	1.39	1.54
200	1.85	2.16	2.47	2.78	3.09
300	2.78	3.24	3.70	4.17	4.63
400	3.70	4.33	4.93	5.56	6.18
500	4.63	5.41	6.17	6.94	7.72
600	5.56	6.49	7.40	8.33	9.27
700	6.48	7.57	8.63	9.72	10.81
800	7.41	8.65	9.87	11.11	12.36
900	8.33	9.73	11.10	12.50	13.90
1000	9.26	10.81	12.33	13.89	15.44

Cubic yards = sq.ft. x thickness (in decimal equivalents of a foot) divided by 27. (Example, 285 sq. ft. x .375'[4½"] divided by 27 = 3.96 cu. yds.)

CHECK: From above tables....200 sq. ft. (4½" thick)......... = 2.78 cu. yds.
                    80 sq. ft...................... = 1.11 cu. yds.
                   05 sq. ft...................... = 0.069 cu. yds.
TOTAL 285 sq. ft...................... = 3.959 cu. yds.

Area Contents in Cubic Yards
Table 11-22

interior angles ([8 — 2] = 6 x 180° = 1080°). Each interior angle of an octagon will be 135° (1080° divided by 8 = 135°), as shown in Figure 11-18. The miter cut on each end of the forms will be 67½' (135° ÷ 2 = 67½°). Figure 11-19 shows how a 2'' x 4'' form can be cut for a 67½° miter. All miter cuts for the forms in any octagon will be 67½°.

Table 11-20 shows the length of each side and the areas of ten octagons. If 2'' x 4'' forms are used, add 0-5/8'' on each end of the form for the miter cut. See Figure 11-21.

Table 11-22 shows the cubic contents of several areas for various depths. Use this table as a quick reference in computing the amount of concrete required for most slabs.

Index

●

Practical References for Builders

Basic Lumber Engineering for Builders

 Beam and lumber requirements for many jobs aren't always clear, especially with changing building codes and lumber products. Most of the time you rely on your own "rules of thumb" when figuring spans or lumber engineering. This book can help you fill the gap between what you can find in the building code span tables and what you need to pay a certified engineer to do. With its large, clear illustrations and examples, this book shows you how to figure stresses for pre-engineered wood or wood structural members, how to calculate loads, and how to design your own girders, joists and beams. Included FREE with the book — an easy-to-use version of NorthBridge Software's *Wood Beam Sizing* program. **272 pages, 8¹/₂ x 11, $38.00**

Estimating Home Building Costs

Estimate every phase of residential construction from site costs to the profit margin you include in your bid. Shows how to keep track of manhours and make accurate labor cost estimates for footings, foundations, framing and sheathing finishes, electrical, plumbing, and more. Provides and explains sample cost estimate worksheets with complete instructions for each job phase. **320 pages, 5¹/₂ x 8¹/₂, $17.00**

Getting Financing & Developing Land

Developing land is a major leap for most builders — yet that's where the big money is made. This book gives you the practical knowledge you need to make that leap. Learn how to prepare a market study, select a building site, obtain financing, guide your plans through approval, then control your building costs so you can ensure yourself a good profit. Includes a CD-ROM with forms, checklists, and a sample business plan you can customize and use to help you sell your idea to lenders and investors. **232 pages, 8¹/₂ x 11, $39.00**

National Construction Estimator

Current building costs for residential, commercial, and industrial construction. Estimated prices for every common building material. Provides manhours, recommended crew, and gives the labor cost for installation. Includes a CD-ROM with an electronic version of the book with *National Estimator*, a stand-alone *Windows*™ estimating program, plus an interactive multimedia video that shows how to use the disk to compile construction cost estimates. **560 pages, 8¹/₂ x 11, $47.50. Revised annually**

Excavation & Grading Handbook Revised

Explains how to handle all excavation, grading, compaction, paving and pipeline work: setting cut and fill stakes (with bubble and laser levels), working in rock, unsuitable material or mud, passing compaction tests, trenching around utility lines, setting grade pins and string line, removing or laying asphaltic concrete, widening roads, cutting channels, installing water, sewer, and drainage pipe. This is the completely revised edition of the popular guide used by over 25,000 excavation contractors. **384 pages, 5¹/₂ x 8¹/₂, $22.75**

Estimating Excavation

How to calculate the amount of dirt you'll have to move and the cost of owning and operating the machines you'll do it with. Detailed, step-by-step instructions on how to assign bid prices to each part of the job, including labor and equipment costs. Also, the best ways to set up an organized and logical estimating system, take off from contour maps, estimate quantities in irregular areas, and figure your overhead. **448 pages, 8¹/₂ x 11, $39.50**

CD Estimator Heavy

CD Estimator Heavy has a complete 780-page heavy construction cost estimating volume for each of the 50 states. Select the cost database for the state where the work will be done. Includes thousands of cost estimates you won't find anywhere else, and in-depth coverage of demolition, hazardous materials remediation, tunneling, site utilities, precast concrete, structural framing, heavy timber construction, membrane waterproofing, industrial windows and doors, specialty finishes, built-in commercial and industrial equipment, and HVAC and electrical systems for commercial and industrial buildings. **CD Estimator — Heavy is $69.00**

Construction Forms & Contracts

125 forms you can copy and use — or load into your computer (from the FREE disk enclosed). Then you can customize the forms to fit your company, fill them out, and print. Loads into *Word* for *Windows*™, *Lotus 1-2-3*, *WordPerfect*, *Works*, or *Excel* programs. You'll find forms covering accounting, estimating, fieldwork, contracts, and general office. Each form comes with complete instructions on when to use it and how to fill it out. These forms were designed, tested and used by contractors, and will help keep your business organized, profitable and out of legal, accounting and collection troubles. Includes a CD-ROM for *Windows*™ and Mac. **400 pages, 8¹/₂ x 11, $41.75**

CD Estimator

If your computer has *Windows*™ and a CD-ROM drive, *CD Estimator* puts at your fingertips 85,000 construction costs for new construction, remodeling, renovation & insurance repair, electrical, plumbing, HVAC and painting. You'll also have the *National Estimator* program — a stand-alone estimating program for *Windows*™ that *Remodeling* magazine called a "computer wiz." Quarterly cost updates are available at no charge on the Internet. To help you create professional-looking estimates, the disk includes over 40 construction estimating and bidding forms in a format that's perfect for nearly any word processing or spreadsheet program for *Windows*™. And to top it off, a 70-minute interactive video teaches you how to use this CD-ROM to estimate construction costs. **CD Estimator is $68.50**

Craftsman Book Company
6058 Corte del Cedro, P.O. Box 6500
Carlsbad, CA 92018

☎ 24 hour order line
1-800-829-8123
Fax (760) 438-0398

Order online
http://www.craftsman-book.com
Free on the Internet! Download
any of Craftsman's estimating costbooks
for a 30-day free trial! http://costbook.com

Name

Company

Address

City/State/Zip
○ This is a residence

Total enclosed_____(In California add 7.25% tax)
*We pay shipping when your check covers your
order in full.*

In A Hurry?
Use your ○ Visa ○ MasterCard
○ Discover or ○ American Express

Card#_____

Exp. date_____Initials_____

Tax Deductible: Treasury regulations make these references
tax deductible when used in your work. Save the canceled
check or charge card statement as your receipt.

10-Day Money Back Guarantee

○ 38.00 Basic Lumber Engineering
for Builders

○ 68.50 CD Estimator

○ 69.00 CD Estimator Heavy

○ 41.75 Construction Forms &
Contracts with a
CD-ROM for *Windows*™
and Macintosh

○ 39.50 Estimating Excavation

○ 17.00 Estimating Home Building
Costs

○ 22.75 Excavation & Grading
Handbook Revised

○ 39.00 Getting Financing &
Developing Land

○ 47.50 National Construction
Estimator with FREE
National Estimator on
a CD-ROM.

○ 19.00 Building Layout

○ FREE Full Color Catalog

Prices subject to change without notice

Mail This Card Today
For a Free Full Color Catalog

Over 100 books, videos, and audios at your
fingertips with information that
can save you time and money. Here you'll find
information on carpentry,
contracting, estimating, remodeling, electrical
work, and plumbing.

All items come with an unconditional 10-day
money-back guarantee.
If they don't save you money, mail them back
for a full refund.

Name

Company

Address

City/State/Zip

Craftsman Book Company / 6058 Corte del Cedro / P.O. Box 6500 / Carlsbad, CA 92018

BUSINESS REPLY MAIL
FIRST CLASS MAIL PERMIT NO. 271 CARLSBAD, CA

POSTAGE WILL BE PAID BY ADDRESSEE

 Craftsman Book Company
6058 Corte del Cedro
P.O. Box 6500
Carlsbad, CA 92018-9892

NO POSTAGE
NECESSARY
IF MAILED
IN THE
UNITED STATES

BUSINESS REPLY MAIL
FIRST CLASS MAIL PERMIT NO. 271 CARLSBAD, CA

POSTAGE WILL BE PAID BY ADDRESSEE

 Craftsman Book Company
6058 Corte del Cedro
P.O. Box 6500
Carlsbad, CA 92018-9892